D0948142

Vegan World Fusion Cuisine

Copyright ©2004 by Thousand Petals Publishing.

All rights reserved. Printed in the United States of America. No part of this book may be used or reproduced in any manner whatsoever without prior written permission from Thousand Petals Publishing, except in the case of brief quotations for the purpose of reviews. For further information please contact:

Thousand Petals Publishing

P.O. Box 1119, Kapaa, HI 96746

www.veganfusion.com

1 (888) 44-LOTUS

Thousand Petals Publishing provides information regarding the vegan lifestyle for educational purposes. The authors and publishers are not offering or dispensing medical advice. Since every individual's health condition and circumstances are unique, the authors and publisher advise that you seek the services of a qualified health care professional before using any information offered in this book for medical purposes.

Thousand Petals Publishing and The Blossoming Lotus Restaurant will be happy to donate copies of this book to non profit educational and charitable organizations. Please see our website for more information.

All recipes presented herein, are thoroughly tested and remain the exclusive property of The Blossoming Lotus Restaurant and Thousand Petals Publishing. They are intended for personal use only.

Please visit our main location:

Blossoming Lotus Restaurant

4504 Kukui Street, Kapa'a, Hawaii 96746

(808) 822-7678 www.blossominglotus.com

For potential commercial application and restaurant franchises, please contact us at www.veganfusion.com

Design & Typography by Adam Prall of Hawaii Link Design

adam@hawaiilink.net (808) 246-9300

Food Photography by Amy Archbold, amayananda@yahoo.com

SECOND EDITION

ISBN 0-9752837-1-5

To Stacy and Misty,
Thanks for everything!
With love,
Chefs of the Lotus

Vegan World
Fusion Cuisine

Words of wisdom & welcome

"Our task must be to free ourselves. . .

by widening our circle of compassion

to embrace all living creatures and the whole of nature

and its beauty...

Nothing will benefit human health

and increase chances of survival for life on Earth

as much as the evolution to a vegetarian diet."

Albert Einstein

BLOSSOMING LOTUS

Vegan World Fusion Cuisine

HEALING RECIPES AND TIMELESS WISDOM
FROM OUR HEARTS TO YOURS

"Never doubt that

a small group of

thoughtful citizens

can change the world.

Indeed it is the only

thing that ever has." —MARGARET MEAD

contents

©michael Neugebauer*

Foreword
Dr. Jane Goodall DBE[†]

Founder, The Jane Goodall Institute
UN Messenger of Peace

WE ARE LIVING AT A CRITICAL TIME IN HUMAN HISTORY. Our population is increasing at a terrifying rate – there are more than six billion human beings on the planet. The gap between the poor and the rich has widened. Millions of people live in degrading poverty on less than $2.00 per day, while the urban elite around the world enjoy increasingly luxurious and quite (environmentally) unsustainable lifestyles. We are facing massive loss of wilderness, desertification, widespread pollution, global warming, extinction of species, violence, war and a whole host of social injustices. It seems that there are destructive forces in the world, arising from greed, ignorance and a lack of respect for other people and other life forms that threaten life on the planet as we know it today. I have three young grandchildren, and when I think of how much of the planet we have destroyed since I was a child, I feel deep shame.

Is there anything that can be done to put the brakes on our plunge to destruction, to reverse direction? Of course there is. The trouble is that as individuals we feel helpless in the face of such massive destruction, misery and injustice. We lose hope and fall into apathy. Yet if each one of us each day considered the ecological and social implications of our actions, if each one of us made ethical choices in what we bought, our business practices, our consumer-driven economy would change overnight. Individual actions, collectively, can—and do—affect policy making. Of course, thanks in part to electronic communication, more and more people have begun to understand this.

Many of us, however, do not fully appreciate the far reaching consequences of what we choose to eat. It is important to understand that transforming grain into animal protein is horribly wasteful, and has serious adverse effects on the environment. On the other hand, a diet based on organically grown plant foods is both healthy and environmentally sustainable. Gradually transitioning towards such a diet would be one of the wisest choices you could make if you are concerned with your health, the health of the planet and the future of our children.

The Blossoming Lotus is a pioneer in bringing this healing awareness into our hearts and homes. Their Vegan World Fusion Cuisine Cookbook serves as a manual for sustainable, nonviolent living, painting a picture of a world without boundaries, where all cultures are celebrated and all people are treated with respect and caring.

The creative and delicious recipes in this book come from all corners of the globe, as do the wisdom quotes and inspirational photography. There is much here that will encourage you and help you discover the sense of well being, wholeness and lightness that results from a vegetarian diet.

Dr. Jane Goodall, 2004

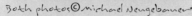

Both photos © Michael Neugebauer

JANE GOODALL began her landmark study of chimpanzees in Tanzania in June 1960, under the mentorship of anthropologist and paleontologist Dr. Louis Leakey. Her work at the Gombe Stream Chimpanzee Reserve would become the foundation of future primatological research and redefine the relationship between humans and animals.

In 1977, Goodall established the Jane Goodall Institute (JGI), which continues the Gombe research and is a global leader in the effort to protect chimpanzees and their habitats. The Institute also is widely recognized for establishing innovative, community-centered conservation and development programs in Africa, and the Roots & Shoots education program with more than 6,000 groups in 87 countries.

Dr. Goodall travels an average 300 days per year speaking about the threats facing chimpanzees, other environmental crises and her reasons for hope that humankind will solve the problems it has imposed on the Earth. She continually urges her audiences to recognize their personal responsibility and ability to effect change through consumer action, lifestyle change and activism.

Dr. Goodall's scores of honors include the Medal of Tanzania, the National Geographic Society's Hubbard Medal, Japan's prestigious Kyoto Prize, the Prince of Asturias Award for Technical and Scientific Research 2003, the Benjamin Franklin Medal in Life Science, and the Gandhi/King Award for Nonviolence. In April 2002 Secretary-General Annan named Dr. Goodall a United Nations "Messenger of Peace." In 2003, Dr. Goodall was named a Dame of the British Empire by Queen Elizabeth II, the equivalent of knighthood.

Her list of publications includes two overviews of her work at Gombe—*In the Shadow of Man* and *Through a Window*—as well as two autobiographies in letters, the spiritual autobiography *Reason for Hope* and many children's books. *The Chimpanzees of Gombe: Patterns of Behavior* is the definitive scientific work on chimpanzees and is the culmination of Jane Goodall's scientific career. She has been the subject of numerous television documentaries and is featured in the large-screen format film, *Jane Goodall's Wild Chimpanzees* (2002).

*Sanctuary chimpanzees. Jane Goodall does not handle wild chimpanzees. †Dame of the British Empire

vegan world fusion cuisine

Blossoming Lotus:
healing ourselves, healing the planet

Aloha and welcome to a transformational journey into new realms of culinary creation. Vegan World Fusion Cuisine is a peaceful and loving approach to food preparation that unites cooking traditions from around the world.

More and more people are affirming that through conscious and wise food choices we can heal our bodies and restore balance to our planet. By honoring the cuisine, art, music and spiritual traditions of the world's cultures we cultivate understanding and peace for all on our precious planet. We trust that you will join us on our journey.

The Blossoming Lotus Café opened its doors on the Hawai'ian Island of Kaua'i on September 9, 2002. We offer an exciting and extensive selection of gourmet Vegan and Live Food cuisine, served in a healing and inspirational setting of world art and music. Our outdoor tropical courtyard is the perfect place to sample our wide selection of healing herbal tea blends and world class desserts. Here you will also find our signature juice bar and bakery where the creations are simply indescribable. Our restaurant and cuisine continue to catch the attention of many, leading *Zento* magazine to describe us as "one of the most innovative and exceptional Vegan restaurants in the world."

A gourmet dining experience at The Blossoming Lotus can be most healing and transcendental. Our cuisine is prepared and served with mindfulness, gratitude and the intention to heal and nurture. We lovingly offer the highest quality ingredients available, selecting those that are organically and locally grown whenever possible.

Here on Kaua'i, we are in the fortunate position of being able to meet travelers from all over the world. Since most people are more open to trying new things while on vacation, we are able to attract those who are seeking a healthier dining alternative but might not normally frequent a Vegan restaurant. Every day we introduce many people to this profound way of eating. When these happy travelers return to their homes, The Blossoming Lotus experience remains as a cherished example of how Vegan cuisine can be transformational, exciting, healthy and delicious.

It is because of you, our island family, friends and worldwide visitors, that we are able to share our vision with the world through this cookbook. This vision is the collective creation of many chefs, artists, healers, musicians and philosophers. It culminates here in the recipes, quotes and images now offered to you. It is our wish for you to experience for yourself the joy of *Vegan World Fusion Cuisine.*

Haleakala Crater, Maui, Hawaii

General Principles in Vegan Natural Food Preparation

A vegetarian diet is one that does not include meat, fish or poultry. There are three types of vegetarian diets. A "lacto-ovo vegetarian" diet includes eggs and dairy products. A "lacto-vegetarian" diet includes dairy products, but not eggs. "Vegan" is a word that is used to describe a diet and lifestyle that does not include the use or consumption of animal-based products. Because it does not include animal products, the phrase "plant based" is sometimes used instead of the word "Vegan". A strict Vegan would not consume honey nor would they wear or use articles containing leather, wool or silk.

On the surface, placing the word "natural" in front of the word "food" seems to be a redundancy. Yet if one were to look at the ingredients listed in many of the "foods" in today's mainstream marketplace, it would become clear why the distinction is an important one. Chemicals, artificial colors, flavors and preservatives are unnecessarily included into many of our foods and therefore into our bodies. "Natural" food preparation is based upon the belief that food is best consumed in as close to its whole, unadulterated state as possible. This means working with fresh fruits, vegetables, nuts and seeds, unprocessed grains, unbleached flours and unrefined oils and sweeteners. It also means leaving out the harmful chemicals and preservatives. The incredible thing is that preparing foods "the natural way" is easier, much healthier, less expensive, more fun and—needless to say—tastes better.

Another principle involved in Vegan natural food preparation emphasizes the connection between eating these "healthier" foods and feeling "healthier". The food you eat is likely to be the most important variable in the healing process. Quite possibly, many of the illnesses that are prevalent today would be prevented, cured or minimized with the aid of appropriate changes in one's diet and lifestyle.

Here, in our cookbook, you will learn how to prepare exciting meals with these pure and simple ingredients. We hope you will feel inspired to share this wisdom with friends and family as you create a more vibrant and healthful life.

Why Vegan

Our food choices have a direct impact upon our health and upon the health of our planet. Most Vegans experience optimal health, increased energy and attunement to their environment.

Much of the information contained in this section is from the landmark book *Diet for a New America*, by John Robbins. Mr. Robbins, who was once the heir to the Baskin-Robbins ice cream franchise fortune, is a pioneer in the Vegan movement. When he began to discover the practices of the meat, dairy and egg industry, he did extensive research, which resulted in the creation of his book. The following information is included to provide a brief

"NEW OPINIONS OFTEN APPEAR FIRST AS JOKES AND FANCIES, THEN AS BLASPHEMIES AND TREASON, THEN AS QUESTIONS OPEN TO DISCUSSION AND FINALLY AS ESTABLISHED TRUTHS." - GEORGE BERNARD SHAW

introduction into some of the reasons why many people choose to adopt a Vegan lifestyle.

Most people who adopt a Vegan lifestyle do so for reasons that would fit into any or all of the following three categories: (1) Health or Medical, (2) Environmental or Political and (3) Moral, Ethical or Religious.

Health or Medical

A great deal of evidence exists indicating that the overconsumption of cholesterol and saturated fats found in animal products leads to heart disease and certain forms of cancer. Other studies have been done suggesting that the over consumption of animal products leads to obesity, diabetes, hypertension, gout and kidney stones.

The modern day method of factory farming is the production method for most of the meat, egg and dairy industries. The conditions on these factory farms necessitates administering various antibiotics, drugs and hormones in order to keep the animals alive as well as to have the animals weigh as much as possible in order to maximize profits. These drugs inevitably make their way into the bodies of the humans that consume them. Mad Cow disease is simply a result of an industry that does not place a high value on the public welfare.

There also seems to be a great deal of evidence indicating that animal products contain higher concentrations of toxic residues from various pesticides and antibiotics. This has resulted in the creation of antibiotic-resistant bacteria. Many human illnesses that were once easily treated with antibiotics are no longer able to be treated with the same dosage or type of antibiotic. This increase in resistance to certain strains of antibiotics is now a global issue that will run out of control unless we adopt a plant based diet.

In their 1995 report, the U.S. Department of Agriculture and the U.S. Department of Health and Services affirmed that all of the body's nutritional needs can be met through a plant based diet. When switching to any form of diet, care is required to ensure that the food one consumes meets all of their personal nutritional needs. Our recipes are designed to ensure this is the case.

Environmental or Political

Many people are now becoming aware of the fact that the Earth has only a limited amount of resources and that these resources must be used wisely. While Earth Day celebrations, awareness of environmental issues, rainforest preservation and global warming initiatives are becoming more widespread, much more still needs to be done. The following is why many people choose to adopt a plant based diet in an effort to conserve and reallocate the Earth's limited resources.

Macchu Piccu, Peru

- Over 60 million people die of starvation every year.

- The livestock population of the U.S. consumes enough grain and soybeans each year to feed over 5 times the human population of the country. Animals are fed over 80% of the corn and 95% of the oats that are grown on our soil.

- Less than half of the harvested agricultural acreage goes to feed people.

- It takes sixteen pounds of grain to produce one pound of meat.

- It requires 3 ½ acres of land per person to support a meat centered diet, 1 ½ acres of land to support a lacto-ovo vegetarian diet and 1/6 of an acre of land to support a Vegan diet.

- If Americans were to reduce meat consumption by just 10 percent, it would free up 12 million tons of grain annually.

- Developing nations use land to raise beef for wealthier nations instead of utilizing that land for sustainable agriculture practices.

- According to the U.S. Department of Agriculture, one acre of land can produce 20,000 pounds of potatoes. This same amount of land can only produce 165 pounds of meat.

- Topsoil is the dark, rich soil that supplies the nutrients to the food we grow. It takes 500 years to produce an inch of topsoil. This topsoil is rapidly vanishing due to clear cutting of forests and cattle grazing practices.

- For each acre of forest land cleared for human purposes, 7 acres of forest is cleared for grazing livestock or growing livestock feed. This includes Federal land that is leased for cattle grazing purposes. This policy greatly accelerates the destruction of our precious forests.

In order to support cattle grazing, South and Central America are destroying their rainforests. These rainforests contain close to half of all the species on Earth and many medicinal plants. Over a thousand species a year are becoming extinct and most of these are from rainforest and tropical settings. This practice also causes the displacement of indigenous peoples who have been living in these environments.

Half of the water used in the U.S. goes to irrigate land growing feed and fodder for livestock. It takes approximately 2,500 gallons of water to produce a single pound of meat. Similarly, it takes approximately 4,000 gallons of water to provide a day's worth of food per person for a meat-centered diet, 1,200 gallons for a lacto-ovo vegetarian diet and 300 gallons for a Vegan diet.

The factory farm industry causes a tremendous amount of ground water pollution due to the chemicals, pesticides and run off waste that is inherent in its practices.

Vegan World Fusion Cuisine

Moral, Ethical
or Religious

Many people adopt a vegetarian diet because of religious or moral beliefs that prohibit the killing of animals. Many of those who adopt a Vegan diet for ethical reasons feel that they do not wish to support practices that inflict harm or suffering on any creature that seems to have the capacity to feel pain.

The small family farm where husbandry practices engendered a certain respect for the animals that were used for food is becoming a thing of the past. Today, most of the world's meat, dairy and egg production occurs on massive factory farms that are owned by agribusiness conglomerates. This has brought about practices that view farm animals solely in terms of their ability to generate profits.

Animals are routinely given chemicals and antibiotics to keep them alive in these conditions. In order to increase the weight of cows, many are fed sawdust, plastic, tallow, grease and cement dust seasoned with artificial flavors and aromas. Dairy cows are forced to remain pregnant most of their lives and are injected with hormones to increase milk production. Male calves born from these cows often are raised to become "veal". This practice consists in confining a newborn calf to a crate that is so small that he or she is unable to turn around. This is to ensure that the flesh remains tender. They are fed diets that are deliberately iron deficient, a practice that induces anemia and allows the flesh to remain white. After four months or so in these conditions, the calf is slaughtered to produce "veal".

For more information on Veganism please contact some of the organizations listed in the Resource Guide in Chapter 13 or visit our web site at www.veganfusion.com.

< Mt. Waialeale, Kauai, Hawaii

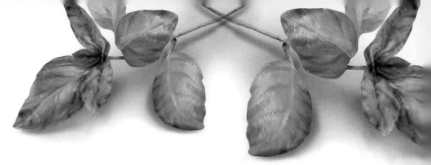

"THERE ARE TWO WAYS TO LIVE YOUR LIFE, ONE IS AS THOUGH NOTHING IS A MIRACLE, THE OTHER IS AS THOUGH EVERYTHING IS A MIRACLE." - ALBERT EINSTEIN

Go Organic

Organic farming represents a cycle of sustainability that starts and ends with the Earth. The flow of this wheel of life is from seed to food to compost and back to the soil. Even though you have heard the term "organic" for many years, we feel it is more important than ever for all of us to focus attention on this movement. The Organic Trade Association defines their trade by stating that "organic farming is based on practices that maintain soil fertility, while assisting nature's balance through diversity and recycling of energy and nutrients. This method also strives to avoid or reduce the use of synthetic fertilizers and pest controls. Organic foods are processed, packaged, transported and stored to retain maximum nutritional value, without the use of artificial preservatives, coloring or other additives, irradiation or synthetic pesticides."

Organic products are grown without the use of powerful and toxic chemical pesticides or fertilizers, many of which have not been fully tested for their effects on humans. Organic farmers employ farming methods that respect the fragile balance of our ecosystem. This results in a fraction of the ground water pollution and topsoil depletion that is generated by conventional methods. Most people have also found the taste and nutrient quality of organic products to be superior to that of conventionally grown food.

Another reason to support organic farmers has to do with the health of the farm workers themselves. Farm workers on conventional farms are exposed to high levels of toxic pesticides on a daily basis. This is believed to bring about many forms of short-term illnesses and often fatal diseases. Finally, by supporting organic farmers, we are supporting small, family farms. This once prevalent method of farming is rapidly disappearing. This is due to the small farmer's inability to compete with the heavily subsidized agribusiness farms that use synthetic soil, pesticides, crop dusters and heavy machinery on lands that encompass thousands of acres.

For more information and to support the organic movement please see the listings in the resource guide in chapter 13 and shop at your local health food store.

The moai statues of Rapa Nui,
Easter Island, Chile

We are what we eat... please choose wisely

GMO Awareness

GMOs (Genetically engineered and Modified Organisms) and genetic engineering pose a profound threat to people, the environment and our agricultural heritage. GMO-Free Kauai aims to raise awareness and educate the public about the health, economic and environmental risks of genetically engineered organisms, while providing meaningful ways to work together and be GMO-free. Please join us in this critical movement to move Hawaiian agriculture away from genetic engineering and towards truly sustainable agriculture. Call us at (808)651-9603, email us at gmofreekauai@care2.com, or visit us on the web at www.gmofreekauai.org. Of course, Kaua'i is but a microcosm of planet Earth. This is a worldwide movement of conscious beings striving to raise awareness on this critical topic. For more info, please contact us at our web site www.veganfusion.com.

Transition Dieting

This cookbook is designed with "transition dieting" in mind. "Transition dieting" acknowledges that most people do not make diet or lifestyle changes overnight and are not willing to instantly sacrifice all of the foods they are accustomed to eating. It affirms that long lasting dietary changes are more likely if made gently, with foods that are delicious and easy to prepare. To honor this, each chapter includes a wide selection of Vegan cuisine, ranging from the heavier "comfort foods" for those beginning to introduce more natural foods into their diet, to living foods selections, which many consider the most pure and healthful form of cuisine. The sample menus on pages 216-217 list the items that are recommended for each stage of the journey to a healthier and lighter diet.

Choose Life... Living Foods

There is a growing interest in preparing foods that have not been cooked. It is coming to be a specialized area within Vegan food preparation. These Living Foods are nutrient rich foods that have not been heated above 116 degrees. This preserves the heat sensitive enzymes and allows for the maximum amount of the naturally occurring life force to remain in the food. Instead of cooking the food, Live Food preparation involves soaking, sprouting and dehydrating to create the flavors desired. People on a Live Food diet report feeling healthier and more vibrant than ever before.

The Blossoming Lotus has been specializing in Live Food preparation since its inception. We include our favorite Live Food recipes in virtually every chapter (look for the lotus 🪷 to find these incredible Live Food items). You might discover, as you prepare the recipes in this book, that you will naturally gravitate towards these delicious items.

$e = mc^2 \ldots$ the Theory of Relativity

Please realize that there are many variables involved in recipe creation and that there is always a measure of flexibility in the recipes. Many factors such as ripeness, sweetness and bitterness can create different tastes. Oven temperatures and blender speeds may vary slightly, altering cooking times and the consistency of dishes. Electric and gas ranges heat food differently, altitude and humidity will affect timing as well. Please develop an intuition for which flavors work for you. Use the recipes as a starting point to explore your own culinary creativity.

The recipes in this book are chosen and designed to assist you in awakening the creative chef within. Each recipe teaches a specific technique in Vegan natural food preparation. By preparing these recipes and learning these general techniques, you will acquire the skills necessary to become a world-class Vegan chef.

Healing Teas & Elixirs

Herbs and teas have been used for healing for thousands of years. The Blossoming Lotus specializes in the offering of international teas and elixirs from around the world. We house over 30 international healing teas designed to compliment our Vegan cuisine. A few of the teas offered include: South American Lapacho, Hawaiian Kava Kava, African Honeybush, South African Rooibos, South American Yerba Mate, Peruvian Maca, Chinese Pu Erh and Japanese Bancha to name a few. By serving these herbal teas, The Blossoming Lotus is spreading the word regarding their incredible healing benefits as well as helping to support indigenous cultures. Enjoy!

Compassion in Action

We aspire to serve as an example of how a business can be run with integrity and compassion. We strive for social and environmental responsibility before looking at the bottom line. We gather as *'ohana*, family, devoted to healing—the healing of our selves, our relations and our precious planet. United with local organic farmers, we are committed to initiating a cycle of sustainability on the island of Kaua'i. Using organic ingredients and composting as much as possible allows us to minimize our impact on our fragile home.

We now wish to share our intentions and practices with the rest of the world. The Blossoming Lotus has created a business model which is an example of how integrity and kindness leads to ultimate success—something you can feel and taste.

Giving Thanks

Please take a moment before preparing or partaking of the recipes. Take a breath and give thanks. Send love to all those involved in the wheel of life from seed to table. Give thanks for the bounty of the Earth that provides for all of our needs. Feel the appreciation of working with natural and organically grown ingredients. Appreciate the low impact that plant based diets have upon our fragile home and the other living creatures that bless us with their presence. Give thanks for the indigenous peoples, clean water, pure air, fertile soil and the flourishing rainforests that your actions are supporting.

Aloha

The word *aloha* is made up of two parts. *Alo* means "to share" and *ha* means "breath". *Aloha* may be translated as "to share breath," or, more poetically, "to share the breath of life." When this sharing of the breath of life is combined with a love and respect for the Earth and a sense of grateful stewardship it is called *aloha 'aina*.

The Blossoming Lotus serves as an example of how this positive aloha 'aina vibration can thrive in a commercial setting. Treat yourself to a unique dining experience of international, organic gourmet Vegan and Live Food cuisine in a healing environment of world art and music. It is our sincere hope that you will be inspired as you prepare these dishes to create a similar environment in your own home. Mahalo (Give Thanks) for sharing in our space, together we are creating the world in which we wish to live—a world where our children can live in peace.

In Love and Light, the Chefs of the Lotus

2

santori summer rolls page

appetizers
snacks
spreads

ROASTED RED PEPPER HUMMUS

BABA GANOUSH

SUMMER ROLLS WITH PEANUT SAUCE

SPINACH STUFFED MUSHROOMS

MANGO CHUTNEY

PINEAPPLE MACADAMIA SALSA

SALSA FRESCA

PAPAYA PINE NUT SALSA

ANTIPASTO

GUACAMOLE

BBQ TEMPEH KEBOBS
 WITH GRILLED VEGETABLES

BASIL PATÉ

SUNDRIED TOMATO PATÉ

CASHEW CHEEZ

DEHYDRATED FLAX CRACKERS

LIVING CHARD ROLLS

SUNFLOWER SEED DIP

CARROT ALMOND PATÉ NORI ROLLS

ALOHA PATÉ

RADICAL ROASTED RED PEPPER HUMMUS

20 min prep / 35 minutes cooking / 6-8 servings

3 C	Garbanzo beans, cooked & well drained (page 209)
1 large	Red bell pepper (1 C roasted)
¾ C	Tahini, roasted (creamy)
¼ C	Lemon juice, fresh squeezed
3 Tbl	Nama shoyu
1 Tbl	Olive oil
2 tsp	Cumin powder, toasted (page 194)
1 ½ tsp	Garlic, minced
¾ tsp	Sea salt, or to taste
¾ tsp	Black pepper, ground to taste
¼ tsp	Cayenne pepper

loving preparation

1. Preheat oven to 400°. Roast bell pepper according to instructions on page 193.
2. Place pepper in food processor with lemon juice, shoyu and olive oil and process until blended well.
3. Add garbanzo beans and remaining ingredients and process until smooth.

serving suggestion and variations

⤳ Serve with toasted pita triangles or as part of a Mideast platter with Live Tabouli (page 153) or Couscous Salad (page 80) or replace red pepper with one of the following:

⤳ *Garlic Lover's* 1½ C roasted garlic, 1½ tsp minced fresh garlic.

⤳ *Sundried Tomato Basil* ½ C sundried tomatoes, soaked & drained, 2 Tbl basil, minced.

⤳ *Calamata Rosemary* 1½ Tbl fresh rosemary, minced, ¾ C Calamata olives, chopped.

BATHSHEBA'S BABA GANOUSH

20 min prep / 35 min cooking / 2-3 servings

2 medium	Eggplant (1 ½ C roasted)
3 Tbl	Olive oil
3 Tbl	Tahini, roasted (creamy)
¾ tsp	Cumin powder, toasted
3 Tbl	Lemon juice, fresh squeezed
1 ½ Tbl	Italian parsley, minced
2 tsp	Nama shoyu
1 ½ tsp	Garlic, minced
½ tsp	Mirin
½ tsp	Sea salt, or to taste
½ tsp	Black pepper, ground to taste
Pinch	Cayenne pepper

loving preparation

1. Preheat oven to 375°. Slice eggplant in half, place face down on well oiled baking sheet and roast until a knife can easily pass through any part of the eggplant, approximately 35 minutes.
2. Combine with remaining ingredients in food processor and process until smooth.

"WHAT'S SO FUNNY ABOUT PEACE, LOVE AND UNDERSTANDING?" - ELVIS COSTELLO

SATORI SUMMER ROLLS

40 minutes / 8 rolls

8 sheets	Rice paper
•	Hot water
2 c	Rice mixture (see below)
¾ c	Rice noodles, cooked
¾ c	Carrots, shredded
16 leaves	Basil, fresh
16 leaves	Mint, fresh

Rice Mixture

2 c	Brown rice, cooked (page 206)
½ c	Coconut milk
1 Tbl	Nama shoyu
Pinch	Crushed red pepper flakes

loving preparation

1. Combine rice mixture ingredients in a large bowl and mix well.
2. Fill a shallow pan half full with hot water. Place a rice paper sheet in the hot water and remove when soft, approximately a minute. Lay individually on a clean, natural-fiber towel.
3. Place ¼ c of rice mixture on the bottom portion of the rice paper. Flatten to form into a small rectangle. Top with a small amount of rice noodles, a small amount of carrots, 2 mint leaves and 2 basil leaves. Fold sides toward center and roll up. Rolls should be thin and tightly rolled. Place in a container and cover with a clean, slightly moist towel until ready to serve.

serving suggestion & variations

↬ Slice diagonally and serve with Peanut Sauce (this page).
↬ Add a variety of vegetables such as sunflower seed sprouts, grated daikon radish or sliced avocado.

PRIMAL PEANUT SAUCE

10 minutes / 2 ½ cups

1 ¾ c	Coconut milk
⅓ c	Peanut butter
2 ½ Tbl	Maple syrup, or to taste
2 Tbl	Nama shoyu, or to taste
½ tsp	Curry paste (page 197)
¼ tsp	Crushed red pepper flakes

loving preparation

1. Place all ingredients in a blender and blend until smooth.

variations

↬ Replace peanut butter with almond butter or other nut butter.

SOCRATES SPINACH STUFFED MUSHROOMS

25 min prep / 20 min cooking / 12 – 15 mushrooms

12-15	Stuffing mushrooms
1 recipe	Lemon Herb Marinade (page 195)
1 Tbl	Olive oil
¼ C	Shallots, minced
½ C	Portabello mushrooms, diced
1 small bunch	Spinach, steamed & drained to yield ½ C (page 193)
¼ C	Tomato, chopped
1 tsp	Basil, minced
1 tsp	Italian parsley, minced
1 ½ tsp	Nutritional yeast

¾ tsp	Nama shoyu (optional)
½ tsp	Mirin
½ tsp	Garlic, minced
Pinch	Crushed red pepper flakes
•	Sea salt, to taste
•	Black pepper, ground to taste
3 Tbl	Bread crumbs (page 93) for garnish
3 Tbl	Pine nuts, toasted (page 194) for garnish

loving preparation

1. Preheat oven to 375°. Wipe clean stuffing mushrooms, remove any stems and place in a shallow baking dish with Lemon Herb Marinade for 20 minutes or longer.
2. While mushrooms are marinating, place oil in a small sauté pan on medium high heat. Add shallots and portabello mushrooms and cook for 5 minutes, stirring frequently. Add tomatoes and spinach and cook for 3 minutes, stirring occasionally. Add remaining ingredients, except pine nuts and bread crumbs, mix well and remove from heat.
3. Spoon a small amount of mixture into each mushroom, top with breadcrumbs and pine nuts, bake until mushrooms are slightly soft, approximately 10 minutes. Be careful not to overcook.

serving suggestions

↬ Serve on its own or serve with a dipping sauce of Roasted Red Pepper Sauce (page 60), Nut Cheez (page 29) or Live Alfreda Sauce (page 82).

Greek Orthodox Monastery of Rousanou, Meteora, Greece

"THERE WILL BE NO END TO THE TROUBLE OF STATES,

OR OF HUMANITY ITSELF, UNTIL PHILOSOPHERS BECOME KINGS IN THIS

WORLD, OR UNTIL THOSE WE NOW CALL KINGS AND RULERS REALLY AND

TRULY BECOME PHILOSOPHERS, AND POLITICAL POWER AND PHILOSOPHY

THUS COME INTO THE SAME HANDS." - PLATO

MAHADEV'S MANGO CHUTNEY

20 min prep / 20 min cooking / 2-3 servings

2 Tbl	Sesame oil		1 ½ tsp	Mirin
½ tsp	Cumin seed		1 ½ tsp	Nama shoyu
½ tsp	Brown mustard seed		2 Tbl	Sucanat
1 small	Yellow onion, diced (¾ c)		2 Tbl	Cilantro, minced
1 Tbl	Ginger, peeled & minced		½ tsp	Sea salt
1 ½ tsp	Jalapeño pepper, seeded, minced		¼ tsp	Coriander powder
3 medium	Mango, firm, chopped (3 c)		¼ tsp	Black pepper, ground to taste
¼ c	Red bell pepper, diced		Pinch	Cardamom powder
1 ½ tsp	Apple cider vinegar, raw		Pinch	Cayenne pepper

loving preparation

1. Place oil in a 3 qt saucepan on medium high heat. Add cumin and mustard seeds and cook for one minute, stirring constantly. Add onion and jalapeño, cook for 5 minutes, stirring frequently.
2. Add mango, bell pepper, apple cider vinegar, mirin and shoyu, cook for 5 minutes on low heat, stirring frequently. Add remaining ingredients, remove from heat and serve.

"AH! HOW WONDERFUL! BENEATH THE BANYAN TREE, THE

DISCIPLES ARE ELDERS, THE PRECEPTOR IS YOUNG.

THE INSTRUCTION GIVEN BY THE PRECEPTOR IS SILENCE,

AND THE DOUBTS OF THE DISCIPLES ARE DISPELLED."

- HYMN TO DAKSHINAMURTI

PELE'S PINEAPPLE MAC NUT SALSA

35 minutes / 6 cups

1 large	Pineapple, ripe
¾ C	Macadamia nuts, dry roasted, chopped (page 194)
½ C	Red bell pepper, diced
¼ C	Red onion, diced
2 Tbl	Lime juice, fresh squeezed
2 Tbl	Cilantro, minced & packed firm
1 Tbl	Cumin powder, toasted (page 194)
1 Tbl	Mirin
1 ½ tsp	Jalapeño, seeded & diced
1 ½ tsp	Garlic, minced
1 ½ tsp	Chili powder
½ tsp	Sea salt, or to taste
½ tsp	Hot sauce, or to taste (page 214)
Pinch	Cayenne pepper

loving preparation

1. Preheat grill. Skin & cut pineapple into ½" slices and grill until there are charmarks on both sides, flipping occasionally. Chop into ¼" cubes, approx. 5 C.
2. Place with the remaining ingredients in a large mixing bowl and mix well.

SANTIAGO'S SALSA FRESCA

15 minutes / 2 ½ cups

4 small	Roma tomatoes, chopped (2 C)
½ C	Red onion, diced
2 Tbl	Cilantro, minced
2 Tbl	Lime juice, fresh squeezed
1 tsp	Jalapeño, seeded & minced
½ tsp	Garlic, minced
½ tsp	Sea salt, or to taste
¼ tsp	Black pepper, ground to taste
¼ tsp	Chili powder
¼ tsp	Cumin powder
Pinch	Cayenne pepper

loving preparation

1. Place all ingredients in a large mixing bowl and mix well.

PILANI'S PAPAYA PINE NUT SALSA

20 minutes / 2 cups

2 C	Papaya, ripe & firm, cleaned & chopped into ½" cubes
¼ C	Red onion, diced
¼ C	Pine nuts, toasted (page 194)
2 Tbl	Cilantro, minced
2 Tbl	Lime juice, fresh squeezed
1 tsp	Jalapeño, seeded & minced (optional)
½ tsp	Garlic, minced (optional)
½ tsp	Chili powder
•	Cumin powder, toasted
Pinch	Cayenne pepper
•	Sea salt, to taste
•	Black pepper, ground to taste

loving preparation

1. Place all ingredients in a large mixing bowl & mix well.

variations

↬ For **Roasted Corn and Garlic Salsa**, replace papaya with 2 C roasted corn, 1 C roasted garlic (page 193) and 1 C of chopped tomato.

serving suggestions

↬ Serve as part of a Feista Platter with Guacamole (page 26), topped with Sour Crème (page 196), baked blue corn tortilla chips and Flax Seed Crackers (page 30).
↬ Serve over grilled tempeh or tofu cutlet.

ATHENA'S ANTIPASTO PLATTER

45 minutes / 8 servings

8 slices	Brushcetta (see below)
1 recipe	Tapenade (see below)
1 large	Red bell pepper, roasted & sliced into eight ½" strips (page 193)
8 rings	Grilled onion, sliced (page 194)
1 cutlet	Tofu, tempeh or ulu, grilled & sliced into 8 uniform pieces (page 194)
4 large	Artichoke hearts, cooked & quartered (page 213)
8	Greek olives

Tapenade Spread

1 C	Kalamata or other olives
1 Tbl	Olive oil
1 Tbl	Lemon juice, fresh squeezed
1 Tbl	Nutritional yeast
2 tsp	Capers
1 ½ tsp	Garlic, fresh minced

Bruschetta

1	Whole grain baguette, sliced thin
1 recipe	Basting sauce (page 196)
1 Tbl	Garlic, minced (optional)
•	Sea salt, to taste
•	Black pepper, ground to taste

Dipping Sauce

¼ C	Olive oil
1 Tbl	Balsamic vinegar
2 Tbl	Fresh herbs, minced (try basil, parsley or your favorite)
1 tsp	Lemon juice, fresh squeezed
¼ tsp	Garlic, minced (optional)
•	Sea salt, to taste
•	Black pepper, ground to taste

loving preparation

1. For **Bruschetta**, preheat oven to 400°, place bread slices on a well oiled baking sheet, brush liberally with basting sauce, and top with minced garlic, salt and pepper to taste. Place in oven and bake until top is crispy golden, approximately 10 minutes.
2. For **Tapenade**, place all ingredients in food processor and pulse chop until olives are just finely minced. Timing is important. Please do not over process or it will turn into a uniform paste.
3. Spread a small amount of tapenade on each brushetta. Top with sliced, roasted red bell pepper and grilled onion.
4. Place artichoke heart on piece of grilled tofu, tempeh or ulu. Top with greek olive, held together with a toothpick. Serve with dipping sauce or other sauce of choice.

serving suggestion & variations

- Be creative and imaginative in your display. Serve with a dipping sauce of choice such as Peanut (page 21), BBQ (page 26) or Sweet and Sour (page 125).
- Replace tapenade with another spread such as Hummus (page 20), Sour Crème (page 196) or Pesto (page 113 or 140) and serve over flax crackers topped with chopped tomatoes and chopped fresh basil or other herbs.
- Bell peppers and onion may be replaced with sundried tomatoes, roasted garlic cloves or other roasted or grilled veggies, cut to the appropriate size for the toast.
- Smoked fresh coconut meat (page 212) is wonderful as a topping combined with roasted red pepper.

GRAÇIAS À DIOS GUACAMOLE

15 minutes / 2 ¼ cups

2 medium	Avocados, chopped (1 ½ c)
1 c	Tomato, diced, or salsa of your choosing
¼ c	Red onion, diced
3 Tbl	Lime juice, fresh squeezed
2 Tbl	Cilantro, minced
1 ½ tsp	Jalapeño pepper, seeded & minced
1 tsp	Garlic, minced
1 tsp	Nama shoyu (optional)
½ tsp	Sea salt, or to taste
¼ tsp	Black pepper, ground to taste
¼ tsp	Chili powder
Pinch	Cayenne pepper
1 Tbl	Sour crème (optional, page 196)

loving preparation

1. Place all ingredients in a large mixing bowl and mix well.

serving suggestions

- Serve as a dip for corn chips or Flax Seed Crackers (page 30).
- Add as a filling for Baba B's Burrito (page 86).
- Use as a topping for Grilled Tempeh Mexicana (page 117).

BODHISATTVA'S BBQ TEMPEH KEBOBS

30 min prep / 15 min cooking / 6-8 kebobs

6-8	Kebob skewers
8 oz	Tempeh, ¾" cubes
1 medium	Bell pepper, 1" chop
½ medium	Red onion, quartered
6-8 medium	Cherry tomatoes
1 large	Portabello mushroom, 1" cubes
1 recipe	Shoyu Marinade (page 195)

BBQ Sauce

¼ c	Barley malt syrup
¼ c	Catsup (page 197)
2 Tbl	Safflower oil
2 tsp	Apple cider vinegar, raw
2 tsp	Vegetarian Worcestershire sauce
1 tsp	Stone ground mustard
½ tsp	Chili powder
½ tsp	Paprika
¼ tsp	Liquid smoke (optional, see *Glossary*)
Pinch	Cayenne pepper, or to taste

loving preparation

1. Combine BBQ sauce ingredients in a medium size bowl and whisk well. Place tempeh and vegetables in the bowl, mix well and allow to marinate for 20 minutes, stirring occasionally.
2. Decoratively arrange tempeh and vegetables on skewers, finishing each with a cherry tomato. Grill until char marks appear and tempeh and vegetables are cooked through, approximately 15 minutes. Baste with Basting Sauce (page 196) as grilling and top with remaining BBQ sauce before serving.

Mt. Everest, Nepal

SAL KENT'S BASIL ALMOND PATÉ

20 minutes / 2 cups

1 c	Almonds
1 c	Basil, tightly packed
¼ c	Filtered water
¼ c	Olive oil
2 Tbl	Lemon juice, fresh squeezed
1 Tbl	Nama shoyu
2 tsp	Garlic, minced
•	Sea salt, to taste
•	Black pepper, ground to taste
•	Cayenne pepper, to taste

loving preparation

1. Soak almonds according to method on page 202.
2. Place almonds in a food processor and process until smooth.
3. Add remaining ingredients and process until smooth.

SUN RU'S SUNDANCE SUNDRIED TOMATO PATÉ

35 minutes / 2½ ccups

1¼ c	Almonds
¾ c	Sundried tomatoes
⅔ c	Sundried tomato soak water
½ c	Basil, tightly packed
2 Tbl	Lemon juice, fresh squeezed
2 tsp	Nama shoyu, or to taste
1 tsp	Garlic, minced (optional)
¼ tsp	Sea salt, or to taste
¼ tsp	Black pepper, ground to taste
Pinch	Cayenne pepper
1½ Tbl	Flax oil

loving preparation

1. Soak almonds according to method on page 202.
2. Soak tomatoes in warm filtered water for 20 minutes. Drain and set aside ⅔ c of the soak water.
3. Place almonds in a food processor and process until smooth.
4. Add remaining ingredients and process until smooth.

serving suggestions

꙳ Enjoy on its own with a salad, or use as a spread in Live Nori Rolls (page 32) or as a spread for a Live Sandwich (page 112).

"YOU GOT TO GET IN TO GET OUT." - PETER GABRIEL

28

CONQUERING LION CASHEW CHEEZ

20 min prep / 6 hrs-overnight culturing / 3-4 servings

2 c	Cashews	1 tsp	Garlic, minced (optional)
1 c	Filtered water	1 tsp	Nama shoyu, or to taste
⅓ c	Red bell pepper, diced	¼ tsp	Sea salt, or to taste
2½ Tbl	Green onion, diced	Pinch	Crushed red pepper flakes
2 Tbl	Cilantro, minced		

loving preparation

1. Blend cashews with filtered water until *very* smooth. Place in a ½ gallon open-mouthed glass jar. Cover tightly with plastic wrap and secure with a rubber band. Cover with a towel and allow to sit in a warm place overnight.
2. Pour cashew mixture into a large mixing bowl, combine with remaining ingredients and mix well.

variations

- Delicious when made with macadamia nuts or pine nuts.
- Blend 1 c of chopped red pepper with cultured cashew mixture, before adding the remaining ingredients.
- Replace cilantro with other fresh herbs.
- Add ¼ c grated carrots or beets.
- Replace bell pepper with other fresh veggies.

serving suggestion

- Use as a dip for Flax Crackers (page 30).
- Use as a spread in Live Nori Rolls (page 32) or scoop into a salad.

CONQUERING LION BREAKS EVERY CHAIN

DEVA SHAKTI'S DEHYDRATED FLAX CRACKERS

1 hour prep / 12 hrs dehydrating / 2 trays

Savory

2 c	Flax seeds
½ c	Sundried tomatoes, soaked in 1 c luke warm water until soft
1¼ c	Sunflower seeds or pumpkin seeds, soaked & drained (page 202)
1 Tbl	Nama shoyu, or to taste
1 tsp	Lemon juice, fresh squeezed
1 tsp	Sea salt, or to taste
½ tsp	Black pepper, ground to taste
½ tsp	Crushed red pepper flakes
¼ c	Fresh mixed herbs, chopped (experiment with basil, dill, oregano, parsley, thyme or your favorite)

Rosemary Lavender

2 c	Flax seeds
1¼ c	Almonds or macadamia nuts, soaked & drained (page 202)
½ c	Shitake mushrooms soaked in 1 c water
1 Tbl	Black sesame seeds
1 Tbl	Nama shoyu, or to taste
1 Tbl	Sage, minced (½ Tbl dry)
2 tsp	Rosemary, minced (1 tsp dry)
2 tsp	Lavender flowers
1 tsp	Sea salt, or to taste
½ tsp	Black pepper, ground to taste

Sweet

2 c	Flax seeds
2 c	Walnuts or cashews, soaked & drained (page 202)
½ c	Dried figs or other dried fruit soaked in 1 c filtered water
½ c	Dates, soaked in water until soft, then drained
1 Tbl	Fresh mint, minced (½ Tbl dry)
1 tsp	Sea salt, or to taste
1 tsp	Ginger, peeled & minced
1 tsp	Anise seeds (optional)

loving preparation

1. For each variety, place flax seeds in a large mixing bowl with 2 ½ c of filtered water and allow seeds to soak until all liquid is absorbed and seeds are gelatinous, at least 30 minutes.
2. Place all other ingredients including soak water in food processor and process until smooth. Place in large mixing bowl with flax seeds and mix well.
3. Spread thinly and evenly on teflex dehydrator sheets, place in dehydrator and dehydrate at 115° for 6 hours. Flip and transfer to a mesh screen for remaining 6 hours to ensure even dehydrating.

serving suggestion

- Serve with Nut Cheez (page 29) or any of the Live Food patés, or other spreads and dips such as hummus (page 20), guacamole (page 26) and salsa (page 24).
- Spread a thicker layer, dehydrate longer until crispy, and use as a flax cracker pizza crust for live pizza (page 113).

variations

- Needless to say, flax crackers are a staple for today's Vegan. Experiment with adding various herbs and spices to each batch. Highlighting an herb or spice in a dish allows you to discover each one's individual flavor and unique quality; try **Indian** spices such as cumin powder, curry and cilantro. **Mexican** spices such as chili powder, cumin powder, jalapeño and cilantro.

EVER LIVING
EVER GIVING CHARD ROLLS

15 minutes / 1 serving

1 large	Chard leaf, rinsed well
¼ C	Live foods paté (pages 28 & 32)
1 Tbl	Nut Cheez (page 29)
1 slice	Avocado
Sprinkle	Mung beans sprouts
1 Tbl	Carrots, grated

loving preparation

1. Lay out a chard leaf on a clean flat surface. Place a small scoop of paté towards the bottom of the leaf in the center, form into a small rectangle.
2. Top with Nut Cheez, avocado, mung sprouts, and carrots. Fold in sides and roll away from you, like a burrito, until all the filling is enclosed and roll is as firm as possible. Slice in half and enjoy with Cucumber Mint Dressing (page 57) or sauce of choice.

variations

- Experiment with different patés, Nut Cheez and veggies. Amounts of paté, Nut Cheez and veggies used will depend upon size of chard leaf.
- Chard leaf may be replaced with collards, cut into squares and used as the "bread layers" for a live club sandwich.

"WE MUST NOT ALLOW THE CLOCK AND THE CALENDAR TO BLIND US TO THE FACT THAT EACH MOMENT OF LIFE IS A MIRACLE AND MYSTERY." - H.G. WELLS

JAI TO THE MOST HIGH
SUNFLOWER SEED DIP

15 minutes / 2-3 servings / soaking time

1 C	Sunflower seeds
¼ C	Lemon juice, fresh squeezed
½ C	Filtered water
2 medium	Sundried tomatoes, soaked in warm water
2 Tbl	Red bell pepper, diced
1 Tbl	Green onion, diced
1 Tbl	Olives, sliced thin
2 tsp	Basil, minced
2 tsp	Italian parsley, minced
1 tsp	Apple cider vinegar, raw
1 tsp	Nama Shoyu, or to taste
½ tsp	Garlic, minced (optional)
¼ tsp	Oregano, fresh minced
¼ tsp	Sea salt, or to taste
¼ tsp	Black pepper, ground to taste

loving preparation

1. Soak sunflower seeds according to method on page 202.
2. Soak sundried tomatoes for 20 minutes. Drain & chop small and place in a large mixing bowl.
3. Place soaked and drained sunflower seeds, lemon juice, water and garlic in food processor and process until smooth.
4. Place all ingredients in the large bowl and mix well. For best results allow to sit for a few hours before serving.

variations

- Serve as a stuffing in a large tomato or colored bell peppers as the main component of a large mixed green salad.
- Top with Nut Cheez (page 29). It can also be served as a spread for sandwiches or Live Nori Rolls (page 32).

CARPE DIEM CARROT ALMOND PATÉ NORI ROLLS

20 minutes prep / 4 servings

4 sheets	Nori, sundried for sushi
1 recipe	Cashew or Macadamia Cheez (optional, page 29)
•	Salad greens, avocado, sprouts, grated carrots and beets and assorted veggies for fillings

Carrot Almond Paté

1 C	Almonds
1 C	Carrots, chopped
2 Tbl	Filtered water
2 Tbl	Lemon juice, fresh squeezed
1 Tbl	Ginger, peeled and minced
1 tsp	Turmeric root, fresh peeled and minced (optional, please do not substitute dry powder for fresh root)
1 tsp	Dill, minced (½ tsp dry)
½ tsp	Nama shoyu, or to taste (optional)
Pinch	Cayenne pepper
•	Sea salt, to taste
•	Black pepper, ground to taste

loving preparation

1. Soak almonds according to method on page 202.
2. Place *Paté* ingredients in food processor and process until smooth.
3. Place nori sheet on bamboo mat if you wish. Spread ½ C of pate on nori sheet, top with 2 Tbl of Nut Cheez (optional) and wrap fillings of choice. Experiment with amount of filling to create the perfect size roll.
4. Moisten the top portion of the sheet with water, roll away from you, creating as firm of a roll as possible. Slice diagonally in half. For dipping, serve with your choice of live dressing or sauce.

serving suggestion

⚬ Serve in stuffed veggies like tomato, cucumber or zucchini.

AMMACHI'S ALOHA PATÉ

45 minutes / 3-4 servings

½ C	Almonds
½ C	Cashews or macadamia nuts
½ C	Sunflower seeds
⅓ C	Carrot, chopped
⅓ C	Beet, chopped
2 Tbl	Leek, rinsed well & diced
¼ C	Daikon radish, diced
¼ C	Green bell pepper, diced
1 Tbl	Basil, Italian parsley or cilantro, minced
½ tsp	Garlic, minced (optional)
•	Sea salt, to taste
•	Black pepper, ground to taste
dash	Nama shoyu (optional)

loving preparation

1. Place all ingredients in food processor and process until smooth. A small amount of water may be added to ensure ease in processing.

serving suggestions

⚬ For best results allow to sit for several hours or overnight before serving.
⚬ This is a relatively "heavy" paté, good for those just transitioning to Live Foods.
⚬ Use as a sandwich spread or as a spread on Raw Nori Rolls with avocado, sprouts, Nut Cheez (page 29) and grated veggies.

3

Sister Jah Love Roasted Squash Soup, page 47

soups

BROCCOLI BISQUE

MIDEAST CHICKPEA

POTATO FENNEL LEEK

SPLIT PEA & ROASTED PARSNIP

MINESTRONE

COCO PURPLE POTATO

ROASTED SQUASH

BLACK BARLEY CORN

FIRE ROASTED GAZPACHO

CHICKEN-FREE NOODLE SOUP

ROASTED RED PEPPER & TOASTED PINE NUT

BLACK BEAN

LIVE CORN CHOWDER

LIVE GARDEN VEGGIE

LIVE LAVENDER-INFUSED CARROT GINGER

LIVE MELON SOUP

BHAKTI'S BROCCOLI BISQUE

25 min prep, / 20 minutes cooking / 3-4 servings

5 c	Filtered water or vegetable stock	2 tsp	Sea salt, or to taste
3 ½ c	Broccoli flowerettes	1 tsp	Dill, fresh minced (½ tsp dry)
1 medium	Onion, chopped	Pinch	Crushed red pepper flakes
1 c	Cashews, roasted, (page 194)	•	Black pepper, ground to taste
½ c	Celery, sliced thin	•	Nama shoyu, to taste (optional)
1 Tbl	Garlic, minced		

loving preparation

1. Add filtered water or stock, broccoli, onion, celery and garlic to a 3 qt pot and cook over medium high heat until all veggies are just soft, approximately 20 minutes, stirring occasionally.
2. Remove from heat, allow to cool 10-15 minutes, place in a blender (we recommend a Vita-Mix, see page 192), add cashews and very carefully blend until smooth. Blend in batches, being careful to fill blender only half full. Start with low speed initially, slowly increase speed until desired consistency is reached. Return to pot, add remaining ingredients and stir well.

variations

↬ *Hearty Broccoli Bisque* Add ¾ c of corn or ¾ c coarsely chopped broccoli after blending for more of a textured soup. Allow broccoli to cook through before serving.
↬ *Kali's Cauliflower Bisque* Substitute cauliflower for broccoli and add 1 Tbl of nutritional yeast before blending.
↬ *Creamy Vegetable* Replace broccoli with other veggies like zucchini or corn for a creamy vegetable soup.

other ideas

↬ Experiment with different herbs.
↬ Replace cashews with other toasted nuts or seeds or replace nuts with same measure of coconut milk, soy or rice milk.

"YOUR SACRED SPACE IS WHERE YOU CAN FIND YOURSELF AGAIN AND AGAIN." - JOSEPH CAMPBELL

SHALOM ALECHEM MID EAST CHICK PEA SOUP

20 min prep / 25 min cooking / 4–5 servings

6 c	Filtered water or vegetable stock		1 tsp	Cumin powder, toasted (page 194)
2 c	Onion, chopped		1 tsp	Sea salt, or to taste
1 c	Celery, sliced thin		½ tsp	Black pepper, ground to taste
3 Tbl	Garlic, minced		Pinch	Cayenne pepper
5 c	Chick peas (garbanzo beans)		3 Tbl	Nama shoyu, or to taste
	cooked (page 209)		1 Tbl	Lemon juice, fresh squeezed
¾ c	Tahini, roasted		1 Tbl	Italian parsley, minced

loving preparation

1. Place onion, celery, garlic and water or stock in a 3 qt pot and cook over medium high heat for 20 minutes, stirring occasionally.

2. Add 3 c chickpeas and remaining ingredients except parsley, remove from heat and allow to cool 10-15 minutes. Place in a Vita-Mix blender and blend until smooth. Be careful when blending hot liquids not to fill the blender too full. Return to pot, add parsley and remaining 2 c of chick peas, stir well and cook on low heat for 5 minutes, stirring frequently. Garnish with chopped green onion and a thinly sliced lemon wedge. Serve with warm pita bread.

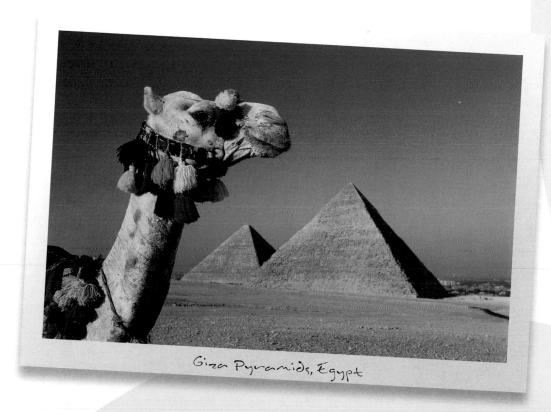

Giza Pyramids, Egypt

ST. PATRICK'S POTATO FENNEL LEEK SOUP

25 min prep / 20 min cooking / 4-5 servings

2 Tbl	Olive oil
1 c	Leek, sliced thin
½ c	Fennel bulb, chopped
2 Tbl	Garlic, minced
6 c	Filtered water or vegetable stock
2 medium	Potatoes, rinsed, chopped (2 ½ c)
1 c	Soy milk
1 Tbl	Italian parsley, minced
2 tsp	Nama shoyu, or to taste
2 tsp	Sea salt, or to taste
½ tsp	Black pepper, ground to taste
Pinch	Cayenne pepper

loving preparation

1. Place oil in a 3 qt pot on medium heat. Add leek, garlic and fennel, cook for 3 minutes, stirring frequently. Add potatoes and water and cook until soft, approximately 20 minutes, stirring occasionally. Add soy milk.
2. Remove from heat and allow to cool 10-15 minutes. Carefully blend in batches, filling the blender half way. Return to pot, add seasonings and stir well.

"MAY WE LIVE IN PEACE WITHOUT WEEPING. MAY OUR JOY OUTLINE THE LIVES WE TOUCH WITHOUT CEASING. AND MAY OUR LOVE FILL THE WORLD, ANGEL WINGS TENDERLY BEATING." - AN IRISH BLESSING

SAHIB'S SPLIT PEA & ROASTED PARSNIP SOUP

20 min prep / 30 min cooking / 4-6 servings

2 c	Parsnip, ½" cubes
2 Tbl	Olive oil
1 ½ c	Onion, diced
¾ c	Celery, diced
¾ c	Carrot, ½" cubes
2 Tbl	Garlic, minced
1 c	Split peas, green or yellow
8-10 c	Filtered water or vegetable stock
3 Tbl	Nama shoyu, or to taste
1 Tbl	Italian parsley, minced
1 tsp	Sea salt, or to taste
½ tsp	Black pepper, ground to taste
¼ tsp	Crushed red pepper flakes
2 drops	Liquid smoke (optional)

loving preparation

1. Preheat oven to 375°. Add parsnips and 1 Tbl of olive oil to a well oiled baking sheet. Mix well and bake until the parsnips are just soft, approximately 20 minutes, stirring occasionally to ensure uniform cooking.
2. While parsnips are cooking, place 1 Tbl of olive oil in a 5 qt pot over medium heat, add onion, celery, carrot and garlic, cook for 5 minutes, stirring occasionally
3. Add 6 c of water or stock and split peas, and cook until peas are soft, approximately 20 minutes, stirring occasionally. Slowly add remaining water or stock, allowing peas to absorb liquid and attain the perfect consistency.
4. Add remaining ingredients, including parsnips, and stir well.

St. Patrick's Potato Fennel Leek soup

GIA BOMBIA'S MOMMA MIA MINESTRONE

45 min prep / 40 min cooking / 8-10 servings

2 Tbl	Olive oil		½ C	Parsnip, roasted, ½" cubes
1 medium	Onion, chopped (1 C)			(optional, page 193)
¼ C	Fennel bulb, diced		½ C	Carrots, chopped
2 Tbl	Garlic, minced		½ C	Zucchini, chopped
1 tsp	Fennel seed		½ C	Summer squash, chopped
1 tsp	Rosemary, fresh, minced		¼ C	Nama shoyu, or to taste
1 tsp	Thyme, fresh, minced		2 Tbl	Tomato paste
	(½ tsp dried)		1 C	Elbow pasta or rotini, wheat-free
7 C	Filtered water or vegetable stock		2 Tbl	Italian parsley, minced
	(page 200)		1 Tbl	Basil, minced
2 C	Crushed tomatoes		1 Tbl	Balsamic vinegar
	or chopped Roma tomatoes		2 tsp	Nutritional yeast
1 C	Garbanzos, cooked (page 209)		2 tsp	Oregano, minced (1 tsp dry)
1 C	Kidney beans, cooked (page 209)		1 tsp	Sea salt, or to taste
1 C	Red potatoes, ½" cubes		½ tsp	Black pepper, ground to taste
½ C	Celery, chopped			

loving preparation

1. Place oil in a large pot on medium heat. Add onion, fennel bulb, garlic, fennel seed, thyme and rosemary, cook for 5 minutes, stirring occasionally.
2. Add filtered water or stock, tomatoes, beans, potato, celery, parsnip, carrot and squashes, cook until vegetables are just soft, approximately 25 minutes, stirring occasionally.
3. Add tomato paste, pasta & herbs and cook until pasta is done, approximately 10 minutes, stirring occasionally.

serving suggestions

- Top with additional nutritional yeast before serving.
- Serve with Focaccia Bread (page 104) cut into triangles. Baste with Basting Sauce (page 196) and minced garlic while baking.

KALALAU'S COCO ULU SOUP

15 min prep / 25 min cooking / 5 servings

5 ½ C	Filtered water or vegetable stock
1 ½ C	Ulu (breadfruit), marinated, grilled & sliced into ½" cubes (page 194)
1 medium	Onion, sliced (1 c)
1 medium	Purple potato, chopped (1 c)
¾ C	Celery, sliced thin

½ C	Carrots, sliced thin
4 tsp	Garlic, minced
1 ¾ C	Coconut milk
¼ C	Nama shoyu, or to taste
½ tsp	Black pepper, ground to taste
½ tsp	Crushed red pepper flakes
1 Tbl	Cilantro, minced
•	Sea salt, to taste

loving preparation

1. Combine water or stock, ulu, onion, potatoes, celery, carrots and garlic in a 3 qt pot and cook on medium high heat for 20 minutes, stirring occasionally. Add coconut milk and cook for 5 more minutes, stirring occasionally. Add remaining ingredients, stir well and remove from heat.

Kalalau Valley, Kaua'i, Hawai'i

"FIRST KEEP THE PEACE WITHIN YOURSELF, THEN YOU CAN ALSO BRING PEACE TO OTHERS." - THOMAS A. KEMPIS

KALALAU TRAIL
- A WILDLAND TRAIL -
CAUTION: UNEVEN FOOTING BECAUSE OF PROTRUDING ROOTS AND ROCKS, LOOSE DIRT AND ROCKS, MUD AND SLIPPERY SURFACES. TRAIL IS NARROW &/OR STEEP IN PLACES. USE APPROPRIATE FOOTWEAR.
PROCEED AT YOUR OWN RISK.
DEPT. OF LAND & NATURAL RESOURCES

SISTAH JAH LOVE ROASTED SQUASH SOUP

20 min prep / 35 min cooking / 5-6 servings

1 small	Butternut or buttercup squash (1 ½ C cooked)		2 Tbl	Maple syrup, or to taste
1 large	Garnet yam, peeled & chopped (2 C)		3 Tbl	Nama shoyu
1 medium	Onion, chopped (1 C)		½ tsp	Curry paste (page 197)
1 C	Celery, sliced thin		1 small	Cinnamon stick
2 Tbl	Garlic, minced		•	Sea salt, to taste
4 ½ C	Filtered water or vegetable stock		•	Black pepper, ground to taste
2 ½ C	Coconut milk			

loving preparation

1. Preheat oven to 375°. Rinse the butternut squash, slice lengthwise and remove the seeds. Place face down on a lightly-oiled baking sheet and bake until a knife can pass through it easily, approximately 30 - 35 minutes. Remove from oven and allow to cool. Scoop the inside of the squash into a large blender.

2. While squash is cooking, place the yams, onions, celery, garlic, coconut milk, filtered water and cinnamon stick in a 3 qt pot, cook on medium high heat until yams are thoroughly cooked, approximately 30 minutes, stirring occasionally. Remove from heat and allow to cool 10-15 minutes.

3. Remove cinnamon stick, add nama shoyu and maple syrup, place in blender with squash and blend according to instructions on page 36. Add salt and pepper to taste, mix well and enjoy.

4. Garnish with black sesame seeds and a leaf of mint or cilantro. The flavor of this soup may vary according to the sweetness of the yams and squash, add maple syrup to taste.

Sunset on the Ganges River, India

"ALBERT CAMUS ONCE SAID 'LIVE TO THE POINT OF TEARS.' THAT'S WHAT I WANT TO DO. I WANT TO SO EXPERIENCE THE EXQUISITENESS OF LIFE THAT I AM MORE AND MORE IN AWE." - R . R .

B.G.'S BLACK BARLEY CORN SOUP

20 min prep / 55 min cooking / 4-5 servings

4 C	Filtered water or vegetable stock		1 ½ C	Corn, fresh or frozen
1 C	Black barley		3 Tbl	Nama shoyu, or to taste
6 ½ C	Filtered water or vegetable stock		2 tsp	Garlic, minced
1 ½ C	Onion, sliced		1 Tbl	Miso paste
½ C	Celery, sliced thin		1 tsp	Thyme, fresh, minced (½ tsp dry)
½ C	Shitake mushrooms, sliced		•	Sea salt, to taste
½ C	Carrots, sliced thin		•	Black pepper, ground to taste
½ C	Red bell pepper, sliced			

loving preparation

1. Place black barley (see *Glossary*) and 4 C of filtered water or vegetable stock in a small pot and bring to a boil. Reduce heat, cover and simmer until barley is soft and plump, approximately 50 minutes. Drain well and set aside.
2. While barley is cooking, add 6 ½ C filtered water or vegetable stock, onion, celery, mushrooms and carrots to a 3 qt pot, cook over medium heat for 20 minutes, stirring occasionally. Add red pepper and corn, cook for 10 more minutes, stirring occasionally.
3. Place miso in a small bowl with 1 C of the broth from the pot and stir until smooth. Return to pot. Add remaining ingredients including black barley and stir well. As with all soups, please do not boil.

CARPE DIEM

SURYA'S FIRE ROASTED GAZPACHO

40 minutes / 4-5 servings

4 C	Tomato juice, fresh
4 large	Roma tomatoes, grilled (1 ½ C chopped, page 194)
⅔ C	Filtered water or vegetable stock
⅔ C	Cucumber, peeled, seeded & diced
⅔ C	Corn, fresh or frozen
½ C	Green bell pepper, diced
⅓ C	Red onion, diced
3 Tbl	Lime juice, fresh squeezed
3 Tbl	Cilantro, minced
1 Tbl	Nama shoyu, or to taste
1 Tbl	Basil, minced
1 ¼ tsp	Cumin powder, toasted
1 tsp	Garlic, minced
1 tsp	Jalapeño pepper, seeded & minced
½ tsp	Chili powder
½ tsp	Hot sauce (optional, page 214)
Pinch	Cayenne pepper
•	Sea salt, to taste
•	Black pepper, ground to taste

loving preparation

1. Place tomatoes and juice in blender and blend until smooth. Place in a large mixing bowl with remaining ingredients and mix well. Serve chilled, the colder the better. Goes great with Korn Bread (page 108).

variations

- Commercially-available Spicy Tomato Vegetable Juice may replace tomato juice, and canned fire roasted tomatoes may replace grilled tomatoes.
- For a 🪷 Live Gazpacho, do not grill the tomatoes, roast the jalapeño pepper or toast the cumin powder and use freshly-juiced tomatoes.

GRANDMOTHER MOON'S CHICKEN-FREE NOODLE SOUP

20 min prep / 35 min cooking / 4-5 servings

8 C	Filtered water or vegetable stock
1 ½ C	Onion, chopped
¾ C	Celery, sliced thin
¾ C	Carrot, sliced thin
¾ C	Parsnip, sliced thin
2 Tbl	Garlic, minced
1 ½ C	Chicken-style seitan, ½" chop (see *Glossary*)
1 C	Thin noodle pasta, uncooked (see *Glossary*)
2 Tbl	Nama shoyu, or to taste
1 ½ Tbl	Italian parsley, minced
1 Tbl	Dill, minced (1 ½ tsp dry)
•	Sea salt, to taste
•	Black pepper, ground to taste

loving preparation

1. Place water or stock, onion, carrot, parsnip, celery and garlic in a large pot, cook over medium heat for 20 minutes, stirring occasionally.
2. Add seitan and cook for 5 minutes, stirring occasionally. Add remaining ingredients, reduce heat to low and cook until pasta is done, approximately 8 minutes, stirring occasionally.

"I WENT TO THE WOODS BECAUSE I WANTED TO LIVE DELIBERATELY, TO FRONT ONLY THE ESSENTIAL FACTS OF LIFE, AND SEE IF I COULD NOT LEARN WHAT IT HAD TO TEACH, AND NOT, WHEN I CAME TO DIE, DISCOVER THAT I HAD NOT LIVED. I WANTED TO LIVE DEEP." —HENRY DAVID THOREAU

Surya's Fire Roasted Gazpacho

ROASTED RED PEPPER & PINE NUT SOUP

30 min prep / 20 min cooking / 5-6 servings

4 medium	Red bell peppers (3 C roasted)
6 C	Filtered water or vegetable stock
1 ½ C	Onions, chopped
¾ C	Celery, chopped
½ C	Shitake mushrooms, sliced thin
4 tsp	Garlic, minced
1 Tbl	Miso paste, mellow variety or one of your favorites
6 Tbl	Nama shoyu, or to taste
½ tsp	Black pepper, ground to taste
½ tsp	Sea salt, or to taste
3 Tbl	Italian parsley, minced
½ C	Pine nuts, toasted for garnish (page 194)

loving preparation

1. Preheat oven to 400°. Roast bell peppers according to instructions on page 193.
2. While peppers are roasting, place water or stock, onions, celery, mushrooms and garlic in a 3 qt pot, cook over medium high heat for 20 minutes, stirring occasionally. Remove from heat, allow to cool 10-15 minutes.
3. Place in the blender with peppers and remaining ingredients, except the pine nuts and parsley, and blend according to instructions on page 36.
4. Garnish liberally with parsley & pine nuts. As with all soups, please do not boil.

CORAZON DE CRISTO BLACK BEAN SOUP

20 min prep / 20 min cooking / 4-5 servings

6 C	Filtered water or vegetable stock
1 ½ C	Onion, diced
1 C	Carrots, diced
½ C	Celery, sliced thin
4 tsp	Garlic, minced
2 tsp	Jalapeño, roasted, seeded & minced, (page 193)
3 ½ C	Black beans, cooked (page 209)
¼ C	Red bell pepper, diced
1 tsp	Sea salt, or to taste
1 tsp	Chili powder
¾ tsp	Black pepper, ground to taste
½ tsp	Cumin powder, toasted
¼ tsp	Oregano, dry
6 Tbl	Nama shoyu, or to taste
2 Tbl	Cilantro, minced

loving preparation

1. Add water or stock, onion, garlic, celery, jalapeño and carrots to a 3 qt pot, cook on medium high heat until carrots are soft, approximately 15 minutes, stirring ocassionally.
2. Add beans, bell peppers and spices, cook for 5 minutes, stirring occasionally. Add shoyu and cilantro, stir well and enjoy.

serving suggestions

꙳ Serve with a dollop of Sour Crème (page 196).

"ALL THAT I AM, ALL THAT WE ARE, SHINING IN LOVE LIKE AN INFINITE STAR. ONE WITH THE ALL, ALL BECOMES ONE. ALL HAS BEEN HERE SINCE CREATION BEGAN. BREAK DOWN THE WALLS OF ILLUSION AND FEAR, SEEK FOR THE TRUTH & THE TRUTH SHALL APPEAR" - SHIMSHAI

AIYAH'S GARDEN LIVING CORN CHOWDER

30 min prep / 3-4 servings

2 ½ c	Filtered water
3 c	Corn, fresh
1 c	Avocado, mashed
¼ c	Celery, diced
¼ c	Onion, diced
1 Tbl	Nama shoyu, or to taste
1 tsp	Ginger, peeled & minced
1 tsp	Garlic, minced (optional)
1 tsp	Sea salt, or to taste
½ tsp	Jalapeño, seeded & minced
¼ tsp	Black pepper, ground to taste
Pinch	Cayenne pepper
2 tsp	Cilantro, minced
½ c	Red bell pepper, diced

loving preparation

1. Place 2 c of corn and all remaining ingredients except cilantro and red bell pepper in a blender and blend until smooth.
2. Pour into serving bowls. Top with cilantro, bell pepper and remaining 1 c of corn. Serve chilled.

Mt. Kailash, Tibet

DEAN'S DRAGON LIVE GARDEN VEGGIE SOUP

30 min prep / 2-3 servings

3½ c	Filtered water or fresh vegetable juice
½ c	Mushrooms, diced
½ c	Zuchinni, diced
½ c	Carrots, grated
¼ c	Jicama, diced
¼ c	Red bell pepper, diced
¼ c	Celery, diced
¼ c	Daikon radish, diced
3 Tbl	Red onion, diced (optional)
2½ Tbl	Nama shoyu, or to taste
1½ Tbl	Fresh herbs, minced, your favorites
1 tsp	Garlic, minced (optional)
1 tsp	Ginger, peeled & minced
Pinch	Cayenne pepper
•	Black pepper, ground to taste
•	Sea salt, to taste
•	Crunchy sprouts for garnish

loving preparation

1. Place all ingredients in a large mixing bowl and mix well. For optimal flavor, refrigerate soup for a few hours before serving.

serving suggestions

↝ Top with a small scoop of Live Alfreda Sauce (page 82) or nutritional yeast, and crunchy sprouts. This soup may be enjoyed cold or at room temperature. Serve with Flax Crackers (page 30) or Manna Bread (page 112).

variations

↝ Experiment with different vegetable juices as the base, try different seasonal veggies and herbs.

JOIE DE VIVRE LAVENDER INFUSED CARROT GINGER SOUP

30 minutes / 2-3 servings

3 ½ C	Carrot juice, fresh (approx. 3 ½ lbs carrots)	2 Tbl	Nama Shoyu (optional)
½ C	Macadamia nuts	1 Tbl	Lemon juice, fresh squeezed
¼ C	Avocado, mashed	½ tsp	Dill, fresh (¼ tsp dry)
2 Tbl	Ginger, juiced	½ tsp	Curry powder (optional)
2 Tbl	Lavender flowers, dried & soaked in ½ C warm water	Pinch	Cayenne pepper
		•	Sea salt, to taste
		•	Black pepper, ground to taste

loving preparation

1. Soak lavender in warm water for 15 minutes. Strain well, discard flowers and place water in a blender. Add remaining ingredients except dill, salt and pepper, blend until smooth. Add dill, salt and pepper, stir well and enjoy the joy of it all.

serving suggestion

↪ Garnish with grated carrots, beets, zucchini, jicama or daikon radish. Sprinkle with black sesame seeds. Enjoy cold or at room temperature.

variations

↪ Replace carrot juice with other veggie juices. Experiment with different nuts, seeds and herbs.

Lourdes Basilica, France

"WHAT WISDOM CAN YOU FIND THAT IS GREATER THAN KINDNESS?" - JEAN-JACQUES ROUSSEAU

REMARKABLE MELON SOUP

20 minutes / 2 servings

1 large	Melon (honeydew, crenshaw or cantaloupe, etc) chopped small (4 c)
1 c	Coconut water, fresh

2 Tbl	Lime juice, fresh squeezed
Pinch	Chili powder
Pinch	Cayenne pepper
Pinch	Cinnamon powder
•	Agave nectar, to taste
•	Blueberries and mint leaves for garnish

loving preparation

1. Place all ingredients in a blender and blend until smooth. Serve chilled and top with blueberries and mint leaves.

suggestions

ᦓ Sweetness of the soup will vary according to fruit. More or less coconut water may be added to reach the desired consistency.

ᦓ Slice a melon in half, scoop out the seeds and use as a bowl for the soup. Garnish with fresh fruit and top with shredded coconut.

4

dressings & sauces

DRESSINGS

THOUSAND ISLAND

PECAN VINAIGRETTE

LIVE LEMON MISO TAHINI

GREEN GODDESS

SESAME SHITAKE

CAESAR

ROASTED RED PEPPER VINAIGRETTE

LIVE CILANTRO LIME VINAIGRETTE

LIVE PAPAYA SEED RANCH

LIVE CUCUMBER MINT

MAPLE BALSAMIC

LIVE FLAX OIL

LIVE TOMATO BASIL

LIVE LEMON HERB

SAUCES

THAI COCONUT

MARINARA

ROASTED RED PEPPER

SPINACH MUSHROOM

CURRY

CRANBERRY

ROASTED SQUASH

MUSHROOM GRAVY

BLACK BEAN

LIVE CARROT GINGER

LIVE TOMATO

LIVE ALMOND HERB

108 MATAJI'S 1,000 ISLAND DRESSING

10 minutes / 1 ½ cups

½ C	Vegan mayonnaise (page 196)
½ C	Catsup (page 197)
¼ C	Dill relish or kosher dill pickles, finely diced
1 tsp	Garlic, minced
½ tsp	Dill, fresh minced (or ¼ tsp dry)

loving preparation

1. Combine all ingredients in a large mixing bowl and mix well.

PEACEFUL PECAN VINAIGRETTE

20 minutes / 3 ½ cups

1 C	Filtered water
1 C	Pecans, toasted (page 194)
½ C	Safflower or sunflower oil
1 Tbl	Maple syrup or agave nectar
5 tsp	Apple cider vinegar, raw
1 Tbl	Nama shoyu, or to taste
¼ tsp	Garlic, minced (optional)

loving preparation

1. Place all ingredients in a blender and blend until smooth.

variation

↬ Mix 1 part Toltec Pecan Dressing with 1 part Maple Balsamic (page 57) for Baba B's Favorite Maple Pecan Dressing.

ILAKA'S LEMON MISO TAHINI DRESSING

10 minutes / 2 ¼ cups

1 C	Filtered water
⅔ C	Tahini, raw
3 Tbl	Nama shoyu, or to taste
3 Tbl	Lemon juice, fresh squeezed
1 Tbl	Miso paste, your favorite
1 Tbl	Cilantro, minced
2 tsp	Maple syrup or agave nectar
¼ tsp	Cayenne pepper, or to taste

loving preparation

1. Place all ingredients in a blender and blend well.

variations

↬ For a thick miso tahini dip, add water slowly until a desired consistency is reached.

GARVIN'S GALACTIC GREEN GODDESS

15 minutes / 2 ½ cups

⅔ C	Soy or rice milk
1 C	Vegan mayonnaise, (page 196)
1/3 C	Basil, fresh, minced & tightly packed
2 Tbl	Italian parsley, fresh, minced
1½ Tbl	Apple cider vinegar, raw
1½ Tbl	Nama shoyu, or to taste
¼ tsp	Black pepper, ground to taste
¼ tsp	Sea salt, or to taste
Pinch	Cayenne pepper

loving preparation

1. Place all ingredients in a blender and blend well.

"THE WINE OF REALITY OVERFLOWETH THE CHALICE OF REASON." - D. GERSH, THE BOOK OF DAMONISMS

SACRED SESAME SHITAKE DRESSING

15 minutes / 3 cups

2 C	Filtered water
½ C	Toasted sesame oil
¼ C	Grilled shitake mushrooms, diced (page 194)
¼ C	Sesame seeds
2 Tbl	Apple cider vinegar, raw
1 Tbl	Miso paste
1 Tbl	Nama shoyu, or to taste
2 tsp	Maple syrup or agave nectar
•	Sea salt, to taste
•	Black pepper, ground to taste
Pinch	Cayenne pepper

loving preparation

1. Place all ingredients in a medium sized bowl and whisk well.

Seven Sacred Pools, Maui, Hawai'i

LIFE IS SHORT AND WE HAVE NEVER TOO MUCH TIME FOR GLADDENING THE HEARTS OF THOSE WHO ARE TRAVELING THE DARK JOURNEY WITH US. OH BE SWIFT TO LOVE, MAKE HASTE TO BE KIND." - HENRI FREDERICK AMIEL

GIVE UNTO CAESER SALAD DRESSING

10 min dressing / 20 min croutons / 1 ¾ cup dressing, 4 C croutons

	Dressing		*Croutons*
12.3 oz	Silken tofu, soft	5 slices	Multigrain bread (4 C), in ½" cubes
¼ C	Filtered water	2 Tbl	Olive oil
3 Tbl	Lemon juice, fresh squeezed	1 Tbl	Italian parsley, minced
1 Tbl	Nutritional yeast	1 Tbl	Basil, minced
2 tsp	Vegetarian Worcestershire sauce	2 tsp	Nutritional yeast
1 ½ tsp	Garlic, minced	1 tsp	Oregano, minced (½ tsp dry)
1 ½ tsp	Dijon mustard	1 tsp	Thyme, minced (½ tsp dry)
2 tsp	Nama shoyu	•	Sea salt, to taste
1 tsp	Capers	•	Black pepper, ground to taste
¾ tsp	Sea salt, or to taste		
½ tsp	Black pepper, ground to taste		

loving preparation

1. Preheat oven to 375°. Combine *Crouton* ingredients in a large mixing bowl and mix well. Spread onto a well oiled baking sheet and bake until bread is crispy, approximately 15 minutes.
2. Combine all *Dressing* ingredients in a blender and blend until smooth.

serving suggestion

꙳ Toss dressing with chopped romaine lettuce, top with croutons.

"LOVE IS THE BEAUTY OF THE SOUL" - ST AUGUSTINE

RUDRA'S ROASTED RED PEPPER VINAIGRETTE

15 minutes + roasting time for 3 ½ cups

2 C	Filtered water
1 medium	Red bell pepper, roasted
½ C	Safflower or olive oil
2 Tbl	Apple cider vinegar, raw
4 tsp	Nama shoyu, or to taste
1 Tbl	Miso paste, mellow red or your favorite variety
2 tsp	Maple syrup or agave nectar
¼ tsp	Sea salt, or to taste
¼ tsp	Black pepper, ground to taste
Pinch	Cayenne pepper

loving preparation

1. Roast bell peppers according to instructions on page 193.
2. Place all ingredients in a blender and blend well.

EL SIGNOR'S CILANTRO LIME VINAIGRETTE

15 minutes for 3 cups

¾ C	Filtered water
½ C	Olive oil
¼ C	Cilantro, minced & tightly packed
¼ C	Lime juice, fresh squeezed
1 Tbl	Apple cider vinegar, raw
1 ½ tsp	Nama shoyu, or to taste
1 tsp	Maple syrup, or Agave nectar
¾ tsp	Jalapeño, seeded & minced
½ tsp	Chili powder
¼ tsp	Garlic, minced (optional)
Pinch	Cayenne pepper
•	Sea salt, to taste
•	Black pepper, ground to taste

loving preparation

1. Place all ingredients in a blender and blend well.

"GIVE LIGHT AND THE DARKNESS WILL DISAPPEAR OF ITSELF." - ERASMUS

"LET FOOD BE THY MEDICINE AND LET THY MEDICINE BE FOOD." - HIPPOCRATES

PUNA'S PAPAYA SEED RANCH DRESSING

15 minutes / 2½ cups

1 ¼ C	Filtered water
1 C	Macadamia nuts
1 Tbl	Lemon juice, fresh squeezed
1 Tbl	Papaya seeds, fresh
1 Tbl	Apple cider vinegar, raw
1 tsp	Nama Shoyu, or to taste
½ tsp	Garlic, minced (optional)
Pinch	Cayenne pepper, or to taste
•	Sea salt, to taste
•	Black pepper, ground to taste

loving preparation

1. Place all ingredients in a blender and blend until smooth.

variations

⤳ Add 1 tsp of fresh herb like cilantro, basil, Italian parsley or dill.

⤳ Try adding 2 tsp of nutritional yeast for a nutty flavor.

INNER LIGHT CUCUMBER MINT DRESSING

15 minutes / 2 ¾ cups

1 medium	Cucumber, peeled, seeded & chopped (1 ¼ C)
1 C	Filtered water or coconut water
¼ C	Cashews or macadamia nuts
2 Tbl	Lemon juice, fresh squeezed
2 tsp	Apple cider vinegar, raw
2 tsp	Mint leaf, minced
½ tsp	Nama shoyu, or to taste
½ tsp	Ginger, peeled & minced
½ tsp	Garlic, minced (optional)
Pinch	Cayenne pepper
•	Sea salt, to taste
•	Black pepper, ground to taste

loving preparation

1. Place all ingredients in a blender and blend until creamy.

variations

⤳ Try replacing mint with other fresh herbs.

⤳ Replace cashews with other soaked nuts or seeds.

UMA'S MAPLE BALSAMIC VINAIGRETTE

5 minutes / 2 cups

2/3 C	Filtered water
½ C	Olive oil
¼ C	Balsamic vinegar
2½ Tbl	Maple syrup
1½ Tbl	Nama shoyu
1 Tbl	Stone ground mustard

loving preparation

1. Place all ingredients in a small bowl and whisk well.

"ONE DOESN'T DISCOVER NEW LANDS WITHOUT CONSENTING TO LOSE SIGHT OF THE SHORE FOR A VERY LONG TIME." – ANDRE GIDE

Puna's Papaya Seed Ranch Dressing

FATIMA'S FLAX DRESSING

10 minutes / ½ cup

¼ C	Flax seed oil
1 Tbl	Filtered water
1 Tbl	Lemon juice, fresh squeezed
1 Tbl	Cilantro or other fresh herbs, minced
1 ¼ tsp	Nama shoyu, or to taste
1 tsp	Apple cider vinegar, raw
½ tsp	Garlic, minced (optional)
dash	Agave nectar
pinch	Cayenne pepper

loving preparation

1. Place all ingredients in a small bowl and mix well.

HOLY GRAIL TOMATO BASIL DRESSING

15 minutes / 2 cups

¼ C	Olive oil
¼ C	Sundried tomatoes, soaked in warm water until soft
¾ C	Sundried tomato soak water
2 Tbl	Basil, fresh, minced
1 Tbl	Apple cider vinegar, raw
2 tsp	Nama shoyu
2 tsp	Lemon juice, fresh squeezed
1 tsp	Italian parsley, minced
Pinch	Cayenne pepper
•	Sea salt, to taste
•	Black pepper, ground to taste

loving preparation

1. Soak sundried tomatoes in water for 20 minutes. Drain & set aside ¾ C soak water.
2. Place all ingredients in blender and blend until smooth.

OHANA OIL-FREE LEMON HERB DRESSING

10 minutes / ½ cup

¼ C	Lemon juice, fresh squeezed
¼ C	Filtered water
2 tsp	Italian parsley, cilantro, basil or fresh herb of your choice, minced
½ tsp	Apple cider vinegar, raw
½ tsp	Nama Shoyu
¼ tsp	Garlic, minced (optional)
¼ tsp	Ginger, peeled & minced (optional)
¼ tsp	Dulse flakes (optional)
pinch	Kelp powder (optional)
•	Sea salt, to taste
•	Black pepper, ground to taste

loving preparation

1. Place all ingredients in a small bowl and whisk well.

variations

↝ Add 2 Tbl of flax oil, olive oil or raw tahini.

"NONVIOLENCE LEADS TO THE HIGHEST ETHICS, WHICH IS THE GOAL OF ALL EVOLUTION. UNTIL WE STOP HARMING ALL OTHER LIVING BEINGS, WE ARE STILL SAVAGES."

- THOMAS EDISON

Sauces

HARI JIWAN'S THAI COCONUT SAUCE

10 min prep / 20 min cooking / 2 cups

1 ¾ C	Coconut milk
2 Tbl	Peanut or almond butter
2 Tbl	Nama shoyu
1 Tbl	Maple syrup or agave nectar
1 tsp	Lime juice, fresh squeezed
1 tsp	Mirin
1 small	Lime leaf (see *Glossary*)
2"	Lemongrass stem (optional)
Pinch	Crushed red pepper flakes
•	Sea salt, to taste
•	Black pepper, ground to taste
2 tsp	Cilantro, minced

loving preparation

1. Place all ingredients except cilantro in a small sauté pan and cook over low heat for 20 minutes, stirring occasionally.
2. Remove lime leaf and lemon grass stem, add cilantro and enjoy.

serving suggestions

- Serve as a sauce for steamed veggies.
- Use in Tropical Ratatouille (page 79) and for Thai Pizza (page 104).

MYSTIC MARINARA

20 min prep / 40 min cooking / 6 cups

1 Tbl	Olive oil
1 ¼ C	Yellow onion, chopped
½ C	Shitake mushrooms, sliced thin
2 Tbl	Garlic, minced
5 C	Fire roasted tomatoes
	OR
8 med	Roma tomatoes, grilled (page 194)
1 ½ C	Tomato juice, fresh
¾ C	Tomato paste
2 Tbl	Nama shoyu, or to taste
1 Tbl	Balsamic vinegar
2 Tbl	Basil, minced
2 Tbl	Italian parsley, minced
1 tsp	Oregano, fresh minced (½ tsp dry)
1 tsp	Thyme, fresh minced (½ tsp dry)
¾ tsp	Sea salt, or to taste
½ tsp	Sucanat
¼ tsp	Black pepper, ground to taste

loving preparation

1. Place oil in a 3 qt saucepan on medium high heat. Add mushrooms, garlic and onion, cook for 5 minutes, stirring frequently. Reduce heat to a simmer, add tomatoes, tomato juice and tomato paste, cook 5 minutes, stirring frequently.
2. Place mixture in the blender and blend until smooth. Return to pot. Add remaining ingredients and simmer over low heat for 20 minutes, stirring occasionally.

serving suggestion

- Use as a sauce for your favorite pizza or pasta. Try over Fennel Calzone (page 107).

"ALL BEINGS TREMBLE BEFORE VIOLENCE. ALL FEAR DEATH, ALL LOVE LIFE. SEE YOUR SELF IN OTHERS. THEN WHOM CAN YOU HURT? WHAT HARM CAN YOU DO?" - BUDDHA

ROMEO'S ROASTED RED PEPPER SAUCE

15 min prep / 2 cups / roasting time

2 medium	Red bell peppers (1 ½ C roasted)
¼ C	Rice milk
2 Tbl	Toasted coconut (page 194)
½ tsp	Nama shoyu, or to taste
½ tsp	Mirin
Pinch	Cayenne pepper (optional)
•	Sea salt, to taste
•	Black pepper, ground to taste

loving preparation

1. Roast bell peppers according to instructions on page 193.
2. Place all ingredients in a blender and blend until creamy.
3. Pour into a small sauce pan and cook on low heat until warm, approximately 5 minutes, stirring frequently.

serving suggestion

- Goes well with Black Rice Polenta (page 143).
- Nice mixed in with Mexican Seitan and Black Bean Salad (page 132).
- Serve over grilled tempeh or tofu cutlets and garnish with toasted coconut flakes.

variations

- Replace rice milk with coconut milk, soy milk or other nut and seed milks (page 204).
- Blend in a small hot pepper.

SAT NAM'S SPINACH MUSHROOM SAUCE

20 minutes prep / 15 min cooking / 4-6 servings

3 C	Soy milk
½ C	Crimini or shitake mushrooms, thinly sliced
½ bunch	Spinach, steamed, well drained & tightly packed to yield ½ C (page 193)
2 Tbl	Olive oil
1 Tbl	Buckwheat flour
1 Tbl	Spelt flour
1 tsp	Nutritional yeast
Pinch	Saffron threads soaked in 2 Tbl water
Pinch	Cayenne pepper
•	Sea salt, to taste
•	Black pepper, ground to taste
•	Nama shoyu, to taste (optional)

loving preparation

1. Place soy milk in a 3 qt pot on medium heat. Add mushrooms and spinach and cook until mushrooms are soft, approximately 7 minutes, stirring frequently.
2. Create a roux (a flour based paste that is used to thicken sauces) by placing oil and flours in a small mixing bowl and whisking well. Slowly add to pot, stirring constantly.
3. Add remaining ingredients and cook until sauce thickens, approximately 5 minutes, stirring occasionally.

serving suggestion

- Try as a sauce over Multigrain Rainbow Casserole (page 147) or Polenta Black Rice Casserole (page 143) or as a sauce for pastas, pizzas and steamed veggies.

"TWO ROADS DIVERGED IN A WOOD. AND I, I TOOK THE ONE LESS TRAVELED BY, AND THAT HAS MADE ALL THE DIFFERENCE." - ROBERT FROST

Queen's Pool, Chiapas, Mexico

GIFT OF GOVINDA CURRY

20 min prep / 20 min cooking / 6 cups

2 Tbl	Sesame oil		1½ Tbl	Nama shoyu, or to taste
1 medium	Onion, sliced thin (1 c)		1 ½ tsp	Curry powder
1 Tbl	Garlic, minced		½ tsp	Cumin powder, toasted (page 194)
1 Tbl	Ginger, peeled & minced		½ tsp	Curry paste (page 197)
2 ¾ c	Coconut milk		¼ tsp	Crushed red pepper flakes
2 Tbl	Maple syrup or agave nectar		1 ½ tsp	Cilantro, chopped

loving preparation

1. Place oil in a 3 qt pot on medium high heat. Add onion, garlic and ginger, cook for 5 minutes, stirring frequently. Add remaining ingredients except cilantro, reduce heat to simmer, cook for 15 more minutes, stirring occasionally. Add cilantro and enjoy.

serving suggestions

- For a stew, grill a tempeh, tofu or ulu cutlet (page 194), slice into small cubes and add to curry sauce.
- For a **Curry Pot**, add 2 c of assorted vegetables to pot when adding coconut milk, cook until veggies are just tender.
- Serve over brown basmati rice, quinoa or your favorite grain.
- Garnish with black sesame seeds and a few cilantro leaves.

variations

- May be served as part of a Taj Mahal Indian Sampler Platter with Dahl (page 149), Bindi Masala (page 78), Chutney (page 23) and Spelt Chapatti (page 110).

"THE PRACTICE OF PEACE AND RECONCILIATION IS THE MOST VITAL AND ARTISTIC HUMAN ENDEAVOR." ~ THICH NHAT HANH

CHRIS CRINGLE'S CRANBERRY SAUCE

10 min prep / 15 min cooking / 2 ½ cups

4 c	Cranberries, fresh or frozen		¾ tsp	Cinnamon powder
1 c	Filtered water		½ tsp	Ginger powder
¼ c	Sucanat		¼ tsp	Allspice powder
¼ c	Orange juice, fresh squeezed		¼ tsp	Nutmeg, ground
2 Tbl	Maple syrup or agave nectar		Pinch	Cardamom powder
1 Tbl	Mirin		¼ c	Pecans, chopped (optional)

loving preparation

1. Place cranberries and filtered water in a 3 qt pot over medium heat and cook for 5 minutes, stirring frequently. Add orange juice, sucanat, maple syrup and cook for 8 minutes, stirring frequently. Add mirin and remaining ingredients, cook for 3 minutes, or until cranberries have "popped" and the sauce thickens.

serving suggestions

- Serve over Grilled Tempeh, Tofu or Ulu (page 194) or serve as part of a holiday feast along with Holiday Loaf (page 126), Wild Rice Pilaf Stuffed Squash (page 77), or Candied Yams (page 212).
- Garnish with fresh mint leaves.

variation

- For a sweeter version, replace water with fruit juice, such as apple or pear.

THREE SISTERS SQUASH SAUCE

10 min prep / 30 min cooking / 2 cups

1 small	Butternut or buttercup squash, roasted (1 c cooked)
1½ c	Coconut, soy or rice milk
•	Sea salt, to taste
•	Black pepper, ground to taste
Pinch	Cayenne pepper
•	Maple syrup or agave nectar, to taste

loving preparation

1. Roast squash according to method discussed on page 42. Place in blender with remaining ingredients and blend well.
2. Slowly add liquid to desired consistency.

"THIS ABOVE ALL, TO THINE OWN SELF BE TRUE." - SHAKESPEARE

AVALON'S MAGIC MUSHROOM GRAVY

10 min prep / 15 min cooking / 3 ½ cups

1 Tbl	Olive oil
1 medium	Onion, ¼" dice (1 C)
¾ C	Shitake mushrooms, sliced thin
1½ Tbl	Garlic, minced
2 C	Filtered water or vegetable stock
¼ C	Nama shoyu, or to taste
Pinch	Nutmeg, ground
Pinch	Cayenne pepper

Roux

2 Tbl	Spelt flour
2 Tbl	Olive oil
1 Tbl	Filtered water

loving preparation

1. Create a *Roux* by placing spelt flour in a small bowl. Add 2 Tbl olive oil and 1 Tbl filtered water and whisk until a thick paste is created. Set aside.
2. Place 1 Tbl of olive oil in a large sauté pan on medium high heat. Add onion and garlic, cook for 5 minutes, stirring occasionally.
3. Add mushrooms and cook for 5 minutes, stirring occasionally. Add remaining ingredients except roux mixture and cook for 5 minutes on low heat, stirring occasionally. Add roux mixture and cook until gravy has a thick consistency, approximately 10 minutes, stirring frequently.

variation

↬ For a lower oil version, replace roux with 3 Tbl of arrowroot powder or kuzu root dissolved in ½ C of cold water.

BLESSED BLACK BEAN SAUCE

20 min prep / 15 min cooking / 4 cups

2 Tbl	Olive oil
½ C	Red onion, sliced
1½ Tbl	Garlic, minced
2 tsp	Jalapeño, seeded & minced
2 C	Black beans, cooked, (page 209)
1 C	Filtered water or vegetable stock
2 Tbl	Nama shoyu, or to taste
1 Tbl	Cilantro, minced
1 tsp	Sea salt, or to taste
½ tsp	Chili powder
½ tsp	Cumin powder, toasted
¼ tsp	Black pepper, ground to taste
½ tsp	Mirin
Pinch	Cayenne pepper

loving preparation

1. Place oil in a 3 qt pot on medium heat. Add onion, garlic and jalapeño, cook for 5 minutes, stirring frequently. Add black beans and remaining ingredients and cook for 10 minutes, stirring occasionally.
2. Remove from heat and place in a blender with remaining ingredients except cilantro, blend until smooth. Add cilantro and mix well. More or less water may be used to create desired consistency.

serving suggestions & variation

↬ Serve over Polenta Black Rice Casserole (page 143), or as a topping for steamed vegetables, grilled tempeh or tofu. Also delicious when topped with Shanti's Sour Crème (page 196).
↬ For a more textured sauce, add ½ C cooked black beans, ¼ C corn and 2 Tbl diced roasted red pepper (page 193) after blending, and mix well.

"THE REAL AND LASTING VICTORIES ARE THOSE OF PEACE AND NOT WAR." - EMERSON

"ALWAYS DO RIGHT. THIS WILL GRATIFY SOME PEOPLE AND ASTONISH THE REST." – MARK TWAIN

CUPID'S CARROT GINGER SAUCE

20 min prep / 10 min cooking / 3 cups

2 c	Carrots, peeled & sliced
1 ½ c	Coconut milk
½ c	Filtered water or vegetable stock
2 Tbl	Ginger, peeled & minced
2 Tbl	Olive oil
2 tsp	Nama shoyu
1 tsp	Dill, fresh, minced (½ tsp dry)
1 tsp	Mirin
Pinch	Cayenne pepper
•	Sea salt, to taste
•	Black pepper, ground to taste

loving preparation

1. Place oil in a 3 qt pot on medium high heat. Add carrots and ginger, cook for 3 minutes, stirring frequently. Add water or stock and cook until carrots are soft, approximately 15 minutes, stirring occasionally.
2. Remove from heat, place in a blender with coconut milk and blend until smooth.
3. Return to pot, add remaining ingredients and mix well.

serving suggestion

☞ Serve as a sauce over steamed vegetables (page 193), Spicy Thai Noodles (page 99) or Polenta Casserole (page 143).

SIMSO'S STRAWBERRY SAUCE

10 min prep / 10 min cook / 2-3 servings

6 medium	Strawberries, chopped (1 c)
7 Tbl	Filtered water
1 Tbl	Agave nectar, maple syrup, brown rice syrup or sucanat
1 tsp	Mirin
½ tsp	Mint, minced
Pinch	Cardamom powder
Pinch	Cinnamon powder

loving preparation

1. Place strawberries and filtered water in a small sauté pan and heat over low heat until strawberries start to break apart, approximately 8 minutes, stirring occasionally.
2. Add remaining ingredients and stir well.

serving suggestions

☞ Fantastic over heated Kava Brownies (page 156), Big Momma Freedom Chocolate Cake (page 157), Tofu Cheezcakes (page 158) or as a dessert sauce for fruit salads.

variations

☞ Experiment with different fruits such as blueberries or mango. A small amount of coconut, soy or rice milk may be added.
☞ You may also vary sweeteners for different flavors.

"THE NEXT MESSAGE YOU NEED IS ALWAYS RIGHT WHERE YOU ARE." - RAM DASS

🪷 LOTUS LIVE TOMATO SAUCE

20 minutes for 2 ½ cups

2 c	Roma tomatoes, chopped
¼ c	Sundried tomatoes soaked in warm water until soft
½ c	Sundried tomato soak water
2 Tbl	Beets, grated
2 Tbl	Olive oil
1 Tbl	Basil, minced
1 Tbl	Italian parsley, minced
1 tsp	Nama shoyu, or to taste
1 tsp	Nutritional yeast
½ tsp	Oregano, minced (¼ tsp dry)
½ tsp	Thyme, minced (¼ tsp dry)
½ tsp	Sea salt, or to taste
¼ tsp	Black pepper, ground to taste
¼ tsp	Sage, minced

loving preparation

1. Soak tomatoes in warm water for 20 minutes. Drain and set aside ½ c of soak water.
2. Place in blender with remaining ingredients and blend until smooth.

serving suggestions

↝ Serve as sauce over Live Zucchini Pasta (page 82), Marinated Live Veggies (page 195) or Live Greek Pizza (page 113).
↝ Top with nutritional yeast.

🪷 AGAPE LIVE ALMOND SAUCE

20 minutes for 3 ¼ cups

1 1/3 c	Almonds
2 c	Filtered water
2 tsp	Fresh herbs of your choosing, minced
½ tsp	Garlic, minced (optional)
¼ tsp	Sea salt, or to taste
¼ tsp	Black pepper, ground to taste
Pinch	Cayenne pepper

loving preparation

1. Soak and peel almonds according to method on page 202. Place in a blender with remaining ingredients and blend until smooth.

serving suggestions

↝ Serve as a sauce for Nori Paté Rolls (page 32) or over Marinated Live Veggies (page 195).
↝ Try as a pizza sauce for Live Pizza (page 113) & top with chopped tomatoes and fresh minced basil.

variations

↝ Experiment with adding a pinch of a spice of your choosing to see how the spice affects the dish.
↝ *Sweet* Blend almonds & water with 3-4 pitted dates.
↝ *Indian* Add a pinch each of cilantro, cumin and curry.
↝ *Mexican* Add cilantro, chili powder and cumin.
↝ *Italian* Basil, oregano, thyme or parsley.
↝ *Native American* Add minced sage or rosemary.

"THE LION AND THE CALF WILL LIE DOWN TOGETHER BUT THE CALF WON'T GET MUCH SLEEP." - WOODY ALLEN

5

Jewel of the Lotus Green Papaya Salad, page 81

salads & sides

TUNA FREE TEMPEH SALAD

COLESLAW

EGG FREE SALAD

APRICOT CORN BREAD STUFFING

ROASTED ROOT VEGETABLES

HERB ROASTED POTATOES

JAMAICAN JERK PLANTAIN

PURPLE POTATO SALAD

AFRICAN KALE AND YAM

ACORN SQUASH W/ WILD RICE PILAF

BINDI MASALA

TROPICAL COCONUT RATATOUILLE

LIVE HEAVENLY ARAME SALAD

COUSCOUS SALAD

ASPARAGUS W/ROASTED PEPPER & DILL

LIVE GREEN PAPAYA SALAD

LIVE FETTUCINI ALFREDA

"CHARLIE'S RELIEF" TUNA-FREE TEMPEH SALAD

20 min prep / 10 min cooking / 3-4 servings

1 lb	Multigrain soy tempeh, quartered
1 ¼ C	Vegan Mayonnaise (page 196)
⅔ C	Kosher dill pickles, diced
⅔ C	Celery, diced
½ C	Red onion, diced
2 Tbl	Nama shoyu
2 Tbl	Italian parsley, minced
1 Tbl	Stone ground mustard
2 tsp	Apple cider vinegar, raw
½ tsp	Garlic, minced
•	Black pepper, ground to taste

loving preparation

1. Place tempeh in a steamer basket in a 3 qt pot and steam for 10 minutes according to method on page 193.
2. Chop tempeh into ⅛" square pieces. Combine with remaining ingredients in a large mixing bowl and mix well.

serving suggestions

↝ Enjoy on its own as a salad or use as a spread for a wrap or sandwich.
↝ Use as filling for **Stuffed Tomatoes**, served cold or for a **Tuna-free Melt**, top with Nut Cheez (page 29) and bake at 350° until cheez melts.

CURANDERO'S COLESLAW

25 min prep / 3-4 servings

2 C	Red cabbage, julienne
2 C	Green cabbage, julienne
1 C	Carrots, grated
2 tsp	Ginger, peeled & minced well
1 C	Vegan mayonnaise (page 196)
2 Tbl	Apple cider vinegar, raw
1 Tbl	Lemon juice, fresh squeezed
1 Tbl	Stone ground mustard
1 tsp	Dill, fresh minced
1 tsp	Celery seed
¼ tsp	Sea salt, or to taste
½ tsp	Black pepper, ground to taste
Pinch	Cayenne pepper
2 Tbl	Nama shoyu (optional)

loving preparation

1. Place cabbages, carrots and ginger in a large bowl and mix well.
2. Place remaining ingredients in a small bowl, whisk well. Combine all ingredients, toss well and enjoy.

"WHAT LIES BEHIND US AND WHAT LIES BEFORE US ARE TINY MATTERS COMPARED TO WHAT LIES WITHIN US." - RALPH WALDO EMERSON

AMAYA'S EGOLESS EGG-FREE SALAD

25 minutes / 3-4 servings

1 lb	Extra firm tofu, crumbled	1 ½ tsp	Apple cider vinegar, raw
¾ C	Celery, diced	1 tsp	Turmeric powder
½ C	Red onion, diced	½ tsp	Garlic, minced
½ C	Vegan mayonnaise, (page 196)	•	Black pepper, ground to taste
1 Tbl	Dill, minced, or ½ tsp dry	•	Sea salt, to taste
2 ½ tsp	Stone ground mustard	2½ Tbl	Nama shoyu

loving preparation,

1. Combine all ingredients in a large mixing bowl and gently mix well. For additional flavor, allow to sit for a few hours before serving.

note

⌐ This wonderful dish acquires a yellow color thanks to the turmeric.

serving suggestions

⌐ Great as a sandwich and wrap filling or in stuffed tomatoes with a salad.

"ALONG MY TRAVELS I WAS DELIGHTED BY THE DIVINE, AND THROUGH MUCH LOVE I BEGAN TO SEE WITH NEW EYES, A BEAUTIFUL WORLD, AN INTERACTIVE UNIVERSE FILLED WITH MAGIC AND MYSTERY THAT IS AS LIMITLESS AS OUR OWN IMAGINATION." - A.A.

AMAZING GRACE APRICOT CORN BREAD STUFFING

15 min prep / 30 min cooking time / 6 cups

2 Tbl	Olive oil
¾ C	Onion, diced
½ C	Celery, diced
2 tsp	Garlic, minced
½ C	Apricots, dried, chopped
½ C	Pecans, toasted (page 194) & chopped
3 Tbl	Carrot juice, fresh
1 Tbl	Nama shoyu
1 Tbl	Sage, fresh, chopped (1 tsp dry)
•	Sea salt, to taste
•	Black pepper, ground to taste
3 ½ C	Korn bread, ½" cubes (page 108)

loving preparation

1. Preheat oven to 350°. Place oil in a large sauté pan on medium high heat. Add onion, celery and garlic, cook for 5 minutes, stirring frequently. Add remaining ingredients except corn bread and cook for 5 minutes, stirring frequently.
2. Remove from heat and place in a large mixing bowl with corn bread, gently mix well.
3. Place in a well oiled 9" x 13" casserole dish. Bake for 20 minutes and serve hot.

serving suggestion

↝ Try as part of a holiday feast with the Kind & Gentle Holiday Loaf (page 126) or Acorn Squash and Wild Rice Pilaf (page 77) and Cranberry Sauce (page 63).

"I AM FOUND BY GRACE. HALLOWED BE THIS PLACE. O HALLOWED BE THIS PLACE, SACRED SPACE, WE'VE ALL BEEN TOUCHED BY HOLY GRACES." – SASHA BUTTERFLY

ROOTS, ROCK, REGGAE ROASTED ROOT VEGETABLES

15 min prep / 50 min cooking / 2-3 servings

3 Tbl	Olive oil
½ C	Filtered water or vegetable stock
6 C	Root Vegetables, chopped (parsnip, beet, sweet potato, carrot, Jerusalem artichoke, celeriac or other root vegetables)
½ C	Fennel bulb, chopped
2 Tbl	Fresh Herbs, minced (parsley, dill, &/or basil)
1 tsp	Sea salt, or to taste
1 tsp	Black pepper, ground to taste
Pinch	Cayenne pepper
2 Tbl	Nama shoyu, or to taste
1 Tbl	Balsamic vinegar

loving preparation

1. Preheat oven to 375°. Rinse vegetables well and chop into ½" cubes. Combine all ingredients, except Nama shoyu and balsamic vinegar, in a 9" x 13" casserole dish and mix well.
2. Bake until all vegetables are cooked through, approximately 50 minutes, stirring occasionally.
3. Remove from oven, cool for 5 minutes, add nama shoyu and balsamic vinegar, mix well.

BILBO'S TATERS

15 min prep / 40 min cooking / 4-5 servings

8 medium	Russet, red bliss, yellow Finn or other potatoes, ½" cubes (8 C)
3 Tbl	Garlic, minced
3 Tbl	Fresh herbs, minced (try parsley, basil, thyme, oregano, dill, rosemary or sage)
¼ C	Olive oil
3 Tbl	Nama shoyu, or to taste
1 tsp	Paprika
¾ tsp	Sea salt, or to taste
1 tsp	Black pepper, ground to taste

loving preparation

1. Preheat oven to 375°. Rinse and scrub potatoes well, chop into ½" cubes and place in large mixing bowl. Add remaining ingredients, except nama shoyu, and toss well.
2. Place in a well oiled 9" x 13" casserole dish and bake until a knife can easily pass though a potato, approximately 35-40 minutes, stirring occasionally.
3. Remove from oven, place in a large mixing bowl, add nama shoyu and mix well.

variations

↬ Top with Sour Crème, (page 196), Mushroom Gravy (page 64), or as a part of a breakfast that includes Tofu Scramble (page 178).

"ALL THAT IS GOLD DOES NOT GLITTER. NOT ALL THOSE THAT WANDER ARE LOST." - J.R.R. TOLKEIN

DADDY DREAD'S JAMAICAN JERK PLANTAIN

15 min prep / 1 hour marinate / 15 min cooking / 2 C

3 medium	Plantains (2 ¼ C, sliced)
½ C	Green onion, diced
4 medium	Scotch bonnet peppers, chopped (3 Tbl)
2 Tbl	Sucanat
2 Tbl	Lime juice, fresh squeezed
1 Tbl	Allspice, ground
1 Tbl	Thyme, dried & ground
1 Tbl	Nama shoyu
1 Tbl	Ginger, peeled & minced
2 tsp	Garlic, minced
1 tsp	Black pepper, ground to taste
¾ tsp	Cinnamon powder
¾ tsp	Nutmeg, ground
•	Sea salt, to taste
3 Tbl	Olive oil

loving preparation

1. Place all ingredients except plantains and 1 Tbl of olive oil in a food processor or blender and process until smooth. Place in a large mixing bowl with plantains and allow to marinate for 1 hour or longer.
2. Place 1 Tbl of oil in a large sauté pan on medium high heat. Add plantains and cook until plantains become soft, approximately 15 minutes, turning frequently and adding water if necessary to prevent sticking.

serving suggestions & variations

↝ For a super irie meal, try serving with rice, red beans, corn on the cob, Mango Chutney (page 23) and Mama Nadia's Roti (page 109).
↝ This is a very spicy dish, mon.

PONO PURPLE POTATO SALAD

15 min prep / 15 min cooking / 3 servings,

2-3 medium	Purple sweet potatoes, ½" cubes (about 3¼ cups)
¾ C	Vegan mayonnaise (page 196)
½ C	Celery, sliced thin
¼ C	Red onion, diced
2 tsp	Apple cider vinegar, raw
2 tsp	Nama shoyu, or to taste
2 tsp	Dill, fresh minced
½ tsp	Garlic, minced
½ tsp	Black pepper, ground to taste
¼ tsp	Crushed red pepper flakes
•	Sea salt, to taste

loving preparation

1. Wash potatoes well. Chop into ½" cubes, place in a steamer basket in a 3 qt pot and steam as described on page 193 until potatoes are just soft, approximately 15 minutes. Please do not overcook.
2. Combine all ingredients except potatoes in a large mixing bowl and whisk well.
3. Add potatoes and *gently* mix well.

variations

↝ Purple sweet potatoes—also known as Okinawan sweet potatoes—are an island delicacy. If you cannot find them, you may experiment with yams or any potato of your choice.

"THANK YOU, LORD, FOR WHAT YOU'VE DONE FOR ME. THANK YOU, LORD, FOR WHAT YOU'RE DOING NOW. THANK YOU, LORD, FOR EVERY LITTLE THING. THANK YOU, LORD, FOR YOU MAKE ME SING." - BOB MARLEY

MOTHER AFRICA'S SPICY KALE AND YAM

20 min prep / 25 min cooking / 3-4 servings

1 large bunch	Kale, 4 c chopped, pressed firm		2 Tbl	Sea salt, or to taste
4 c	Garnet yam, rinsed well, chopped		1 Tbl	Garlic, minced
1 ½ Tbl	Olive oil		1 Tbl	Ginger, peeled & minced
2 c	Purple cabbage, sliced		1 tsp	Serrano chile, seeded & diced
1 ½ c	Onion, chopped		•	African Hot Sauce (page 214), to taste
3 Tbl	Nama shoyu			

loving preparation

1. Rinse and drain kale well. Steam kale and yams according to instructions on page 193. Kale should still be colorful & yams should still have some firmness.
2. While kale and yams are steaming, place oil in a large sauté pan and heat on medium high. Add onion, garlic, ginger and chili pepper, cook for 5 minutes, stirring frequently.
3. Add cabbage and cook for 5 minutes, stirring frequently. Add small amounts of water if necessary to prevent sticking. Place in a large mixing bowl with remaining ingredients, add kale and mix well.
4. Add yams and gently mix well.

Church of St. Mary, Ark of the Covenant in Background, Axum, Ethiopia

MS. AUSTIN'S ACORN SQUASH WITH WILD RICE PILAF

30 min prep / 1 hour cooking / 4 servings

2 medium	Acorn squash		1 Tbl	Italian parsley, minced
1 c	Wild rice (3 c cooked, page 206)		½ tsp	Sage, fresh, minced
4 c	Filtered water or vegetable stock		¼ tsp	Rosemary, fresh, minced
½ tsp	Sea salt		¼ tsp	Thyme, fresh, minced
1 Tbl	Olive oil		1 tsp	Vegetarian Worcestershire sauce (optional)
1 medium	Onion, diced (1 c)			
½ c	Celery, chopped		1 tsp	Nama shoyu, or to taste
1 Tbl	Garlic, minced		¼ tsp	Crushed red pepper flakes
1 c	Pecans, toasted & chopped (page 194)		•	Sea salt, to taste
½ c	Cranberries, dried		•	Black pepper, ground to taste

loving preparation

1. Preheat oven to 375°. Rinse squash well, slice in half, scoop out seeds and place face down on a well oiled baking sheet. Bake until a knife can pass easily through any part of the squash, approximately 45 minutes. Set aside.
2. Place wild rice and 4 c filtered water or stock in a large pot and bring to a boil. Cover, reduce heat to simmer and cook until rice kernels are open and just soft and chewy, approximately 50 minutes. Drain well.
3. While squash and rice are cooking, place oil in a large sauté pan on medium high heat. Add onion, celery and garlic, cook for 5 minutes, stirring frequently. Add remaining ingredients and cook for 5 minutes, stirring frequently. Add water or stock if necessary to prevent sticking. Place in a large bowl with drained wild rice and mix well. Stuff into squash and bake for 10 minutes.

serving suggestion

↬ Serve with Mushroom Gravy (page 64) as part of a festive meal with Cranberry Sauce (page 63) and green salad.

variations

↬ Substitute roasted chestnuts for pecans. Add ½ c corn and ½ c sliced mushrooms.

"A TRUE ARTIST CAN EXPRESS BEAUTY IN ANY MEDIUM." – BEN BIMSTEIN

HINDI'S BINDI MASALA

15 min prep / 20 minutes cooking / 2 servings

1 Tbl	Sesame oil		1 Tbl	Nama shoyu
½ tsp	Cumin seed		1 Tbl	Cilantro, minced
¾ C	Onion, chopped		½ tsp	Sea salt
1 Tbl	Garlic, minced		½ tsp	Turmeric powder
1 Tbl	Ginger, peeled & minced		¼ tsp	Coriander powder
2-3 medium	Tomatoes, chopped (2 cups)		¼ tsp	Crushed red pepper flakes
½ C	Filtered water or vegetable stock		¼ tsp	Garam masala
3 C	Okra with stem and tip removed		Pinch	Cayenne pepper (optional)

loving preparation

1. Place oil in a large sauté pan on medium-high heat. Add cumin seed & cook for 1 minute, stirring constantly. Add onion, garlic and ginger, cook for 5 minutes, stirring frequently. Add tomatoes and filtered water and cook for 5 minutes, stirring frequently. Add okra and cook until okra is soft with some firmness, approximately 8 minutes. Add remaining ingredients and stir well.

variation

↬ Replace okra with zucchini or yam.

serving suggestion

↬ Serve with Dahl (page 149) and Tempeh Curry (page 62).

"THE BEST FORM OF WORSHIP IS TO WORSHIP GOD IN EVERY FORM"

- NEEM KAROLI BABA

Haridwar Temple, India

78

TRANSCENDENTAL TROPICAL RATATOUILLE

20 min prep / 20 min cooking / 2 servings

1 Tbl	Olive oil
1 c	Onion, chopped
1 Tbl	Garlic, minced
1 large	Eggplant (2 c chopped)
1 ¼ c	Zucchini, ½" cubes
¾ c	Red bell pepper, ½" chop
•	Sea salt, to taste
•	Black pepper, ground to taste
1 recipe	Thai Coconut Sauce (page 59)
1 Tbl	Cilantro, minced

loving preparation

1. Place oil in a large sauté pan on medium high heat. Add onion and garlic, cook for 3 minutes, stirring frequently. Add eggplant and cook for 5 minutes, stirring frequently.
2. Add Thai Coconut Sauce, cook for 5 minutes, stirring occasionally. Add zucchini and bell pepper, cook for 5 minutes, stirring occasionally. Remove lime leaf, add cilantro, salt and pepper to taste and mix well.

serving suggestions

↬ Garnish with toasted coconut flakes and serve over rice or quinoa.

note

↬ To remove bitterness from eggplant, slice into ½" slices, and place on a baking sheet. Lightly sprinkle with salt and allow to sit until water beads start to form, approximately 10 minutes. Rinse well, cut into cubes and follow above directions.

DOMO ARIGATO HEAVENLY ARAME SALAD

35 minutes prep / 3-4 servings

Salad

2 c	Purple cabbage, julienned, 2" long
1 c	Carrots, grated
1 c	Corn, fresh
1 c	Red bell pepper, diced
1 c	Arame, soaked in warm water until soft & drained
½ c	Green onion, diced
2 Tbl	Cilantro, minced
4 tsp	Pickled ginger, minced (page 197)

Dressing

½ c	Filtered water
¼ c	Lemon juice, fresh squeezed
2 Tbl	Tahini, raw
2 tsp	Nama shoyu, or to taste
¼ tsp	Sea salt, or to taste
¼ tsp	Black pepper, ground to taste

loving preparation

1. Soak arame for a minimum of 15 minutes. Drain & rinse very well. Remove as much excess liquid as possible.
2. For **Salad** assemble all salad ingredients in a large bowl and mix well.
3. For **Dressing** place all ingredients in a small bowl and whisk well. Add dressing to salad mixture and toss well. Enjoy.

serving suggestions

↬ Serve as a side dish with Live Nori Rolls (page 32) or Nirvana Nori Rolls (page 90).

MT. CARMEL COUSCOUS SALAD

15 min prep / 15 min cooking / 2-3 servings

1 ¾ C	Filtered water or vegetable stock	2 Tbl	Lemon juice, fresh squeezed
1 C	Couscous, medium size, toasted	1 Tbl	Balsamic vinegar
1 C	Tomato, chopped	1 ½ tsp	Garlic, minced
¾ C	Cucumber, seeded & chopped	1 tsp	Dill, minced
3 Tbl	Italian parsley, minced	Pinch	Cayenne pepper
		•	Sea salt, to taste

- Black pepper, ground to taste

"I GET UP, I WALK, I FALL DOWN. MEANWHILE I KEEP DANCING." - HILLEL

Jerusalem, Israel

ANAKIN'S ASPARAGUS

25 minutes / 3-4 servings

12 large	Asparagus spears
1 large	Red bell pepper, julienne (1 cup)
2 Tbl	Olive oil
2 Tbl	Fennel bulb, chopped small
1 Tbl	Garlic, minced
1 Tbl	Lemon juice, fresh squeezed
1 ½ tsp	Dill, minced
1 tsp	Nama shoyu (optional)
1 tsp	Balsamic vinegar, or to taste
Pinch	Crushed red pepper flakes
•	Sea salt, to taste
•	Black pepper, ground to taste

loving preparation

1. Steam asparagus according to method on page 193 until just tender, approximately 6 minutes. Please do not overcook asparagus. Drain well and place on a serving platter.
2. Place oil in a sauté pan on medium high heat. Add bell pepper, fennel and garlic, cook until peppers are just soft, approximately 5 minutes, stirring frequently. Add remaining ingredients, mix well and pour over asparagus.

variations

- Many variations are possible. Try steaming different vegetables like broccoli or cauliflower.
- Other vegetables may be used in the sauté, such as zucchini or mushrooms.
- Dill can be replaced with other fresh herbs.
- Any of the salad dressings or sauces can be added to enhance this dish.
- For a buttery flavor, add 1 Tbl flax oil and 1 tsp of nutritional yeast.

JEWEL OF THE LOTUS GREEN PAPAYA SALAD

35 minutes for 2-3 servings

Salad

1 medium	Green papaya, peeled, seeded & grated (4 cups)
⅔ C	Carrots, peeled & grated
⅔ C	Red cabbage, julienned 1" long
⅔ C	Macadamia nuts, chopped
⅓ C	Celery, sliced thin
3 Tbl	Red bell pepper, diced
2 Tbl	Cilantro, minced
2 Tbl	Ginger, peeled & minced fine

Dressing

⅓ C	Lime or orange juice, fresh squeezed
1 Tbl	Nama shoyu, or to taste
1 tsp	Sea salt, or to taste
½ tsp	Black pepper, ground to taste
¼ tsp	Chili powder
⅛ tsp	Crushed red pepper flakes

loving preparation

1. Combine all *Salad* ingredients in a large bowl and gently mix well.
2. Add all *Dressing* ingredients to a small bowl and whisk well.
3. Toss all ingredients together and enjoy.

"WHEN WILL OUR CONSCIENCES GROW SO TENDER THAT WE WILL ACT TO PREVENT HUMAN MISERY RATHER THAN AVENGE IT." - ELEANOR ROOSEVELT

SHANTI GABRIEL'S LIVE FETTUCCINI ALFREDA

40 minutes prep / 2 servings

Sauce

1 ¼ c	Filtered water
1 c	Macadamia nuts
1 Tbl	Lemon juice, fresh squeezed
2 tsp	Nama shoyu
1½ tsp	Garlic, minced
½ tsp	Apple cider vinegar, raw
1 ½ tsp	Nutritional yeast
Pinch	Cayenne pepper
•	Sea salt, to taste
•	Black pepper, ground to taste

Pasta

1 ½ c	Carrots, thinly julienned or grated
1 c	Zucchini, thinly julienned or spiralized (page 192)
1 c	Gold bar squash, thinly julienned or spiralized
1 c	Red bell pepper, thinly julienned
2 tsp	Basil, chopped
2 tsp	Italian Parsley, chopped

loving preparation

1. Combine all *Sauce* ingredients in a blender and blend until smooth. Combine all *Pasta* ingredients in a medium bowl and mix well.
2. Place pasta on two individual plates and top each one with ½ of the sauce. Garnish with chopped macadamia or pine nuts.

"THE EARTH IS BUT ONE COUNTRY AND HUMANKIND ITS CITIZENS." - BAHA-U-LLA'H

Shanti Gabriel's Live Fettuccini Alfreda

6

Grilled Portabello Mushroom Sandwich, page 93

wraps & sandwiches

GAIA'S GRILLED TEMPEH REUBEN

20 min prep / 10 min cooking / 2 servings

8 oz	Tempeh, sliced in half into two thin cutlets
¼ C	Thousand Island Dressing (page 52)
2 Tbl	Homemade Sauerkraut (page 204)
2	Spelt buns or 4 slices whole grain rye bread
•	Sliced red onion, tomato or fixings of choice

loving preparation

1. *Grill*: Preheat grill. Marinate tempeh cutlets in Shoyu Marinade (page 195) for 10 minutes. Cook until grill marks appear on both sides and tempeh is cooked thoroughly, approximately 10 minutes, brushing cutlets with marinade sauce periodically.
2. *No Grill*: If no grill is available, cutlets can be sautéed in 2 Tbl of oil until golden brown, approximately 8 minutes, or placed on a well oiled baking sheet and baked in a 350° oven until done, approximately 15 minutes.
2. Slice buns in half and toast on grill until warmed. Add your favorite fixings for the reuben of your dreams.

BABA B'S BURRITO

20 min cooking / condiment prep time / 1 serving

½ C	Brown rice, cooked
¼ C	Beans, black or pinto, cooked
2 Tbl	Salsa (page 24)
2 Tbl	Guacamole (page 26)
1 Tbl	Shanti's Sour Crème (page 196)
1 Tbl	Chili sauce (page 197)
1	Tortilla, spelt
•	Lettuce & other salad fixings

loving preparation

1. Lay a tortilla on a clean, dry surface. Place ½ C of rice just beneath the center of the tortilla, flatten slightly, leaving at least one inch of space on either side of the tortilla. Add beans and remaining ingredients.
2. Gently fold an inch or so of each side of the tortilla towards the center. Roll the burrito away from you creating a firm wrap. (For overstuffed, open-faced burritos, do not fold sides of the tortilla).

"HOW FAR THAT LITTLE CANDLE THROWS ITS BEAMS! SO SHINES A GOOD DEED IN A WEARY WORLD"
- SHAKESPEARE

Baba B's Burrito pictured on page 87.

I'O NALANI TARO BURGER

40 min prep / 30 min cooking / 4 servings

1-2 medium	Taro corms (roots, 3 cups mashed)
2 Tbl	Sesame oil
¼ C	Red onion, diced
¼ C	Red bell pepper, diced
2 tsp	Garlic, minced
1 tsp	Rosemary, fresh, minced
¾ tsp	Sea salt, or to taste
¼ tsp	Black pepper, ground to taste
¼ tsp	Crushed red pepper flakes
•	Nama shoyu, to taste
2 Tbl	Olive oil for sautéing burgers

loving preparation

1. Peel taro, cut into ½" cubes, place in a large pot with 10 C of water and cook on medium high heat until taro is soft, approximately 30 minutes, stirring occasionally and adding fresh water if necessary. Rinse, drain well and place in a large mixing bowl and let cool. Mash with fork or masher.
2. While taro is cooking, place oil in a large sauté pan on medium high heat. Add onion, bell pepper and garlic, cook for 5 minutes, stirring frequently. Add to taro with remaining ingredients and mix well.
3. Heat a skillet or griddle on medium high heat. Form taro into 4 equal patties and sauté until golden brown on each side, approximately 4 minutes per side, flipping occasionally to ensure even cooking.

serving suggestions

- Serve on a whole grain bun with 2 Tbl Garlic Herb Spread and all the fixings.
- Serve on a bed of lettuce, top with guacamole.

GARLIC HERB SPREAD

20 min prep / 20 min cooking / 1 ½ cups

¼ C	Garlic cloves
12.3 oz	Silken tofu
1 Tbl	Lemon juice, fresh squeezed
2 tsp	Miso paste, mellow variety or one of your favorites
1 ½ tsp	Nama shoyu, or to taste
1 tsp	Nutritional yeast
1 Tbl	Green onion, diced
1 Tbl	Fresh Herbs, minced (try with parsley, sage, rosemary, thyme, basil, cilantro or dill)
Pinch	Cayenne pepper
•	Black pepper, ground to taste
•	Sea salt, to taste

loving preparation

1. Roast garlic according to method discussed on page 193. Add to food processor with lemon juice, miso paste, shoyu and nutritional yeast, process until smooth.
2. Add to a small mixing bowl with remaining ingredients and mix well.

serving suggestion

- Use as a spread for wraps or sandwiches or as a dipping sauce for chips or veggies.

variations

- Altering the herbs will create different varieties.
- Try adding ¼ C roasted red bell peppers to processor with other ingredients.

HOLY HUMMUS WRAP WITH GRILLED TEMPEH

30 minutes / 2 servings

2	Spelt tortillas
½ C	Hummus (page 20)
½ C	Grilled vegetables (page 194)
1 cutlet	Tempeh or tofu, grilled & marinated (page 194) cut into 4 strips
handful	Organic mixed salad greens
2 Tbl	Carrots, grated
2 Tbl	Beets, grated
2 Tbl	Kalamata olives or artichoke hearts, diced
1 Tbl	Maple balsamic dressing (optional, page 57)

loving preparation

1. Lay two tortillas on a clean flat surface. Spread hummus on center of each tortilla.
2. Place 2 slices of the cutlet on top of the hummus, top with remaining ingredients and wrap. Slice in half and enjoy.

variations

~ Create your own wrap by varying spreads, veggies, cutlets and dressing.

BIG BEN'S BAKED TOFU SANDWICH

30 minutes / 3 servings

1 lb	Tofu, sliced into 3 equal lengthwise cutlets
1 recipe	Shoyu Marinade (page 195)
½ C	Peanut sauce (page 21)
¼ C	Green onion, diced
1 Tbl	Ginger, peeled & minced
6 slices	Whole grain bread
3	Romaine lettuce leaves
1 medium	Tomato, sliced thin
3 slices	Red onion, sliced thin
1	Avocado, sliced thin

loving preparation

1. Preheat oven (preferably a convection oven) to 375°. Place tofu cutlets in Shoyu Marinade for 20 minutes. Remove cutlets and place in a shallow baking dish. Add peanut sauce, green onion and ginger, bake for 20 minutes. Allow to cool before placing on sandwich with remaining ingredients.

tip

~ Cutlets can be prepared 2-3 days in advance and used as needed.

variation

~ Replace peanut sauce with Creamy Tahini Marinade (page 195) and follow above instructions.

"I WILL NOT PLAY TUG O WAR. I WOULD RATHER PLAY HUG O WAR. WHERE EVERYONE HUGS INSTEAD OF TUGS. WHERE EVERYONE GIGGLES AND ROLLS ON THE RUG. WHERE EVERYONE SMILES AND EVERYONE GRINS. AND EVERYONE CUDDLES AND EVERYONE WINS"

- SHEL SILVERSTEIN

NIRVANA'S NORI ROLL

10 minutes for 4 servings

4	Nori sheets
2 c	Brown rice, cooked (page 206)
2 tsp	Ume boshi paste (optional)
½ c	Milarepa's Maki Roll Spread (page 214)
8 oz	Tempeh, grilled (page 194) sliced into ¼" strips
¼ c	Beets, grated
1	Avocado, sliced thin

¼ c	Carrots, grated
1 small	Cucumber, seeded & sliced in ¼" strips
¼ c	Green onion, diced
2 Tbl	Pickled ginger, chopped (page 197)

Dipping Sauce

¼ c	Nama shoyu
½ tsp	Wasabi powder
1 Tbl	Green onion, diced

loving preparation

1. Combine **Dipping Sauce** ingredients in a small bowl and whisk well. Lay out a spread of necessary utensils including sushi rolling mat, spatula and above ingredients.
2. Lay a sheet of nori on a sushi mat. Spread ½ c of brown rice on bottom half portion of sheet. Spread ½ tsp ume boshi paste over rice, top with maki roll spread, and fixings of choice, keeping in mind that the more ingredients added the more challenging it will be to roll. Find your ideal nori roll size. Experiment with color, texture and be as creative as you like.
3. Moisten the top portion of the sheet with water, roll away from you, creating as firm of a roll as possible. Slice diagonally in half. Serve with dipping sauce and pickled ginger.

"THE REVERSE SIDE ALSO HAS A REVERSE SIDE." - JAPANESE PROVERB

Mt. Fuji, Japan

Nirvana's Nori Roll

RABBI MOSHE'S NEAT BALL HERO

20 min prep / 30 min cooking / 10 – 2" balls

2 c	Buckwheat, cooked (page 206).
½ c	Red bell pepper, diced
¼ c	Crimini mushrooms, finely diced
¼ c	Bread crumbs (page 54)
2 Tbl	Tahini
2 Tbl	Nutritional yeast
2 Tbl	Tomato paste
2 tsp	Nama shoyu, or to taste
1 tsp	Garlic, minced
1 tsp	Sea salt, or to taste
•	Black pepper, ground to taste

loving preparation

1. For **Bread Crumbs**, follow crouton instructions on page 54 and process in food processor until fine.
2. Preheat oven to 300°. Place all ingredients in a large mixing bowl and mix well. Form into 2" balls and place on a well oiled baking sheet. Bake until a golden brown crust appears, approximately 30 minutes.
3. Serve on whole grain hero bread with Marinara Sauce (page 59).

GRILLED PORTABELLO MUSHROOM SANDWICH

25 minutes for 1 serving

1	Portabello mushroom, marinated & grilled (page 194)
1	Whole grain spelt bun (page 104)
2 Tbl	Vegan mayonnaise or sour crème (page 196)
1 slice	Red onion, sliced thin
1 slice	Tomato, sliced thin
1 leaf	Romaine lettuce

loving preparation

1. Spread mayonnaise, sour crème or condiment of your choosing on the bottom of the bun. Add portabello and top with your favorite fixings.

Citadel and mud city of Bam, Iran

"THE FUTURE BELONGS TO THOSE WHO BELIEVE IN THE BEAUTY OF THEIR DREAMS." - ELEANOR ROOSEVELT

Praying Goddess Kalalea Mountain, Kauai, Hawaii

Francene Hart

ST. THERESA'S TLC: TENDER LOVING CARE

30 minutes for 1 serving

5 strips	Tempeh strips (page 213)
2 slices	Whole grain spelt bread
1 slice	Tomato, sliced
1 slice	Red onion, sliced thin
½	Avocado, sliced
2 slices	Cucumber

1 leaf	Lettuce
•	Condiment of your choosing, such as Thousand Island Dressing (page 52), Vegan Mayonnaise (page 196) or stoneground mustard

loving preparation

1. Preheat oven to 375°. Place tempeh strips in a well oiled baking sheet and bake for 15 minutes. Flip tempeh and cook for an additional 10 minutes.
2. Place tempeh and remaining ingredients on whole grain bread and slice diagonally.

serving suggestions

↝ Serve with baked tortilla chips and a pickle spear.
↝ Serve with toasted dulse strips for your own DLT.

"LOVE THY NEIGHBOUR AS THYSELF." - MARK 12:31

7

Plato's Live Greek Pizza, page 113

breads pizza pasta

HIMALAYAN STUFFED BREAD

TOLTEC TOFU STUFFING

SPICY THAI NOODLES

MACARONI AND CHEEZ

SOBA AND PEANUT SAUCE

PAD THAI

PASTA PRIMAVERA

SPELT FOCACCIA DOUGH

THAI PEANUT PIZZA

SUNCHOKE & FENNEL STROMBOLI

KORN BREAD

JAMAICAN ROTI

SPELT CHAPATTI

LIVE MANNA BREAD

LIVE GREEK PIZZA

PESTO PERFECTO

SHIVA SHAKTI'S HIMALAYAN STUFFED BREAD

20 min prep / 40 min cooking / 5 servings

2 medium	Garnet yams, ½" cubes (3 c)
2 tsp	Sesame oil
¼ c	Onion, diced
2 tsp	Garlic, minced
1 tsp	Jalapeño, seeded & minced
½ c	Coconut milk, soy milk or rice milk
1 ½ tsp	Cilantro, minced
¾ tsp	Curry powder
½ tsp	Sea salt, or to taste
¼ tsp	Black pepper, ground to taste
1 recipe	Focaccia Dough, (page 104)
•	Olive oil or coconut milk for basting

loving preparation

1. Preheat oven to 400°. Prepare Foccacia Dough. Allow to sit in a cool dry place.
2. Peel and steam yams according to instructions on page 193. Place in a measuring cup and mash down (2 c yield).
3. Place oil in large sauté pan on medium heat. Add onion, garlic and jalapeño, cook until onions are translucent, approx. 8 minutes, stirring frequently. Place in large mixing bowl with mashed yams and remaining ingredients, mix well. Refrigerate until cool, approx. 10 minutes.
4. Divide dough into 5 equal balls. Roll out balls on a clean, dry and lightly floured surface with a rolling pin until each portion is approximately 6" in diameter. Place about ½ c of yam mixture in the center of each portion. Fold in sides, then top & bottom portion of loaf towards center.
5. Place on a well oiled or parchment paper lined baking sheet, with the folded creases face down. Brush with olive oil or coconut milk. Bake until golden brown, approx. 15-20 minutes.

serving suggestions

- Serve with Coconut Curry Sauce (page 62) or Mango Chutney (page 23).

TOLTEC TOFU STUFFING

20 min prep / 40 min cooking / 5 servings

2 Tbl	Olive oil
½ c	Onion, chopped
2 tsp	Garlic, minced (optional)
1 tsp	Jalapeño, seeded & minced
1 lb	Tofu, extra firm, crumbled
¾ c	Black beans, cooked (page 209)
½ c	Corn, fresh or frozen
3 Tbl	Tahini
1½ Tbl	Nama shoyu, or to taste
1 Tbl	Cilantro, minced
1 small	Ancho chili soaked in hot water until soft, seeded & chopped
½ tsp	Cumin powder, toasted (page 194)
½ tsp	Chili powder
Pinch	Cayenne pepper
•	Sea salt, to taste
•	Black pepper, ground to taste

loving preparation

1. Place oil in a large sauté pan on medium high heat. Add onion, garlic and jalapeño, cook until onions are soft, approximately 8 minutes, stirring occasionally. Add tofu and cook for 5 minutes, stirring occasionally. Remove and place in a large bowl with remaining ingredients and mix well.
2. Make focaccia bread and follow step 4 in previous recipe.

serving suggestions

- Chill for at least 10 minutes before using as stuffed bread filling. Serve with salsa and guacamole.
- Can be used as a main course for a Mexican Fiesta Platter.
- Can also serve as a pizza topping. Place on baked Foccacia Crust (page 104) and top with freshly chopped tomatoes and chopped basil.

ONE LOVE SPICY THAI NOODLES

20 min prep / 20 min cooking / 2 servings

6 C	Filtered water
8 oz	Udon, soba or rice noodles
2 Tbl	Toasted sesame oil
1 ½ C	Broccoli flowerettes, in ½" pieces
2 tsp	Garlic, minced
1 ½ C	Red bell pepper, julienned (1 medium pepper)
¼ C	Filtered water for sauté

1 small	Lime leaf, sliced thin (optional)
¼ C	Green onion, diced
3 Tbl	Nama shoyu, or to taste
1 ½ Tbl	Cilantro, chopped
¼ tsp	Cayenne pepper
•	Sea salt, to taste
•	Black pepper, ground to taste
•	Black sesame seeds, for garnish

loving preparation

1. Bring 6 C of filtered water to a boil in a 3 qt pot. Add noodles, reduce heat to simmer and cook until pasta is slightly al dente. Rice noodles cook in a minute or less; udon or soba approximately 5 minutes. Drain, rinse well in cold water and place in a large bowl with a small amount of oil to prevent sticking.

2. While pasta is cooking, add oil, garlic and broccoli to a medium size sauté pan and cook over medium high heat for 3 minutes, stirring frequently. Add ¼ C filtered water, red bell pepper and lime leaf. Cook until broccoli is just soft, approximately 8 minutes, stirring frequently, adding more water if necessary to prevent sticking to the pan. Add to pasta with remaining ingredients and gently mix well. Top with black sesame seeds.

variations

- Add ½ C coconut milk with 1 Tbl peanut butter to above when combining all ingredients together.
- Top with chopped peanuts, toasted coconut and a dash of crushed red pepper flakes.
- As a main course bowl, add 4 oz of grilled tempeh cubes.

Phisanulok Buddha, Thailand

MENEHUNE'S MACARONI & CHEEZ

20 min prep / 20 min cooking / 2 servings

1 ½ c	Elbow noodles, wheat free (3 c cooked)

Vegan Cheez Sauce

1 ½ c	Soy or rice milk
2 Tbl	Rolled oats
2 Tbl	Tahini
2 Tbl	Nutritional yeast
1 tsp	Nama shoyu, or to taste
¾ tsp	Dijon mustard
½ tsp	Garlic, minced
½ tsp	Turmeric powder
•	Sea salt, to taste
•	Black pepper, ground to taste

loving preparation

1. Bring 8 c of water to a boil in a large pot. Add noodles and cook until pasta is slightly al dente, approximately 8 minutes, stirring occasionally. A small amount of olive oil may be added to prevent sticking. Drain well and return to pot.

2. While pasta is cooking, prepare **Cheez Sauce** by placing remaining ingredients in a blender and blending until smooth. Pour into a 3 qt pot and heat over low heat until sauce thickens, stirring frequently, approximately 5 minutes. Add pasta and mix well.

variation

☞ Place in a well oiled casserole dish, top with bread crumbs (page 93) and broil for 7 minutes. Top with additional sauce if necessary.

SERENDIPITY SOBA

30 minutes for 2 servings

8 oz pkg	Soba noodles
5 c	Mixed garden vegetables for steaming (broccoli, red bell pepper, carrots, zuchinni, etc. chopped small)
1 c	Peanut sauce (page 21)
1 Tbl	Toasted sesame oil
1 tsp	Garlic or ginger, peeled & minced
1 Tbl	Cilantro, minced
2 tsp	Crushed red pepper flakes
Pinch	Sea salt
•	Black pepper, ground to taste

loving preparation

1. Bring 8 c of water to a boil in a 3 qt sauce pan. Add soba noodles and cook until slightly al dente, approximately 5 minutes, stirring occasionally. A small amount of sesame oil may be added to prevent sticking. Drain, rinse well in cold water and place in a large mixing bowl.

2. Steam vegetables according to instructions on page 193, add to bowl with soba along with remaining ingredients and mix well. Peanut sauce may be prepared earlier or while vegetables are steaming and soba is cooking. Garnish with black and white sesame seeds.

variations

☞ Replace soba with udon noodles. Vegetables may be stir fried, grilled or roasted.

☞ Replace peanut sauce with other sauce recipes listed in Chapter 4 such as Carrot Ginger (page 66) or Curry (page 62).

"NONVIOLENCE IS THE ANSWER TO THE CRUCIAL POLITICAL AND MORAL QUESTIONS OF OUR TIME: THE NEED FOR US TO OVERCOME OPPRESSION AND VIOLENCE WITHOUT RESORTING TO OPPRESSION AND VIOLENCE. WE MUST EVOLVE FOR ALL HUMAN CONFLICT A METHOD WHICH REJECTS REVENGE, AGGRESSION AND RETALIATION. THE FOUNDATION OF SUCH A METHOD IS LOVE." – MARTIN LUTHER KING, JR.

TARA'S PAD THAI

3-5 min prep / 3-5 min cooking / 4-6 servings

8 oz	Rice noodles (the thicker the better)
1 ½ C	Onion, diced
½ C	Green onions, thinly sliced
1 lb	Tofu, extra firm, ¼" cubes
1 C	Mung bean sprouts
⅓ C	Nama shoyu, or to taste
⅓ C	Lime juice, fresh
¼ C	Sucanat
3 Tbl	Peanut butter

2 Tbl	Sesame oil
2 Tbl	Garlic, minced
1 Tbl	Ginger, peeled & minced
1 Tbl	Tahini
1 Tbl	Tamarind pulp (see glossary)
½ tsp	Curry paste (page 197)
¼ tsp	Crushed red pepper flakes
¼ tsp	Cumin powder
¼ tsp	Coriander, ground
•	Cilantro, to garnish
•	Ground peanuts, to garnish

loving preparation

1. Prepare rice noodles by soaking them in boiling hot water for 3-5 minutes. Drain well and place in a large mixing bowl.
2. Place nama shoyu, lime juice, peanut butter, tahini, sucanat, tamarind pulp, curry paste and spices in a medium mixing bowl and whisk well. Set aside.
3. In a wok or large sauté pan, on medium high heat, sauté garlic, ginger and tofu in 1 Tbl sesame oil until tofu is slightly browned, approximately 5 minutes, stirring frequently and adding small amounts of water if necessary to prevent sticking . Add remaining oil, onion, green onion and cook 5 minutes , stirring frequently.
4. Optionally, at this time, you may add 1 C of water chestnuts, 1 C chopped carrots, and 1 C of broccoli flowerettes, or up to 3 C of assorted vegetables. Add additional water if necessary to prevent sticking. and cook lightly for 5 minutes.
5. Add the peanut sauce mixture and cook until the sauce thickens, approximately 5 minutes, stirring frequently. Add to noodles in large mixing bowl.
6. Gently mix in bean sprouts and garnish liberally with freshly chopped cilantro, ground peanuts and a slice of lime.

The Potala Palace, Lhasa, Tibet

RAHIM'S RASTA PASTA PRIMAVERA

20 min prep / 20 min cooking / 3-4 servings

3 c	Pasta, assorted colors		3 Tbl	Kalamata olives, sliced
3 c	Assorted mixed vegetables, (zuchinni, broccoli, carrots, red cabbage, yellow squash, etc), chopped		2 Tbl	Red onion, diced (optional)
			2 Tbl	Italian parsley, chopped
			2 Tbl	Basil, chopped
			1 tsp	Garlic, minced (optional)
1 c	Maple Balsamic Dressing (page 57)		1 tsp	Nama shoyu (optional), or to taste
½ c	Bell pepper, assorted colors, julienned		Pinch	Cayenne pepper
			•	Sea salt, to taste
¼ c	Hemp seeds		•	Black pepper, ground to taste

loving preparation

1. Bring 8 c of water to a boil in a large pot. Add noodles and cook until pasta is soft with some firmness, approximately 8 minutes, stirring occasionally. A small amount of olive oil may be added to pot to prevent sticking. Remove from heat, drain, rinse under water, drain well and place in a large mixing bowl.
2. Steam vegetables according to method discussed on page 193, run under cold water to prevent further cooking. Add to bowl with pasta and remaining ingredients, mix well.

serving suggestion

↬ Serve cold. Garnish with additional hemp and black sesame seeds.

variations

↬ Experiment with different assorted veggies. Maple Balsamic can be replaced with other dressings such as a Pecan Vinaigrette (page 52) or Green Goddess (page 52).

"I WILL BE GLAD AND REJOICE IN THEE; I WILL SING PRAISE TO THY NAME, O THOU, MOST HIGH." - PSALM 9:2

UNIVERSAL SPELT FOCCACIA DOUGH

35 min prep / 15 min cooking / 6-8 rolls or 2 med pizzas

3 ⅓ C	Spelt flour, sifted well
1¼ C	Filtered water, warm to the touch
⅔ C	Olive oil
2 Tbl	Fresh herbs, minced
	(try sage, parsley, basil & thyme)
¼ C	Corn meal
1 Tbl	Dry active yeast
1 Tbl	Garlic, minced (optional)
1 tsp	Sea salt, or to taste
1 tsp	Sucanat
¼ tsp	Black pepper, ground to taste
Pinch	Crushed red pepper flakes

loving preparation

1. Preheat oven to 375°. Place herbs in a small mixing bowl with olive oil, salt , pepper and crushed pepper, mix well and allow to sit for 20 minutes or longer.
2. Place sucanat and warm water in a large bowl, whisk until sucanat dissolves and add yeast.
3. When yeast starts to bubble, add the oil herb mixture and whisk well. Slowly add flour and corn meal and knead into a ball. Cover bowl with towel. When ball doubles in size, thump down, gently knead into a ball, re-cover with towel and let rise again to twice its size.

variations

- **Pizza** roll onto a well oiled baking sheet or pizza pan. Bake until top is golden brown, approximately 15 minutes, top with desired topping and bake until topping is cooked.
- **Homemade Spelt Rolls** divide dough into 6-8 equal parts, place on well oiled or parchment paper-lined baking sheet and bake until golden brown, approximately 15 minutes.
- **Breadsticks** divide dough into 12 equal portions, roll on a cornmeal dusted surface to form pencil-shaped rolls. Baste with Basting Sauce (page 196) and minced garlic. Bake until golden brown, approx. 10 minutes.

TAT TVAM ASI THAI PIZZA

50 min prep / 30 min cooking / 2 - 14" pizzas

1 recipe	Spelt foccacia dough
2 Tbl	Sesame oil
2 C	Onion, sliced
2 Tbl	Garlic, minced (optional)
2 Tbl	Ginger, peeled & minced
1 lb	Tofu, marinated, ¼" cubes
6 C	Broccoli or other vegetable, such as
	snow peas, steamed (page 193)
1 recipe	Thai Coconut Sauce (page 59)
1 C	Peanuts, dry roasted, no salt, for garnish
6 Tbl	Cilantro, chopped, for garnish

loving preparation

1. Marinate tofu according to instructions in the grilling section on page 194. Steam broccoli or veggies. Prepare Coconut Sauce. Preheat oven to 375°. Prepare *Focaccia Dough*. Divide dough in half and bake to form 2 pizza crusts.
2. Place oil in large sauté pan on medium heat. Add onion, garlic, ginger, cook 3 minutes. While gently stirring, add tofu & steamed veggies, cook for 3 minutes. Add Thai Coconut Sauce, reduce heat to low, cook 5 minutes. Using a slotted spoon, place mixture on top of foccacia dough. Pour small amounts of sauce onto pizzas, taking care not to make crust soggy. Top with cilantro & peanuts, bake 10 minutes.

variations

- For an *Italian* variety, use Marinara Sauce (page 59) or Pesto Sauce (there is nothing like a pesto pizza, page 140) and top with 3 C assorted veggies per pizza.
- Top with chopped tomatoes, basil and kalamata olives. Can also add strips of grilled ulu, tempeh or tofu.
- Create your own designer **Spelt Crusted Pizza**. Be creative. Pizzas can be made using Hummus, (page 20), Black Bean Sauce (page 64) Chili Sauce (page 197) & topped with your favorite ingredients.

"WE ARE JUST TENANTS ON THIS WORLD. WE HAVE JUST BEEN GIVEN A NEW LEASE, AND A WARNING FROM THE LANDLORD." - ARTHUR C. CLARKE

"FROM THE GARDEN ISLAND OF KAUAI... WE WHO LOVE THE LAND OFFER THIS PRAYER. MAY ALL BEINGS HAVE HAPPINESS AND THE CAUSES OF HAPPINESS. MAY ALL SUFFERING AND THE STORMS OF LIFE BE TRANSFORMED IN THE LIGHT OF COMPASSION. MAY PEACE AND UNITY FILL EVERY HEART." - HARMONY

SERGIO'S SUNCHOKE AND FENNEL CALZONE

20 min prep / 40 min cooking / 2 - 6" calzones

1 recipe	Foccacia Dough (page 104)
4 C	Sunchoke or parsnip, ½" cubes
1½ C	Fennel bulb, diced
3 Tbl	Olive oil
1 C	Onion, diced
2 Tbl	Garlic, minced

½ C	Vegan Cheez sauce (page 100)
¼ C	Basil and/or Italian parsley, minced
2 tsp	Balsamic vinegar
2 tsp	Nama shoyu, or to taste
Pinch	Crushed red pepper flakes
•	Sea salt, to taste
•	Black pepper, ground to taste

loving preparation

1. Preheat oven to 375°. Prepare foccacia dough.
2. While dough is rising, place sunchokes or parsnips and diced fennel on a well oiled baking sheet. Roast according to instructions on page 193 and set aside.
3. Place oil in a large saute pan on medium high heat. Add onion and garlic, cook for 5 minutes, stirring frequently. Add cooked sunchokes or parsnips and fennel, cook for 5 minutes, stirring frequently. Add remaining ingredients, mix well, place in a large mixing bowl and refrigerate until cool, approximately 10 minutes.
4. Place foccacia dough on a clean, dry and corn meal dusted surface. Divide in half, roll out with a rolling pin until two 6" x 10" rectangles are formed.
5. Place sunchoke or parsnip mixture in the center of each rectangle, making a smaller shape of about 2" wide x 6" long. Fold the sides in towards the center and then fold the top and bottom portion to seal off the contents, making as tight of a roll as possible. Repeat for second calzone.
6. Lay with the crease side down on a well oiled baking sheet or in a loaf pan. Brush dough with Basting Sauce (page 196) or coconut milk and bake until golden brown on top, approximately 25 minutes.

serving suggestion

↝ Slice to desired size and serve with Vegan Cheez Sauce (page 100), Marinara Sauce (page 59) or Spinach Mushroom Sauce (page 60).

variations

Replace filling with one of the following:
↝ **Indian** Fill with Himalayan Stuffed Bread Filling (page 98).
↝ **Mexican** Fill with Toltec Tofu Stuffing (page 98).

"THERE IS A FORCE WITHIN WHICH GIVES YOU LIFE—SEEK THAT. IN YOUR BODY LIES A PRICELESS GEM—SEEK THAT. IF YOU WANT TO FIND THE GREATEST TREASURE DON'T LOOK OUTSIDE, LOOK INSIDE, AND SEEK THAT."- RUMI

KAYA'S KOSMIC KORN BREAD

15 min prep / 45 min cooking / 9" x 9" baking pan

Dry

2 c	Spelt flour, sifted well
⅞ c	Corn meal
¾ c	Millet or quinoa, toasted (page 194)
2½ Tbl	Baking powder, sifted to remove lumps
¾ tsp	Sea salt

Wet

½ lb	Tofu, firm
1 ¾ c	Filtered water
¾ c	Maple syrup or agave nectar, or to taste
½ c	Safflower oil

loving preparation

1. Preheat oven to 350°. Combine **Dry** ingredients in a large mixing bowl and whisk well. Add **Wet** ingredients to a blender and blend until creamy. Add wet to dry and mix well.

2. Pour into a parchment paper-lined 9" x 9" baking pan and bake until a toothpick comes out clean, approximately 45 minutes, or until top browns and cracks appear.

variations

☞ **Southwest** Add the following to dry mixture: ¼ c ancho chilies, soaked in hot water, seeded and diced; ½ c red bell pepper, diced; ¼ c cilantro, minced; ½ c corn, fresh or frozen.

☞ **Blueberry or Strawberry** Add 1¼ c of berries after all ingredients have been mixed together.

☞ **Cranberry Walnut** Add 1 c fresh cranberries and ½ c chopped walnuts after all ingredients have been mixed together.

☞ **Double Corn Bread** Add 1½ c of corn after all ingredients have been mixed together.

"BLESSED ARE THE MERCIFUL, FOR THEY SHALL RECEIVE MERCY." - MATTHEW 5:7

MAMA NADIA'S CARIBBEAN ROTI

1 hour prep / 45 min cooking / 6 servings

Dough
4 c	Spelt flour
4 tsp	Baking powder
1 ½ c	Filtered water, warm
1 tsp	Sea salt

Filling
1 c	Yellow split peas, dry
1 tsp	Sea salt, or to taste
½ tsp	Black pepper, ground to taste
12 strands	Saffron
1 ½ tsp	Garlic, minced
1 small	Scotch bonnet pepper
1 tsp	Cumin powder, toasted (page 194)

loving preparation

1. For *Dough*, place flour, baking powder, sea salt and water in a large mixing bowl and knead until soft and moist, but not hard. Let sit ½ hour. Shape into 6 balls and let sit an additional 15 minutes.
2. For *Filling*, place peas, sea salt, pepper, saffron, garlic and scotch bonnet in a 3 qt pot on medium high heat with 4 c of water and cook for 20 minutes, stirring frequently. Peas should be firm not soft. Drain water and let peas dry. Place in food processor and process until split peas turn to meal (or grind with a mortar and pestle). The meal should be slightly moist but not wet. Add cumin and sea salt to taste.
3. Roll out balls on a clean, dry, lightly floured surface until approximately 6" round. Place 1 ½ Tbl split pea mixture in center of dough and re-form it back into a ball. Let balls sit 15 minutes.
4. Heat a large flat iron skillet over medium high heat. Roll out balls, about 10" round, carefully with a rolling pin. Be careful not to make holes in the Roti. Brush pan with oil and cook one side of Roti until the other side bubbles up, brush with oil and flip. Enjoy and give thanks.

serving suggestions

- Slice into quarters and serve with Mango Chutney (page 23).

variation

- Add roasted potatoes or root vegetables to Govinda's Curry (page 62), place into center of Roti with a slotted spoon and roll like a burrito.

"A CANDLE LOSES NOTHING BY LIGHTING ANOTHER CANDLE." - JAMES KELLER

PADMA BABA'S SPELT CHAPATTI

35 min prep / 20 min cooking / 4 servings

1 ½ C	Spelt flour		1 tsp	Sea salt, or to taste
½ C	Buckwheat flour		⅔ C	Warm filtered water
			2 tsp	Olive oil

loving preparation

1. Place flours and salt in a large mixing bowl and mix well. Slowly add water, stirring constantly, until dough is thick. Add oil and knead dough on a clean dry surface for a few minutes, adding small amounts of flour as needed. Return to bowl, cover with a clean cloth and allow to sit in a dry warm place for 30 minutes.

2. Lightly oil a skillet or griddle on high heat. Divide the dough into 4 equal balls. Flatten to form 6" circles. Place them on a skillet and cook until each side is golden brown and spotted, flipping occasionally to ensure uniform cooking, approximately 5 - 8 minutes per chapatti. Add additional oil if necessary to prevent sticking.

serving suggestion

- Serve as part of a Taj Mahal Indian sampler platter with Mung Dahl (page 149), Chana Masala (page 148) and Mount Zion Mango Chutney (page 23).

variations & note

- Buckwheat flour may be replaced with spelt or other flours to create a variety of flavors.
- Consistency will vary depending upon flour variety used.

Shivling Peak, India

Padma Baba's
Spelt Chapatti

"CLIMB THE MOUNTAINS AND GET THEIR GOOD TIDINGS. NATURE'S PEACE WILL FLOW INTO YOU AS SUNSHINE FLOWS INTO TREES. THE WINDS WILL BLOW THEIR OWN FRESHNESS INTO YOU... WHILE CARES WILL DROP OFF LIKE AUTUMN LEAVES." - JOHN MUIR

MOUNT SINAI MANNA BREAD

30 min prep / 12 hrs soaking / 2 days sprouting / 12 hrs dehydrating / 1 loaf

2 ¼ C	Wheatberries or spelt berries

Veggie Herb Variety

½ to 1 C	Carrot or other veggies, grated or minced
¼ to ½ C	Carrot or other vegetable juice, fresh
1 ½ Tbl	Fresh herbs, minced (basil, parsley, rosemary, dill, cilantro or one of your favorite combinations)
1 tsp	Garlic, minced (optional)
1 tsp	Ginger, peeled & minced

1 Tbl	Sundried olives, chopped (optional)
½ tsp	Sea salt, or to taste
¼ tsp	Black pepper, ground to taste

Sweet & Yummy Variety

¾ C	Dates, raisins or other dry fruit
½ C	Macadamia nuts, soaked for 3 hours & drained well
¼ tsp	Cinnamon powder
¼ tsp	Cardamom powder
¼ tsp	Sea salt, or to taste

loving preparation

1. Rinse wheat berries and place in a large jar or bowl with filtered water and allow to soak for 12 hours, rinsing and changing water periodically. Remove water and place in a warm dry place. Allow to sprout until sprout is about ½ the size of the berry, approximately 2 days. Rinse and drain periodically according to instructions on page 202.
2. Mix sprouted wheat berries with remaining ingredients. Run mixture through a Champion juicer (with blank—not screen—in place) to yield a uniform puréed dough. Shape into loaf form, about 1½" high. Place on a solid dehydrator sheet and dehydrate at 110° until outside is crisp and inside is slightly moist, approximately 12-15 hours. For dehydrator tips, see page 202.
3. Cut into slices, with a wet knife if necessary, and enjoy with spread of choice, as a side dish with any of your live meals.

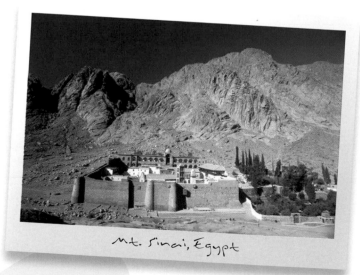

Mt. Sinai, Egypt

variations

- Create a *Paradise Live Veggie Sandwich*, using sprouts, Paté (page 28) or Pesto (page 113), avocado, Cashew or Macnut Cheez (page 29) and grated veggies of choice.
- Can also be used as a bottom for a live pizza. Shape into a circle, approximately ½" thick and dehydrate until most liquid is removed, approximately 16-17 hours.

"...AND GOD SAID, BEHOLD, I HAVE GIVEN YOU EVERY HERB—BEARING SEED WHICH IS UPON THE FACE OF THE EARTH, AND EVERY TREE IN WHICH THE FRUIT OF A TREE YIELDING SEED: TO YOU IT SHALL BE AS MEAT..." - GENESIS 1:29

PLATO'S LIVE GREEK PIZZA

4-6 hours soaking/12-15 hours dehydrating/2-3 servings

Crust

1 c	Raw buckwheat groats, soaked for 4-6 hours
1 c	Macadamia nuts, soaked & drained
3 Tbl	Flax seed, ground
2½ Tbl	Herbs, minced (try basil & parsley)
1 Tbl	Lemon juice, fresh squeezed
Pinch	Crushed red pepper flakes
•	Sea salt, to taste
•	Black pepper, ground to taste
•	Nama shoyu to taste (optional)

Cheez

1 c	Cashew or Macadamia Nut Cheez (page 29)

Sauce

1 c	Live Tomato (page 67) or Live Pesto (following)

Toppings

• Sundried tomatoes, olives, basil, fresh mushrooms or other veggies.

loving preparation

1. Prepare **Nut Cheez** the night before (page 29).
2. Soak buckwheat according to instructions on page 203. draining well, rinsing and replacing water periodically. Rinse and drain well one last time, place in food processor with remaining crust ingredients and process until smooth.
3. Carefully lay out a ½" thin circle layer on a Teflex dehydrator sheet. Dehydrate at 115° until crust is dry, approximately 12-15 hours, flipping once to ensure even drying. Transfer directly to a mesh screen dehydrator tray.
4. Prepare Live Tomato Sauce or the following live pesto sauce. Spread on top of crust, add fresh vegetable toppings.

variation & serving suggestion

⌁ For an alternative crust, flatten Manna Bread (page 112) to form a pizza base and top with above ingredients.
⌁ Top with Alfreda Sauce (page 82).

PESTO PERFECTO

10 minutes / 1 cup

1 c	Basil, tightly packed
¼ c	Cashews, macadamia or pine nuts
¼ to ½ c	Olive oil
2 Tbl	Lemon juice, fresh squeezed
2-3 cloves	Garlic, minced
½ tsp	Nama Shoyu, or to taste (optional)
½ tsp	Sea salt, or to taste
Pinch	Cayenne pepper
•	Black pepper, ground to taste

loving preparation

1. Place all ingredients in food processor and process until smooth.

serving suggestion

⌁ Use as a topping for **Live Pesto Pizza**. Top with sliced roma tomatoes and black sesame seeds. Also good as a live dip or spread.

8

Lao tse's Kung Pao tofu, page 124

tempeh tofu & seitan

BOOKER T'S SOUTHWEST TEMPEH CHILI

35 min prep / 25 min cooking / 5-6 servings

¾ C	Onion, chopped
½ C	Celery, chopped
1 Tbl	Garlic, minced
1 tsp	Jalapeño pepper, roasted, seeded & minced (page 193)
8-12 oz.	Tempeh, cut into ⅛" cubes
4 C	Filtered water or vegetable stock
14.5 oz.	Fire-roasted, crushed tomatoes
1 large	Ancho chili, soaked in water until soft, seeded & minced (2 Tbl)
2 Tbl	Tomato paste
1 Tbl	Barley malt syrup

1½ C	Kidney or black beans, cooked & drained (page 209)
1 ½ C	Corn, fresh or frozen
¾ C	Cashews, roasted, no salt, chopped
6 Tbl	Nama shoyu, or to taste
1 Tbl	Lime juice, fresh squeezed
1 Tbl	Chili powder
1 tsp	Cumin powder, toasted (page 194)
Pinch	Cayenne pepper, or to taste
•	Black pepper, ground to taste
•	Sea salt, to taste
3-4 drops	Liquid smoke (optional)
1½ Tbl	Cilantro, minced

loving preparation

1. Place onion, celery, garlic, jalapeño, tempeh and water or stock in a 3 qt pot and cook over medium heat for 20 minutes, stirring occasionally.
2. Add tomatoes, barley malt syrup, and tomato paste and cook for 10 minutes, stirring occasionally. Add beans and corn and cook for 5 minutes, stirring occasionally. Add remaining ingredients, remove from heat, mix well and enjoy. Flavor improves over time.

serving suggestion

↝ Garnish with a small scoop of Vegan Sour Crème (page 196), additional minced cilantro, and a sprinkle of Toasted Pepitas (page 194). Serve with Southwest Korn Bread (page 108).

variations

↝ This is an oil-free recipe; if you wish to add oil, onion and garlic may be sautéed in 2 Tbl olive oil for 3 minutes as part of step 1. For a thicker chili, additional tempeh may be added.

sedona, Arizona

"I DON'T MAKE JOKES. I JUST WATCH THE GOVERNMENT AND REPORT THE FACTS." - WILL ROGERS

MADRE GRANDE'S GRILLED TEMPEH MEXICANA

30 min prep / 15 min cooking / 2 servings

8 oz	Tempeh sliced into cutlets, marinated & grilled (page 194)
1 c	Campañero's Chili Sauce (page 197)

¼ c	Vegan Sour Crème (page 196)
½ c	Salsa (page 24)

loving preparation

1. Preheat grill. Marinate tempeh in Shoyu or Lemon Herb Marinade (page 195) for 10 minutes. Grill tempeh until it becomes golden with visible grill marks, approximately 8 minutes. Flip cutlets and brush with basting sauce periodically.

serving suggestions

⌇ Serve over rice or quinoa and top with chili sauce, vegan sour crème, and salsa.

variations

⌇ If no grill is available, preheat oven to 375°, place marinated tempeh cutlets in a well oiled, 9" x 13" casserole dish and bake until cooked through, approximately 15 minutes. You may also sauté marinated tempeh cutlets on medium heat in a little olive oil or Basting Sauce (page 196). Try using a cast iron skillet for this one. Sauté until golden brown on each side.

THAT'S AMORE TOFU CACCIATORE

30 min prep / 30 min cooking / 3-4 servings

1 lb	Tofu, extra firm
4 c	Marinara Sauce (page 59), or your favorite tomato sauce
1 Tbl	Olive oil
1 medium	Onion, chopped (1 c)
1 Tbl	Garlic, minced
2 small	Carrots, sliced (1 c)
1 medium	Green bell pepper, chopped
½ c	Artichoke hearts, quartered (optional)

2 Tbl	Nama shoyu, or to taste
1 Tbl	Capers
2 tsp	Vegetarian Worcestershire sauce
1 tsp	Balsamic vinegar
½ tsp	Oregano, minced
Pinch	Crushed red pepper flakes
1 tsp	Basil, minced
1 tsp	Italian parsley, minced
•	Sea salt, to taste
•	Black pepper, ground to taste

loving preparation

1. Slice tofu lengthwise to form 3 cutlets. Marinate in Shoyu Marinade (page 195), and grill until char marks appear on both sides. (page 194). If no grill is available, follow instructions on page 194 for roasted tofu cubes.
2. Place oil in a 3 qt pot on medium high heat. Add onion and garlic and cook for 3 minutes, stirring frequently. Add carrots and bell pepper and cook for 10 minutes, stirring frequently, adding water if necessary to prevent sticking. Add tofu and marinara sauce, reduce heat to simmer and cook for 10 minutes, gently stirring occasionally. Add remaining ingredients and mix well.

serving suggestion

~ Serve over brown rice, quinoa or your favorite wheat-free pasta.

variations

~ Tofu may be replaced with tempeh or seitan.

"WHAT YOU ARE LOOKING FOR IS WHAT IS LOOKING." - ST. FRANCIS OF ASSISI

TIMBALINA'S TEMPEH STROGANOFF

35 min prep / 25 min cooking / 4-5 servings

8 oz	Tempeh, cut into ½" cubes
2 Tbl	Olive oil
1 ½ C	Onion, chopped
2 Tbl	Garlic, minced
1 C	Shitake mushrooms, sliced thin
3 C	Crimini mushrooms, halved or quartered
½ tsp	Paprika
Pinch	Cayenne pepper
2 C	Soy milk
2 Tbl	Nama shoyu, or to taste
2 Tbl	Italian parsley, chopped
¼ tsp	Black pepper, ground to taste
•	Sea salt, to taste

loving preparation

1. Preheat oven to 375°. Place tempeh in a large mixing bowl with Shoyu or Lemon Herb Marinades (page 195) for 10 minutes, stirring occasionally. Place tempeh and marinade in a well oiled 9"x13" casserole dish and bake for 20 minutes, stirring occasionally. Remove from oven.
2. Place oil in a 3 qt pot on medium high heat. Add onion and garlic, cook for 5 minutes, stirring frequently. Add shitake mushrooms and 1 C of crimini mushrooms, cook for 10 more minutes, stirring occasionally. Add paprika & cayenne pepper, remove from heat and blend in a large blender with soy milk until smooth. Return to pot.
3. Add tempeh and remaining 2 C of crimini mushrooms and cook over low heat until the mushrooms are cooked, approximately 10 minutes, stirring occasionally. Be sure not to boil. Add remaining ingredients including tempeh, mix well and remove from heat.

serving suggestions and variations

- Serve over 3 C pasta, rice or quinoa. Garnish with a dollop of Sour Crème (page 196), additional chopped Italian parsley and a dash of paprika.
- Tempeh may be replaced with an equivalent amount of tofu or seitan.

"PRAY TO GOD BUT KEEP ROWING TO SHORE."

- RUSSIAN PROVERB

monastery of the Transfiguration, Valaam Island, Russia

BOGART'S MOROCCAN TEMPEH

25 min prep / 25 min cooking / 3-4 servings

2 Tbl	Olive oil
1 Tbl	Garlic, minced
1 c	Onion, chopped
¼ c	Shitake mushrooms, chopped
8 oz	Tempeh cutlet, marinated and grilled (page 194), ½" cubes
¾ c	Filtered water or vegetable stock
2 c	Roma tomatoes, roasted & grilled (page 194)
1 c	Tomato juice, fresh

¼ c	Raisins
¼ c	Orange juice, fresh
¼ c	Almonds, chopped
3 Tbl	Nama shoyu, or to taste
1 Tbl	Mint, minced
¼ tsp	Cinnamon powder
¼ tsp	Coriander powder
Pinch	Cardamom powder
Pinch	Cayenne pepper
•	Sea salt, to taste
•	Black pepper, ground to taste

loving preparation

1. Place oil in a large sauté pan on medium high heat. Add onion, mushroom and garlic, cook for 3 minutes, stirring frequently. Add water or stock and tempeh, cook for 5 minutes, stirring occasionally.
2. Reduce heat to simmer, add tomatoes and remaining ingredients except mint and almonds, cook for 10 minutes, stirring occasionally. Add almonds and mint, mix well and enjoy.

serving suggestion & variations

- Serve with Couscous Pilaf (page 121).
- Grill tempeh cutlets before cutting into cubes.
- Replace tempeh with tofu or seitan.

"ALL KNOW THAT THE DROP MERGES WITH THE OCEAN BUT FEW KNOW THAT THE OCEAN MERGES WITH THE DROP."

- KABIR

CASBAH COUSCOUS PILAF

15 min prep / 10 min cooking / 3-4 servings

1½ C	Couscous		3 Tbl	Kalamata olives, sliced (optional)
1¾ C	Filtered water or vegetable stock		¼ C	Almonds, chopped (optional)
1 Tbl	Italian parsley, minced		Pinch	Crushed red pepper flakes
1 tsp	Mint, minced		•	Sea salt, to taste
¼ C	Pomegranate seeds (optional)		•	Black pepper, ground to taste

loving preparation

1. Place couscous in a large mixing bowl. Bring water or stock to a near boil. Pour into bowl with couscous and cover with a lid until all liquid is absorbed, approximately 8 minutes. Fluff with a fork, add remaining ingredients and gently mix well.

variations

꙳ Substitute millet or quinoa for couscous and follow grain cooking instructions on page 206.

"NOW IS THE TIME TO REALIZE THAT ALL YOU DO IS SACRED." - HAFIZ

NOOANDA'S PISTACHIO BLUE CORN CRUSTED TEMPEH

25 min prep / 20 min cooking / 4 cutlets

16 oz	Tempeh, sliced into 4 cutlets
1 Tbl	Filtered water
2 tsp	Nama shoyu
1 recipe	Creamy Tahini Marinade (page 195)

Crust

1 c	Pistachios, roasted no salt
½ c	Blue corn chips, crumbled
2 Tbl	Blue corn meal
1 Tbl	Coconut, shredded & toasted (page 194), optional
1 tsp	Cilantro, minced
½ tsp	Cumin, toasted
¼ tsp	Chili powder
Pinch	Crushed red pepper flakes
•	Sea salt, to taste

loving preparation

1. Preheat oven to 350°. Place nama shoyu and water in a 9" x 13" casserole dish, add tempeh cutlets and allow to sit for 5 minutes before flipping. Let sit for another 5 minutes. Prepare *Creamy Tahini Marinade* and pour over tempeh cutlets. Let sit for at least 20 minutes. Cutlets may also be marinated the day before the dish is prepared. Place dish in the oven and bake for 10 minutes.
2. While tempeh is marinating and baking, place crust ingredients in food processor and process until chopped fine.
3. Remove tempeh from oven, cover liberally with crust mixture, return to oven and bake for an additional 10 minutes. Remove from oven, slice cutlets into 1" strips and serve while hot.

serving suggestion

- Serve with quinoa or brown rice and Roasted Red Pepper Sauce (page 60), Mushroom Gravy (page 64) or Spinach Mushroom Sauce (page 60).
- Serve as an appetizer with dipping sauce of choice. Try it with Peanut (page 21), Sweet and Sour (page 125) or BBQ Sauce (page 26).

variations

- Replace tempeh with tofu or ulu.
- For a *Toasted Pecan Coconut Crust*, replace pistachios with pecans and increase coconut to 2 Tbl.

Greek Orthodox Church,
Island of Santorini, Greece

LAO TSE'S KUNG PAO TOFU

35 min prep / 20 min cooking / 4-5 servings

Tofu
¼ C	Filtered water
2 Tbl	Nama shoyu
1 lb	Tofu, extra firm, ½" cubes
1 Tbl	Sesame oil

Vegetable Medley
1 C	Onion, sliced
½ C	Red bell pepper, diced
¼ C	Shitake mushrooms, sliced thin

1 Tbl	Ginger, peeled & minced
1 small	Bok choy, sliced
¼ C	Filtered water or vegetable stock
1 C	Purple cabbage, julienne, 2" strips
½ C	Snow peas
¼ C	Cashews, whole
2 Tbl	Italian parsley, chopped
¼ tsp	Crushed red pepper flakes
1 tsp	Hot sauce (page 214)
•	Sea salt, to taste
•	Black pepper, ground to taste

loving preparation

1. Preheat oven to 375°. Combine all tofu ingredients in a bowl and let sit for at least 20 minutes. Place on a well oiled baking sheet or casserole dish and bake until golden brown, approximately 20 minutes (convection ovens work great for this purpose). Place in a large mixing bowl.
2. Place oil in a large sauté pan on medium high heat. Add onion, pepper, mushroom and ginger and cook for 5 minutes, stirring frequently. Add bok choy and water or stock and cook for 5 minutes, stirring occasionally. Add cabbage and snow peas, cook for 5 minutes, stirring occasionally.
3. Place vegetables and remaining ingredients in mixing bowl with tofu cubes, gently mix well. Serve over white or brown basmati rice.

variations

↬ Countless variations are possible. Tempeh or seitan may be used instead of tofu. Different marinades and sauces may be used for tofu. Rice may be replaced with other grains and even beans. Different vegetables of your liking may be used.

"THE MORE ONE KNOWS, THE MORE ONE FORGIVES." - CONFUCIOUS

SANG WU'S SWEET AND SOUR TEMPEH

20 min prep / 20 min cooking / 4 servings

Tempeh

1 lb	Tempeh or tofu, marinated, grilled, ½" cubes (page 194)

Sweet & Sour Sauce

2 Tbl	Sesame oil
1 small	Onion, diced
2 Tbl	Ginger, peeled & minced
¼ C	Red bell pepper, diced
1 C	Filtered water
17 oz	Apricot preserves, sugar-free
2 Tbl	Arrowroot powder, or kuzu root starch , dissolved in ¼ C cold water
5 Tbl	Nama shoyu, or to taste
2 Tbl	Apple cider vinegar, raw
1 Tbl	Miso paste, mellow
1 Tbl	Mirin
¼ tsp	Crushed red pepper flakes
2 tsp	Cilantro, minced
2 tsp	Black sesame seeds

loving preparation

1. Place sesame oil in a 3 qt pot on medium heat. Add onion, ginger and bell pepper, cook for 3 minutes, stirring occasionally. Add water and apricot preserves, cook for 10 minutes, stirring occasionally.

2. Add arrowroot or kuzu and water mixture, stir for 2 minutes. Add remaining ingredients except tempeh or tofu, cook for 3 minutes, stirring constantly. Add tempeh or tofu and mix well. Garnish with black sesame seeds.

serving suggestions

❧ Omit tempeh and use as a *Sweet And Sour Sauce* for dipping.
❧ Try it with Nori Rolls (page 90).

"A JOURNEY OF A THOUSAND MILES MUST BEGIN WITH ONE STEP." - LAO TSU

KIND AND GENTLE HOLIDAY LOAF

30 min prep / 45 min cooking / 5 loaves

10 sheets	Spelt Phyllo dough (see *Glossary*)		½ C	Walnuts, toasted & chopped (page 194)
¼ C *or more*	Corn oil for basting		8 oz	Seitan, ½" chopped
			1 C	TVP, soaked in 1 C hot filtered water or vegetable stock (page 200)
	Filling		¾ C	Sour crème (page 196)
2 Tbl	Olive Oil		1 Tbl	Italian parsley, minced
1 C	Onion, diced		1 Tbl	Nutritional yeast
2 Tbl	Garlic, minced		4 tsp	Nama shoyu, or to taste
¾ C	Crimini Mushrooms, chopped		1 tsp	Sage, minced
½ C	Celery, sliced thin		•	Sea salt, to taste
			•	Black pepper, ground to taste

loving preparation

1. Preheat oven to 350°. Place TVP and water or stock in a medium bowl until liquid is absorbed, approximately 10 minutes.
2. Place oil in a large sauté pan. Add onion and garlic, cook for 3 minutes, stirring frequently. Add celery, mushrooms and walnuts, cook for 5 minutes, stirring frequently. Add seitan and TVP, cook 7 minutes, stirring frequently. Place in a large mixing bowl with remaining filling ingredients and mix well. Allow to cool.
3. Lay phyllo dough on a clean dry surface. Fold sheet into quarters, lightly baste with corn oil. Repeat with one more sheet of phyllo. Scoop 1 C of filling in center of phyllo square. Fold in sides and roll away from you, forming as tight of a "burrito" roll as possible. Repeat process for remaining phyllos. Place on a well oiled baking sheet, brush one more time with corn oil and bake until golden brown, approximately 20 minutes.

serving suggestions

- ✐ Serve with Spinach Mushroom Sauce (page 60) or Mushroom Gravy (page 64) and Sour Crème (page 196).
- ✐ Can be included in a holiday feast that includes Roasted Squash Soup (page 42), Cranberry Sauce (page 63) and Apricot Corn Bread Stuffing (page 72).

"HAVE PATIENCE WITH ALL THINGS, BUT FIRST OF ALL, WITH YOURSELF." - ST. FRANCIS DE SALES

PICASSO'S PAELLA

30 min prep / 1 hr 10 min cooking / 2-3 servings

2 Tbl	Olive oil		1 c	Chick peas, cooked (page 209)
¾ c	Onion, diced		½ c	Artichoke hearts, quartered
1 Tbl	Garlic, minced		¼ c	Kalamata olives, chopped
½ c	Bell pepper, diced		3 Tbl	Nama shoyu, or to taste
8 oz	Chicken-style seitan, ½" chop		1 Tbl	Italian parsley, minced
3 ¾ c	Filtered water or vegetable stock		½ tsp	Paprika
2 c	Brown rice, uncooked		½ tsp	Sea salt, or to taste
1 c	Roma tomatoes, roasted or grilled & chopped (page 194)		¼ tsp	Black pepper, ground to taste
1 c	Tomato based vegetable juice, fresh		½ tsp	Saffron threads, soaked in 2 Tbl hot water

loving preparation

1. Preheat oven to 375°. Place oil in a large sauté pan on medium high heat. Add onion, garlic, and bell pepper, cook for 3 minutes, stirring frequently. Add seitan and cook 5 minutes, stirring frequently.
2. Place contents of sauté pan in a deep 9"x13" casserole dish with water or stock, rice, tomatoes and vegetable juice. Mix well, cover and bake until most liquid is absorbed, approximately 50 minutes.
3. Add seasonings, mix well, cover, cook for 10 minutes. Remove from oven and enjoy. Rice should be soft and completely cooked. Dish should be moist but not watery.

"HE IS MAD PAST RECOVERY, BUT YET HE HAS LUCID INTERVALS." - MIGUEL DE CERVANTES

THOUSAND PETALS TEMPEH STIR FRY

30 min prep / 20 min cooking / 2-3 servings

8 oz	Tempeh		2 tsp	Nama shoyu, or to taste
2 Tbl	Sesame oil, or ¼ c filtered water		½ tsp	Mirin
½ c	Onion, half moon slices		3 Tbl	Fresh herbs, minced
1 Tbl	Garlic, minced			
1 Tbl	Ginger, peeled & minced			*Garnish*
3 c	Assorted rainbow garden veggies		2 Tbl	Sesame seeds
	(broccoli, bell pepper, snow peas,		2 Tbl	Flax oil
	cauliflower, carrots, zucchini		2 tsp	Nutritional yeast
	etc) ½" to 1" chop			

loving preparation

1. Marinate tempeh in Shoyu or Lemon Herb Marinades (page 195) for 10 minutes and grill or roast according to instructions on page 194. Cut into ½" cubes.
2. Add sesame oil or water to a wok on medium high heat. Add onion, garlic and ginger, cook for 5 minutes stirring frequently. Add mixed vegetables and cook until just tender, approximately 15 minutes, stirring occasionally and adding small amounts of water if necessary to prevent sticking. Add grilled tempeh cubes, shoyu, mirin and herbs, gently mix well and enjoy.
3. Garnish with sesame seeds, flax oil and nutritional yeast.

serving suggestion

⟿ Serve over rice or quinoa, or udon noodles.

variations

⟿ *Indian Flair* Add small amounts of cumin powder, curry and cilantro to taste.

⟿ *Mexican Treat* Add chili powder, cumin powder, and some minced jalapeño.

⟿ *Italian Style* Try basil, parsley, rosemary, sage, fennel and thyme.

⟿ *Country and Western* Add BBQ Sauce (pace 26).

⟿ *Asian Delight* Add Sweet & Sour Sauce (pace 125).

"HE WHO KNOWS THAT ENOUGH IS ENOUGH WILL ALWAYS HAVE ENOUGH." - LAO-TZU

SICILIAN SEITAN WITH SUNDRIED TOMATOES AND PINE NUTS

20 min prep / 15 min cooking / 2-3 servings

2 Tbl	Olive oil		½ C	Sundried tomato soak water
1 ½ C	Onion, sliced thin		½ C	Pine nuts, toasted (page 194)
2 Tbl	Garlic, minced		3 Tbl	Nama shoyu, or to taste
1 lb	Seitan, chicken style, ½" cubes		2 Tbl	Basil, minced
½ C	Soy milk		1 ½ Tbl	Balsamic vinegar
¾ C	Sundried tomato soaked in hot water		1 Tbl	Italian parsley, minced
			¼ tsp	Crushed red pepper flakes
			Pinch	Cayenne pepper

loving preparation

1. Place oil in a large sauté pan on medium high heat. Add onion and garlic, cook for 3 minutes, stirring frequently. Add seitan and sundried tomato soak water, cook for 8 minutes, stirring occasionally. Add chopped sundried tomatoes and remaining ingredients and stir well.

variation

↝ Serve as a main dish with a side green salad. Serve as an appetizer, filling small pastry shells with seitan and topping with Live Alfreda Sauce (page 82).

SAMURAI SEITAN WITH BROCCOLI AND GARLIC

20 min prep / 15 min cooking / 3-4 servings

2 Tbl	Sesame oil		1 C	Filtered water or vegetable stock
1 C	Onion, sliced		3 C	Broccoli, small flowerettes
1 C	Green bell pepper, sliced thin		1 ½ C	Snow peas
½ C	Shitake or oyster mushrooms, sliced thin		¼ C	Nama shoyu, or to taste
2 Tbl	Garlic, minced		2 Tbl	Mirin
1 lb	Seitan, ½" cubes		1½ Tbl	Vegetarian Worcestershire
			2 Tbl	White sesame seeds, for garnish

loving preparation

1. Place oil in a large sauté pan on medium high heat. Add onion and garlic, cook for 3 minutes, stirring frequently. Add water or stock, pepper, mushroom, seitan, broccoli, cook for 8 minutes, stirring occasionally. Add snow peas and remaining ingredients, cook for 3 minutes, stirring frequently. Remove from heat and enjoy.

"TRUTH IS ALWAYS EXCITING. SPEAK IT, THEN, LIFE IS DULL WITHOUT IT." - PEARL S. BUCK

FARM-FRIENDLY SEITAN SALAD

20 min prep / 5 min cooking / 3-4 servings

1 Tbl	Olive oil		¼ C	Kalamata olives, chopped
2 tsp	Garlic, minced		1 Tbl	Stone ground mustard
1 lb	Seitan, chicken style, chopped		2 tsp	Nama shoyu, or to taste
1 C	Vegan mayonnaise (page 196)		2 tsp	Mirin
¾ C	Celery, diced		1 ½ tsp	Dill, minced (or ¾ tsp dry)
½ C	Red onion, diced		1 tsp	Apple cider vinegar, raw
½ C	Artichoke hearts, diced		½ tsp	Black pepper, ground to taste

loving preparation

1. Place oil in a large sauté pan over medium high heat, add seitan and garlic, cook for 5 minutes, stirring frequently and adding small amounts of water if necessary to avoid sticking to the pan.
2. Combine with remaining ingredients in a large mixing bowl and mix well.

serving suggestions

- Serve stuffed in a large tomato, use as a filling for wraps and sandwiches or enjoy on its own with an organic salad.

"ONLY AFTER THE LAST TREE HAS BEEN CUT DOWN, ONLY AFTER THE LAST RIVER HAS BEEN POISONED, ONLY AFTER THE LAST FISH HAS BEEN CAUGHT, ONLY THEN, WILL YOU FIND THAT MONEY CANNOT BE EATEN." - CREE PROPHECY

Farm-Friendly Seitan Salad

MARVELOUS MEXICAN SEITAN AND BLACK BEAN FIESTA

20 min prep / 15 min cooking / 2-3 servings

2 Tbl	Olive oil
1 tsp	Cumin powder
1 medium	Red onion, diced (1 c)
1 small	Green bell pepper, diced (½ c)
1½ Tbl	Garlic, minced
1 tsp	Jalapeño, seeded & minced
1 lb	Seitan, chicken style, chopped
1 c	Black beans, cooked (page 209)

2-3 medium	Roma tomatoes, grilled, chopped (page 194)
1 c	Corn, fresh or frozen (optional)
½ c	Pepitas (pumpkin seeds), toasted (page 194)
2 Tbl	Cilantro, minced
1 Tbl	Lime juice, fresh squeezed
1 Tbl	Nama shoyu, or to taste
½ tsp	Sea salt, or to taste
¼ tsp	Black pepper, ground to taste

loving preparation

1. Place oil in a large sauté pan on medium high heat. Add cumin and cook for 1 minute, stirring constantly. Add onion, bell pepper, garlic and jalapeño and cook for 5 minutes, stirring frequently. Add seitan and cook for 8 minutes, stirring occasionally.
2. Remove from heat, place in a large mixing bowl with remaining ingredients and mix well.

serving suggestion

- Top with Chili Sauce (page 197) or Roasted Red Pepper Sauce (page 60) and a dollop of Sour Crème (page 196).
- Serve warm over a bed of fresh greens.

variations

- For an oil-free version, sauté in ¼ c filtered water, adding more water if necessary to prevent sticking.

"SOLITUDE IS THE FURNACE OF TRANSFORMATION." HENRI NOUWEN

Teotehuacan (Place of the Gods), Mexico

KING JANAKA'S MAPLE GLAZED SEITAN

10 min prep / 20 min cooking / 2-3 servings

2 Tbl	Olive oil
1/4 C	Filtered water or vegetable stock
1 lb	Seitan, chicken style
1 1/2 C	Onion, sliced thin
1/2 C	Red bell pepper, diced
1/4 C	Ginger, peeled & minced
1/4 C	Maple syrup
1/4 C	Nama shoyu, or to taste
1 tsp	Dill, minced
1/2 tsp	Rosemary, minced
1/4 tsp	Cayenne pepper, or to taste

loving preparation

1. Place oil in a large sauté pan on medium high heat. Add onion and ginger and cook for 3 minutes, stirring frequently. Add maple syrup, seitan and water or stock and cook for 8 minutes, stirring occasionally.
2. Reduce heat to low, add remaining ingredients and cook for 5 minutes, stirring occasionally.

serving suggestion

- Serve as a main course with steamed veggies and a side salad.

variations

- Many variations are possible. Add 2 C of sauce, such as Thai Coconut (page 59), Carrot Ginger (page 66) or another of your choosing.
- Replace dill and rosemary with other fresh herbs.
- Add 1/2 C coconut, soy or rice milk.

HOMEMADE SEITAN

3 1/2 hours / 2 lbs

9 C	Whole wheat flour
5 1/2 C	Filtered water
7 C	Akashic Soup Stock (page 200)
1/4 C	Nama shoyu, or to taste

loving preparation

1. Mix flour and water together in a large mixing bowl. Knead for 5 minutes. Work dough by thumping approximately 300 times. Cover dough with cold water and let sit for 45 minutes. Knead dough slowly until water becomes thick with starch.
2. With colander, drain off the water, then repeat with warm water, then cold, then warm… six times. After the fifth rinse you will begin to see the dough become very sticky. After the sixth rinse run the gluten dough under cold water to rinse off the starch and bran. Pull the gluten apart while rinsing.
3. Bring a medium pot of water to a boil. Pull off 2" pieces and drop into boiling water. When they rise to the top like dumplings, scoop out and drop into a bowl filled with cold water. Remove from cold water and place gluten balls in a large pot with Akashic Vegetable Stock and Nama shoyu, bring to a near boil, reduce heat to medium and simmer for 1 1/2 hours.

notes

- This will keep for 1 week in the refrigerator.
- Use in all of the recipes that call for seitan, or create your own dishes. Some people have allergies to wheat, specifically the gluten content. We include this recipe for those transitioning towards a plant based diet from an animal based one.

"YOU GROW UP THE DAY YOU HAVE YOUR FIRST REAL LAUGH AT YOURSELF." - ETHEL BARRYMORE

9

Om Great Spirit Black Rice Polenta Casserole, page 143

casserole grain & bean

THE WHOLE ENCHILADA CASSEROLE

1 hr prep / 45 min cooking / 9" x 13" casserole

12	Blue corn tortillas (or 6 large spelt or whole grain tortillas)		3 Tbl	Tahini
			2 Tbl	Cilantro, minced
			2½ Tbl	Nama shoyu, or to taste
	Filling		1 Tbl	Nutritional yeast
2 Tbl	Olive oil		1½ tsp	Chili powder
1 ½ C	Onion, diced		1 tsp	Cumin powder, toasted (page 194)
¾ C	Green pepper, diced		¼ tsp	Cayenne pepper
2 Tbl	Garlic, minced		•	Sea salt, to taste
1 tsp	Jalapeño, seeded & minced		•	Black pepper, ground to taste
1 ½ lbs	Tofu, extra firm, crumbled			
1 ½ C	Tomato, chopped (or your favorite salsa)			*Sauces & Toppings*
			4 C	Chili Sauce (page 197)
1 C	Black beans, cooked (page 209)		1 ½ C	Nut Cheez (page 29)
			½ C	Black olives, chopped, or to taste
			2 Tbl	Cilantro, chopped

loving preparation

1. Preheat oven to 350° Place oil in a large sauté pan on medium high heat. Add onion, pepper, garlic and jalapeño, cook for 5 minutes, stirring frequently, adding small amounts of water if necessary to prevent sticking. Add tofu and cook for 5 minutes, stirring frequently. Place mixture in a large mixing bowl with remaining filling ingredients and mix well. Set aside.
2. Prepare Chili Sauce and Nut Cheez (these can be prepared a day in advance if necessary).
3. Lightly oil a 9"x13" casserole dish. Layer with ⅓ of your tortillas, top liberally with chili sauce and ½ of the tofu mixture. Top with ½ of Nut Cheez. Repeat with ⅓ more of your tortillas, followed by another liberal spread of chili sauce. Top with remaining ½ of tofu mixture and ½ of Nut Cheez. Finish with last ⅓ of your tortillas and another liberal portion of chili sauce. Bake for 35 minutes. Top with olives and cilantro, allow to cool for 10-15 minutes before serving.

serving suggestion

↣ Serve with a dollop of Sour Crème (page 196), Salsa (page 24), and/or Guacamole (page 26) and top with chopped olives and a sprig of cilantro.

variations

↣ Try adding 1 C of chopped seitan while sautéing.

"REALITY IS NOTHING BUT A COLLECTIVE HUNCH." - LILY TOMLIN

THE GOOD SHEPHERD'S PIE

45 min prep / 1 hour 10 min cooking / 9" x 13" casserole

10-12 medium	Potatoes, ½" cubes (approx 12 c)		¾ c	Corn, fresh or frozen
1 c	Coconut, rice or soy milk		¼ c	Tahini
2 Tbl	Olive oil		4 tsp	Nama shoyu (optional)
¾ c	Onion, diced		1 Tbl	Basil, fresh, minced (1 ½ tsp dry)
1 Tbl	Garlic, minced		1 Tbl	Italian parsley, fresh, minced
¾ c	Carrots, ½" cubes		1 ½ tsp	Sea salt, or to taste
½ c	Celery, sliced thin		1 tsp	Thyme, fresh minced (½ tsp dry)
½ c	Red bell pepper, diced		1 tsp	Sage, fresh minced (½ tsp dry)
½ c	Mushrooms, sliced thin		2 tsp	Barley malt syrup
2 lbs	Tofu, extra firm, crumbled		½ tsp	Black pepper, ground to taste
¾ c	Peas		½ tsp	Crushed red pepper flakes
			¼ tsp	Cayenne pepper, or to taste

loving preparation

1. Preheat oven to 350°. Place potatoes in a large pot with filtered water. Bring to a boil and cook until potatoes are soft, approximately 15 minutes. Drain well, place in a large mixing bowl with coconut milk and mash well. Add salt and pepper to taste. Set aside.
2. While potatoes are cooking, place oil in a large sauté pan on medium high heat. Add onion and garlic, cook for 3 minutes, stirring frequently. Add carrots, celery, bell pepper and mushrooms, cook for 10 minutes, stirring frequently. Add water if necessary to prevent sticking. Add tofu and cook for 5 minutes, stirring frequently. Place in a large mixing bowl with remaining ingredients except potatoes and mix well.
3. Place tofu vegetable mixture in a well oiled 9"x13" casserole dish. Top with mashed potatoes, using a spatula to create a smooth surface. Score pretty designs on top with a fork. Bake until slightly golden brown and completely cooked, approximately 25 minutes. Cool for 10-15 minutes.

serving suggestion

↬ Serve with Mushroom Gravy (page 64) and a dollop of Sour Crème (page 196).

variations

↬ Potato layer may be placed on the bottom, topped with the tofu layer. Once refrigerated, this creates a more solid foundation, and allows for different sized pieces to be cut and served individually.

↬ For Southwest Shepherd's pie, add 2 Tbl minced cilantro, 1 Tbl minced ancho chilies, and 1 c of corn to mashed potato mixture. Add 1½ tsp chili powder and 1 tsp of toasted cumin powder to tofu mixture and serve with Chili Sauce (page 197) instead of mushroom gravy. Top with a dollop of Salsa (page 24) and Vegan Sour Crème (page 196).

SUPER SHAKTI'S SPANIKOPITA

1 hour prep / 40 min cooking / 9"x13" casserole dish

1 ½ lb	Tofu, extra firm, crumbled		¼ C	Garlic, minced
1 pkg	Phyllo sheets, spelt variety (see *Glossary*)		¼ C	Nama shoyu, or to taste
			2 Tbl	Italian parsley, minced
6 C	Spinach, rinsed well		2 Tbl	Basil, minced
2 C	Onion, diced		1 Tbl	Nutritional yeast
2 Tbl	Olive oil		1 ½ tsp	Oregano, minced
¾ C	Garbanzo beans, cooked (page 209), drained & mashed		1 ½ tsp	Thyme, minced
			1 tsp	Rosemary, fresh minced
¾ C	Tahini, roasted		½ tsp	Sea salt, or to taste
½ C	Kalamata olives, chopped		½ tsp	Black pepper, ground to taste
			¼ C	Corn or olive oil for basting

loving preparation

1. Steam spinach lightly for 3-5 minutes (page 193).
2. Preheat oven to 350°. Place 2 Tbl oil in a large pot on medium high heat. Add onions and garlic, cook 5 minutes, stirring frequently. Add the tofu and cook for 10 minutes, stirring frequently. Add the remaining ingredients, except the phyllo dough and corn oil, cook an additional 5 minutes, stirring frequently. Remove from heat.
3. Lightly oil a 9"x13" casserole dish. Place ⅓ of the phyllo dough (7 sheets) on the bottom of the dish, one sheet at a time, lightly oiling each sheet with corn or olive oil using a small pastry brush. Place half of the tofu mixture on top of the phyllo dough.
4. Repeat step 2, using 7 sheets of the phyllo dough and the remaining ½ of the tofu mixture. Top with the remaining phyllo dough, lightly brush with oil, and bake until phyllo is golden brown, approximately 20 minutes. Allow to cool 10-15 minutes before serving.

serving suggestions

➺ Serve with Goddess Dressing (page 52), Roasted Red Pepper Sauce (page 60) or Spinach Mushroom Sauce (page 60).

Moonrise over the Parthenon, Athens, Greece

"THE SOUL'S COMMUNICATION OF TRUTH IS THE HIGHEST EVENT IN NATURE... AND THIS COMMUNICATION IS AN INFLUX FROM DIVINE MIND INTO OUR MIND." - PLOTINUS

PRESTO MANIFESTO LASAGNA

50 min prep / 40 min cooking / 9" x 13" casserole

20 oz	Spelt, rice or other whole-grain lasagna noodles		½ tsp	Black pepper, ground to taste
			½ tsp	Crushed red pepper flakes

Filling			*Garnish*	
1 Tbl	Olive oil		3-4	Tomatoes, medium, ½" slice
1 ½ C	Onion, diced		2 Tbl	Black sesame seeds
5 tsp	Garlic, minced			
2 lbs	Tofu, extra firm, crumbled		*Pesto*	
5 C	Grilled vegetables (zucchini, eggplant, bell peppers, portabello mushrooms or your favorites)		2 ½ C	Basil, tightly packed
			¾ C	Olive oil
			½ C	Macadamia or pine nuts
6 Tbl	Tahini, roasted		3 Tbl	Lemon juice, fresh squeezed
¼ C	Nama shoyu		1 Tbl	Garlic, minced
2 Tbl	Basil, fresh, minced		2 tsp	Nama shoyu, or to taste
2 Tbl	Italian parsley, minced		½ tsp	Sea salt, or to taste
1 Tbl	Nutritional yeast		½ tsp	Black pepper, ground to taste
1 tsp	Sea salt, or to taste		Pinch	Cayenne pepper

loving preparation

1. Preheat oven to 350°. Boil water in a large pot. Add a drop of olive oil and lasagna noodles. Reduce heat to medium high and cook until pasta is al dente (just soft with a hint of firmness), approximately 8 minutes, gently stirring occasionally. Rinse noodles in colander, place on a plate to dry with a small amount of olive oil to prevent sticking.
2. Grill vegetables according to instructions on page 194. Slice thin and set aside.
3. For *Filling*, place 1 Tbl of oil in a large sauté pan on medium high heat. Add onion and garlic, cook for 5 minutes, stirring frequently. Reduce heat to medium, add tofu, cook for 5 mintues, stirring occasionally. Place in a large mixing bowl with remaining filling ingredients and mix well.
4. For *Pesto*, place ingredients in food processor and process until smooth.
5. Lightly oil a 9" x 13" casserole dish. Place a layer of noodles on bottom. Cover with 1/3 of pesto mixture. Top this with ½ of the tofu mixture and then ½ of the grilled veggies. Repeat with a layer of pasta, 1/3 of the pesto mixture, the last half of the tofu mixture and then the last half of the grilled veggies. Finish with another layer of pasta, topped with the last ⅓ of pesto. Garnish with sliced tomatoes and black sesame seeds. Bake until lasagna is thoroughly heated, approximately 30 minutes. As with all casseroles, allow to cool for a minimum of 10-15 minutes.

variations

↝ If no grill is available, slice veggies into small pieces and add to sauté pan after onions have cooked for 5 minutes and before tofu is added. Cook veggies, stirring frequently and adding additional water if necessary to prevent sticking. Many varieties of lasagna can be made. Replace pesto with Marinara Sauce (page 59) or Live Alfreda Sauce (page 82). Add a layer of Cashew or Macadamia Cheez (page 29) for an even cheezier lasagna.

QUE BELLA ASPARAGUS RISOTTO

20 min prep / 25 min cooking / 3-4 servings

2 Tbl	Olive oil		1 Tbl	Tahini
¼ C	Shallots, diced		1 Tbl	Mirin
1 C	Arborio rice		1 ½ tsp	Basil, minced
2 Tbl	Lemon juice, fresh squeezed		1 ½ tsp	Italian parsley, minced
3 ½ C	Filtered water or vegetable stock		½ tsp	Sea salt, or to taste
4-6 large	Asparagus, steamed until just soft, sliced, 1 ½ C (page 193)		¼ tsp	Black pepper, ground to taste
¾ C	Coconut, soy or rice milk		¼ tsp	Saffron strands soaked in 2 Tbl warm filtered water
2 Tbl	Nutritional yeast		Pinch	Crushed red pepper flakes
			•	Nama shoyu, to taste (optional)

loving preparation

1. Place oil in a large sauté pan on medium high heat. Add shallots and cook for 3 minutes, stirring constantly. Add rice and cook for 2 minutes, stirring constantly. Reduce heat to medium, add lemon juice and stir well. Slowly add water or stock, stirring constantly, cook until all liquid is absorbed, approximately 20 minutes.
2. Add remaining ingredients including steamed and sliced asparagus, gently mix well and enjoy.

variations

෴ For roasted squash risotto, replace asparagus with 1 C of roasted squash (page 42)

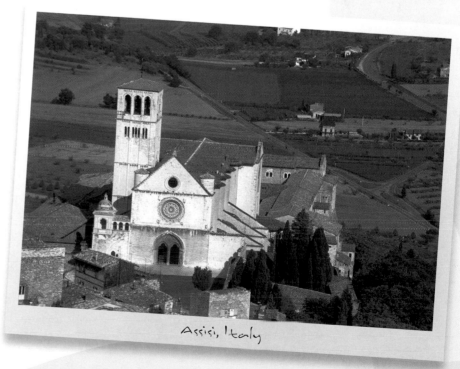

Assisi, Italy

"FOR IT IS IN GIVING THAT WE RECEIVE." -ST. FRANCIS OF ASSISI

SAMADHI LOTUS COCO RICE

35 min prep / 50 min cooking / 9" x 13" casserole

2 c	Brown basmati rice (approx. 4 c cooked)
3 c	Filtered water or vegetable stock
2 ⅓ c	Coconut milk
2 tsp	Cumin seed
2 tsp	Brown mustard seed
2 Tbl	Toasted sesame oil
1 1/3 c	Onion, diced
4 tsp	Garlic, minced

2-3 bunches	Spinach or other greens, rinsed, steamed & drained well (2 c cooked & pressed firm, page 193)
1 c	Cashews, toasted until golden brown, (page 194)
1 c	Garbanzo beans, cooked (page 209)
2½ Tbl	Nama shoyu, or to taste
3 Tbl	Cilantro, minced
2 tsp	Curry powder
½ tsp	Crushed red pepper flakes
Pinch	Cayenne pepper
•	Sea salt, to taste
•	Black pepper, ground to taste
4	Phyllo sheets, spelt
•	Toasted sesame oil for basting

loving preparation

1. Preheat oven to 350°. Add rice, water and 1 c of coconut milk to a large pot and bring to a boil. Cover, reduce heat to simmer and cook until liquid is absorbed, approximately 35 minutes.

2. While rice is cooking, place oil in a large sauté pan on medium high heat. Add cumin seed and mustard seed and cook for 1 minute, stirring constantly. Add onion and garlic and cook for approximately 5 minutes, stirring frequently. Remove from heat and place in a large bowl. Add remaining ingredients including 1⅓ c coconut milk and mix well. Add cooked rice and mix well.

3. Place mixture in a well oiled 9"x 13" casserole dish. Top with four sheets of phyllo dough, lightly brushing each layer with oil before adding another layer . Bake for 15 minutes or until golden brown.

serving suggestion

- Serve with Live Alfreda Sauce (page 82) or Goddess Dressing (page 52).
- For the original Samadhi Lotus Blossoms, follow rolling instructions for Satori Summer Rolls (page 21), using ⅓ c mixture in each rice paper roll. Serve with Peanut Dipping Sauce (page 21).

The Holy Dhama Temple of Badrinath, India

142

OM GREAT SPIRIT BLACK RICE POLENTA CASSEROLE

35 min prep / 1 hour cooking / 9" x 13" casserole

5 c	Filtered water or vegetable stock		1 Tbl	Basil, minced
1 ½ c	Forbidden black rice or sweet black rice (see *Glossary*)		1 Tbl	Italian Parsley, minced
1 tsp	Sea salt, or to taste		½ tsp	Oregano, minced
6 c	Filtered water or vegetable stock		½ tsp	Thyme, minced
2 c	Polenta		½ tsp	Sage, minced
1 c	Coconut, soy, rice, oat or almond milk (optional)		½ tsp	Rosemary, minced
¼ c	Sundried tomatoes, soaked until soft, drained & chopped		2 tsp	Sea salt, or to taste
			•	Nama shoyu to taste (optional)
			•	Crushed red pepper flakes to taste
			•	Black pepper, ground to taste

loving preparation

1. Bring 5 c of water to a boil in a 3 qt pot, add black rice and 1 tsp of salt, cover and simmer on low heat until liquid is absorbed, approximately 60 minutes, stirring occasionally.
2. While rice is cooking, bring 6 c of water or stock to a boil in another 3 qt pot. Reduce heat to simmer and whisk in polenta, being careful that it does not boil over. Add coconut milk and whisk until liquid is absorbed and polenta is smooth. Add remaining ingredients to polenta and stir well.
3. Preheat oven to 350°. When black rice is done cooking, pour into a well oiled 9" x 13" casserole dish. Allow rice to cool slightly and then pour polenta mixture on top of it. Bake in oven until top is golden brown, approximately 10 minutes.

serving suggestion

୬ Serve as a main course with garden salad, Roasted Red Pepper Sauce (page 60) or the Black Bean Sauce (page 64).

variation

୬ Experiment with adding assorted sautéed vegetables, such as ½ c onion finely chopped, ¼ c fennel bulb finely chopped, ¼ c shitake mushrooms, chopped small and ¼ c red bell pepper, diced. Mix in with polenta and follow above instructions.

"MAY YOUR LIFE BE LIKE A WILDFLOWER, GROWING FREELY AND JOYFULLY IN THE BEAUTY OF EACH DAY." – NATIVE AMERICAN PROVERB

DOCTOR D'S BUCKWHEAT PILAF

15 min prep / 20 min cooking / 2-3 servings

1 c	Buckwheat groats, roasted (kasha)		1 c	Red bell pepper, diced
1 ¾ c	Filtered water or vegetable stock		3 Tbl	Green onion, diced
3 Tbl	Toasted sesame oil		¾ c	Carrot, grated
1 Tbl	Garlic, minced		2 Tbl	Nama shoyu, or to taste
1 small	Lime leaf, sliced very thin		1 Tbl	Cilantro, minced
			½ tsp	Crushed red pepper flakes, or to taste

loving preparation

1. Place water or stock in a 3 qt pot and bring to a boil on high heat. Add buckwheat, cover, reduce heat to simmer and cook until kasha is tender and liquid is absorbed, approximately 15 minutes. Gently fluff with a fork and place in a large mixing bowl.
2. While buckwheat is cooking, place 1 Tbl of sesame oil in a medium size sauté pan on medium high heat. Add garlic, lime leaf and red bell pepper, cook for 8 minutes, stirring frequently, adding small amounts of water as necessary to prevent sticking. Add to bowl with remaining ingredients and mix well.

variation

> Add a handful of rinsed & chopped kale and ½ c of cubed tofu while cooking buckwheat.

DOWN-HOME BLACK-EYED COLLARDS

15 min prep / 15 min cooking / 2 servings

1 Tbl	Olive oil		2 Tbl	Nama shoyu, or to taste
1 ½ c	Onion, sliced thin		2 tsp	Thyme, fresh minced (1 tsp dry)
1 Tbl	Ginger, peeled & minced		2 tsp	Oregano, fresh minced (1 tsp, dry)
1 Tbl	Garlic, minced		½ tsp	Vegetarian Worcestershire sauce
½ c	Carrots, sliced thin		½ tsp	Black pepper, ground to taste
½ c	Filtered water or vegetable stock		¼ tsp	Liquid smoke
6 c	Collard greens, chopped ½"		Pinch	Cayenne pepper
1 ¼ c	Black eyed peas, cooked (page 209)		•	Sea salt, to taste

loving preparation

1. Place oil in a 3 qt pot on medium high heat. Add onion, ginger, garlic and carrots, cook for 5 minutes, stirring occasionally.
2. Add collards and water or stock, reduce heat to low, and cook for 10 minutes, stirring occasionally. Add remaining ingredients, cook for 5 minutes. Remove from heat and enjoy.

serving suggestion

> Goes well with Korn Bread (page 108).

"IT'S JUST NOT FUNNY IF YOU DON'T HAVE A SENSE OF HUMOR." - WAVY GRAVY

KAHUNA'S ULU LASAGNA

2 hours prep / 1 hr 10 min cooking / 9" x 13" casserole

1 large	Ulu

Sauce
5 c	Mystic Marinara Sauce (page 59)

Cheez
1 ½ c	Cashews or macadamia nuts
¾ c	Filtered water
1 ½ tsp	Sea salt, or to taste
3 Tbl	Lemon juice, fresh squeezed
3 Tbl	Nutritional yeast

Vegetables
2 Tbl	Olive oil
1 c	Onion, sliced (optional)
2 tsp	Garlic, minced
2 c	Mushrooms, sliced thin
2 medium	Zucchini, sliced thin, (2 c)
1 large	Bell pepper, sliced (¾ c)
1 large bunch	Spinach or kale, rinsed & drained very well, (4 c)
•	Sea salt, to taste
•	Black pepper, ground to taste
•	Cayenne pepper to taste
•	Nama shoyu, to taste (optional)

loving preparation

1. Preheat oven to 350°. Prepare Mystic Marinara Sauce. Place all *Cheez* ingredients in a blender and blend until very smooth, set aside.
2. Cut off ulu stem and cut in half lengthwise. Place in a large pot filled with filtered water. Bring to a boil until knife goes through any part of the ulu, approximately 20 minutes. Remove and run under cold water. Slice thinly into ¼" slices.
3. While the ulu is cooking, place 2 Tbl of olive oil in a large sauté pan on medium high heat. Add onions and garlic, cook for 3 minutes, stirring frequently. Add mushroom, zucchini, pepper and spinach, cook until veggies are cooked through, approximately 10 minutes, stirring occasionally and adding water if necessary to prevent sticking. Add salt, pepper, cayenne and shoyu to taste.
4. Place ¼ c of sauce on bottom of a 9"x 13" casserole dish. Cover with ulu pieces ("noodles"). Spread on ⅓ of Cheez. Layer in ½ of the vegetables. Then layer ⅓ of the sauce. Repeat. Top the layers with the last of the Cheez and bake for 40 minutes. Allow to cool for at least 10-15 minutes before serving.

info

∾ For more information on ulu (breadfruit), please see page 201.

"LET US JUST KEEP LOVING ONE ANOTHER. SHARING OUR MEDICINE WITH EACH OTHER. WE'RE ALL LEARNING WHAT IT MEANS TO BE REAL. SO JUST ACCEPT ALL THAT COMES AND TOGETHER WE WILL HEAL." - MANAKA

ISLE OF MU RAINBOW CASSEROLE

30 min prep / 60 min cooking / 9" x 13" casserole

White

¾ C Sushi rice cooked in 1 C coconut milk & 2 C filtered water

Black

¾ C Black rice cooked in 2 ½ C filtered water or vegetable stock

Orange

¾ C Millet cooked in 2 C fresh carrot juice & 1 C filtered water or vegetable stock

Red

¾ C Quinoa cooked in 1 ½ C fresh beet juice & 1 ½ C filtered water or vegetable stock

Yellow

¾ C Polenta
2 ½ C Filtered water or vegetable stock
¼ C Coconut, soy or rice milk (optional)
2 Tbl Fresh herbs, minced (basil, parsley, dill, cilantro or your favorite)
• Cayenne pepper, to taste
• Sea salt, to taste
• Black pepper, ground to taste

loving preparation

1. Preheat oven to 350°. For white, black, orange, and red layers, please cook in separate pots according to the method discussed on page 206. Season each layer with salt, pepper and cayenne to taste.
2. For polenta layer, bring water or stock to a boil in a 3 qt pot. Reduce heat to low and slowly whisk in polenta, adding coconut milk and herbs as mixture begins to thicken. Season with salt, pepper and cayenne to taste.
3. Spread cooked grains, alternating colors, into a well oiled 9" x 13" casserole dish, using either the white, black or yellow layer as the bottom one. Please wait until a layer has some firmess to it through cooling—approximately 5 minutes—before adding another layer. Place in oven and bake for 15 minutes. Allow to cool for at least 10-15 minutes before serving.

serving suggestion

ॐ Top with Carrot Ginger Sauce (page 66), Spinach Mushroom Sauce (page 60) Mushroom Gravy (page 64) or sauce of choice, or top with a layer of Pesto (page 113 or 140), sliced tomatoes and a sprinkle of black sesame seeds.

"MAKIA—CONCENTRATION—ENERGY FLOWS WHERE ATTENTION GOES." - HUNA PRINCIPLE

MARTIN'S KASHA VARNISHKES

15 min prep / 20 min cooking / 2-3 servings

8 c	Filtered water
3 c	Bow tie pasta
2 Tbl	Olive oil
1 medium	Onion, diced
2 tsp	Garlic, minced
¾ c	Buckwheat, roasted (kasha)
1 Tbl	Flax seed, ground
1 ¾ c	Filtered water or vegetable stock
2 Tbl	Italian parsley, minced
Pinch	Cayenne pepper
•	Sea salt, to taste
•	Black pepper, ground to taste
1 Tbl	Flax oil

loving preparation

1. Bring 8 c of water to a boil in a 3 qt pot. Add bow tie pasta, reduce heat to medium and cook until soft but firm, approximately 8 minutes. Remove from heat, drain well and place in a large mixing bowl.
2. While pasta is cooking, place oil in a large sauté pan on medium high heat. Add onion and garlic, cook for 3 minutes, stirring frequently. Add kasha and flax seeds, cook for 2 minutes, stirring constantly. Slowly add 1 ¾ c water or stock, stirring constantly.
3. Reduce heat to simmer and cook until all liquid is absorbed, approximately 15 minutes. Gently fluff with a fork, add to bowl with pasta. Add remaining ingredients and mix well.

SAT CIT ANANDA'S CHANA MASALA

20 min prep / 35 min cooking / 3-4 servings

1 ½ tsp	Brown mustard seeds
1 ½ tsp	Cumin seeds
2 Tbl	Toasted sesame oil
2 c	Onion, chopped
2 Tbl	Garlic, minced
2 Tbl	Ginger, peeled & minced
1 c	Tomatoes, chopped
1 c	Filtered water
1 ½ c	Coconut milk
3 c	Garbanzo beans, cooked (page 209)
¼ c	Nama shoyu, or to taste
1 ½ tsp	Cinnamon powder
1 ½ tsp	Coriander, ground
1 tsp	Cardamom powder
1 tsp	Cumin powder
½ tsp	Thyme, minced
½ tsp	Black pepper, ground to taste
⅛ tsp	Clove powder
2 Tbl	Cilantro, minced
•	Sea salt, to taste

loving preparation

1. Place brown mustard seed and cumin seeds in a large sauté pan or 3 qt pot on medium high heat. Heat until seeds pop, approximately 1 minute, stirring constantly. Add oil, onion, garlic, and ginger and cook for 5 minutes, stirring frequently.
2. Add tomatoes and cook for 5 minutes, stirring occasionally. Reduce heat to simmer, add water, shoyu, spices, coconut milk and beans, cook 25 minutes, stirring occasionally. Top with cilantro and lovingly serve.

variations

- Add 2 c various garden veggies, finely chopped, while cooking.

"THEY GO FROM STRENGTH TO STRENGTH." - PSALMS 84:7

MAHATMA'S MUNG DAHL

20 min prep / 35 min cooking / 4-5 servings

6 C	Filtered water or vegetable stock		1 Tbl	Cumin seed, toasted (page 194)
1 C	Mung beans, sorted & rinsed well		1 tsp	Cumin powder, toasted
1 medium	Onion diced		½ tsp	Curry powder
1 medium	Carrot, cubed		¼ tsp	Sea salt, to taste
½ C	Celery, thinly sliced		¼ tsp	Black pepper, ground to taste
1 Tbl	Garlic, minced		Pinch	Cayenne pepper
1 Tbl	Ginger, peeled & minced		2 Tbl	Cilantro, minced
1 Tbl	Jalapeño, seeded & minced		⅓ C	Nama shoyu, to taste

loving preparation

1. Rinse beans and place in a medium sized pot with 6 C of water or stock on medium high heat. Add onion, carrot, celery, garlic, ginger and jalapeño, cook on medium high heat until beans are soft, approximately 30 minutes, stirring occasionally.
2. Add shoyu and remaining ingredients, except cilantro, and cook for an additional 5 minutes, stirring occasionally.
3. Add cilantro, remove from heat and enjoy (beans should be rinsed and soaked overnight or for several hours beforehand to improve digestibility; please see page 209 for soaking techniques).

Bathers in Ganges River, Varanasi, India

JOHN BARLEYCORN'S SALAD

20 min prep / 45 min cooking / 4-5 servings

8 large	Brussel sprouts, steamed (page 193) & quartered
2 ½ C	Filtered water or vegetable stock
1 C	Pearl barley
1 C	Corn, fresh
¼ C	Red bell pepper, diced
¼ C	Green onion, diced
2 Tbl	Flax oil
1 Tbl	Italian parsley, minced
1 ½ tsp	Tarragon, fresh minced
Pinch	Cayenne pepper
Pinch	Crushed red pepper flakes
•	Sea salt, to taste
•	Black pepper, ground to taste

loving preparation

1. Place water and barley in a medium pot and bring to a boil over high heat. Reduce heat to simmer, cover and cook until barley is tender and liquid is absorbed, approximately 45 minutes.
2. Fluff grains with a fork, add to a large mixing bowl with remaining ingredients and mix well.

ARJUNA'S RAINBOW PATÉ

1 hour prep / 5-6 servings

2 C	Sundried Tomato Paté, (page 28)
2 C	Carrot Almond Paté (page 32)
2 C	Basil Almond Paté (page 28)

loving preparation

1. Prepare patés according to instructions for each recipe. Use each one as a layer for a three level paté creation or divide each batch in half to create a six layer dish.

serving suggestion

↝ Serve on a bed of clean collards or chard.
↝ Top with Nut Cheez (page 29), Live Tomato Sauce (page 67) or Live Alfreda Sauce (page 82).
↝ Form paté in various geometric shapes and creatively decorate with raw vegetables or sprouts for the ultimate live food casserole.

"IN ALL PEOPLE I SEE MYSELF, NOT ONE MORE AND NOT ONE A BARLEY-CORN LESS." - WALT WHITMAN, SONG OF MYSELF

IZZI'S LIVE LASAGNA

1 hour 20 minutes prep / 9" x 13" casserole

Cheez

3 C	Cashew Cheez (page 29)
½ C	Red bell pepper, diced
1 Tbl	Basil, fresh minced
1 Tbl	Oregano, fresh minced
1 Tbl	Rosemary, fresh minced
1 tsp	Nama shoyu, or to taste
½ tsp	Sea salt, or to taste
½ tsp	Jalapeño, seeded & minced

Sauce

6 medium	Roma tomatoes, seeded
1/3 C	Sundried tomatoes, soaked in warm water until soft
1 Tbl	Olive oil
1 tsp	Sea salt, or to taste
1 ½ tsp	Nama shoyu, or to taste
½ tsp	Black pepper, ground to taste
¼ C	Fresh herbs, minced (basil, oregano, rosemary or your favorites)
¼ tsp	Crushed red pepper flakes

"Noodles"

3-5 large	Zucchini, sliced thin
5-10 large	Portabello mushrooms, sliced thin
1 bunch	Chard, stems removed

loving preparation

1. Begin the **Cashew Cheez** the night before. The next day add all cheez ingredients to a large mixing bowl, mix well and set aside.
2. For **Sauce**, place all ingredients, except fresh herbs in a blender and blend until smooth. Stir in herbs and set aside.
3. Slice zucchinis and mushrooms into thin "lasagna" **Noodles**. Press slices between dry towels to remove excess moisture. Experiment with vegetable peelers, cheez cutters or a mandolin to get uniform thickness.
4. In a 9" x 13" casserole dish begin layering with 2-3 chard leaves and 1/3 of zucchini, then spread on 1/3 of the Cheez, then 1/3 of the mushrooms and sauce. Repeat until all ingredients have been used. Top with Cashew Cheez and sprinkle with basil for an authentic lasagna look.

"SIMPLY PUT, IT'S ALL ABOUT LOVE." - SHANTI GABRIEL

ZAPHOD'S UNIVERSAL CHI LIVE TABOULI

overnight soaking / 24 hours sprouting / 20 minutes prep / 2 servings

1 C	Winter wheat berries, soaked			
1 ½ C	Tomato, chopped	1 Tbl	Flax oil
¼ C	Red Onion, diced	1 Tbl	Lemon juice, fresh squeezed
2 Tbl	Italian parsley, minced	½ tsp	Garlic, minced (optional)
2 tsp	Mint, chopped	•	Sea salt, to taste
		•	Black pepper, ground to taste

loving preparation

1. Place wheatberries and at least 4 C of filtered water in a medium size bowl in a cool dry place. Soak overnight. Place in a collander. Rinse, drain well and return to bowl. Allow to sprout for 24 hours, rinsing & draining periodically (page 202).
2. Place in a large mixing bowl with remaining ingredients and mix well. Allow flavors to mingle for 20-30 minutes before enjoying.

variations

꙾ For a cooked tabouli, cook 1 C of bulghar wheat according to method on page 206. Place in a large mixing bowl with remaining ingredients and mix well.

INCAN TEMPLE SPROUTED QUINOA SALAD

1 hr soaking / 48 hours sprouting / 30 min prep / 2-3 servings

1 C	Quinoa	1 recipe	Shoyu Marinade (page 195)
2 C	Assorted vegetables, diced	1 Tbl	Fresh herbs, minced (try parsley,
	(red onion, red bell pepper,		basil, oregano, thyme, dill or
	portabello mushroom, zuchinni,		your favorite)
	carrots, etc)	2 Tbl	Olives, sliced
		Pinch	Crushed red pepper flakes
		•	Sea salt, to taste
		•	Black pepper, ground to taste

loving preparation

1. Place quinoa and at least 4 C of filtered water in a medium size bowl in a cool, dry place. Sprout according to instructions on pages 202-203.
2. Place all vegetables in a bowl with Creamy Tahini Marinade and allow to sit for at least 30 minutes, up to several hours. Add sprouted quinoa and remaining ingredients, mix well.

serving suggestion

꙾ Serve with a mixed garden vegetable salad and dressing of choice.
꙾ Spread a small amount of Nut Cheez (page 29) in a scooped out tomato. Place quinoa salad on top of cheez, and top with Papaya Seed Ranch Dressing (page 57), Live Alfreda Sauce (page 82) or dressing of choice.

10

Dream Weaver's
Live Fruit Pie, pages 174-5

desserts

KAVA BROWNIES

CHOCOLATE CAKE

VEGAN CHEEZCAKE W/PINEAPPLE TOPPING

CARROT CAKE

FRUIT COBBLER

MAPLE GINGER COOKIES

CAROB COUSCOUS CAKE

NO-BAKE COOKIES

WONDER BARS

HALVAH

RICE PUDDING

MANGO GINGER BARS

BAKLAVA

MINT CHOCOLATE CHIP COOKIES

OIL-FREE MUFFINS

BANANA CHOCOLATE CUSTARD

PUMPKIN PIE WITH MAPLE WHIP

LIVE BLISS BALLS

LIVE PARFAITS

LIVE PIES

I LOVE KALI MA'S KAVA BROWNIES

20 min prep / 45 min cooking / 9" x 13" baking pan

Dry

2 c	Sucanat
2 c	Spelt flour
1 1/3 c	Chocolate chips
⅔ c	Cocoa powder
1½ Tbl	Arrowroot powder
½ tsp	Baking soda
¼ tsp	Sea salt, or to taste

Kava Tea

2 tsp	Kava kava
1/3 c	Filtered water, hot

Wet

½ c	Hot water
3 Tbl	Applesauce, sugar-free
3 Tbl	Raisins
2 tsp	Flax seeds, ground
2 tsp	Vanilla extract, alcohol free

loving preparation

1. Preheat oven to 350°. Steep kava in filtered water for 20 minutes. Strain and save liquid.
2. Place *Dry* ingredients in a large mixing bowl and mix well. Place *Wet* ingredients in a blender and blend until smooth. Combine all ingredients including *Kava Tea* and mix well.
3. Place batter into a parchment paper-lined 9" x 13" baking pan, bake until top is slightly crispy and a toothpick comes out of the center dry, approximately 40-45 minutes. (If you poke a chocolate chip, try again). Allow to cool and top with shredded toasted coconut before serving.

variations

- Serve warm with soy or hemp "ice cream."
- Replace chocolate chips and cocoa powder with carob.
- Top with pieces of environmentally-friendly sugar free chocolate.
- For *Peanut or Almond Butter Fudge Brownies*, combine 1 c of nut butter and ¾ c maple syrup in a large mixing bowl and mix well. Pour ½ of brownie batter into the baking pan and bake for approximately 15 minutes. Layer nut butter mixture on top of this, pour in remaining batter and continue to bake for 30 minutes.

"O, NIGHT THAT GUIDED ME, O, NIGHT MORE LOVELY THAN THE DAWN, O, NIGHT THAT JOINED BELOVED WITH LOVER, LOVER TRANSFORMED IN THE BELOVED!" - ST. JOHN OF THE CROSS

BIG MOMMA FREEDOM CHOCOLATE CAKE

15 minutes prep / 40 min cooking / 9" x 13" cake

Dry

2 ½ C	Spelt flour
2 C	Sucanat
¾ C	Cocoa Powder
1 ½ tsp	Baking soda
½ tsp	Sea salt, or to taste
½ tsp	Cinnamon powder

Wet

6 Tbl	Safflower oil
2 ¼ C	Filtered water
2 Tbl	Apple cider vinegar, raw
1 tsp	Vanilla extract, alcohol free

Frosting

2 C	Chocolate chips
12.3 oz	Silken firm tofu or ripe avocado
2 Tbl	Maple syrup
1 ½ tsp	Vanilla extract, alcohol free

loving preparation

1. **Cake** Preheat oven to 350°. Place dry ingredients in a large mixing bowl and mix well. Combine wet ingredients in a small bowl. Add wet to dry and mix well. Pour into a parchment paper lined 9" x 13" baking pan and bake until a toothpick comes out clean, approximately 35-40 minutes.
2. **Frosting** Place chocolate chips in a double boiler on medium heat until chips are melted, stirring frequently. Combine with remaining ingredients and blend or food process until smooth and creamy. Refrigerate until it thickens.
3. Cool cake before frosting. Garnish with toasted coconut flakes, strawberries, toasted pecans and/or chocolate chips.

variations

- Replace chocolate chips and cocoa powder with carob chips and carob powder.

Lake Titicaca, island of the moon, & holy mountains of Ancohuma & Illampu, Bolivia

SHAKA'S VEGAN CHEEZCAKE

20 min prep / 1 hour baking / 45 min cooking & cooling / 10" cake

Filling

2 lbs	Tofu, firm
1 c	Sucanat
½ c	Soy milk
½ c	Maple syrup
1/3 c	Lemon juice, fresh squeezed
4 Tbl	Nutritional yeast
2 ½ Tbl	Arrowroot powder
2 Tbl	Vanilla extract, alcohol free
½ tsp	Sea salt, or to taste

Crust - Dry

2 c	Spelt flour
¼ c	Sucanat
1 Tbl	Arrowroot powder
1 tsp	Baking powder
¼ tsp	Cardamom powder
¼ tsp	Sea salt, or to taste

Crust - Wet

1/3 c	Safflower oil
2 Tbl	Maple syrup
2 Tbl	Apple juice, fresh
1 tsp	Vanilla extract, alcohol free

loving preparation

1. Preheat oven to 350°. For *Crust*, place dry ingredients together in a large mixing bowl and mix well. Place wet ingredients in another bowl & mix well. Add wet to dry, mixing well with hands, crumbling the ingredients together repeatedly. Press into the bottom of a 10" spring form pan. Bake for 5 minutes.

2. Place all *Filling* ingredients in a large blender and blend until smooth. Pour on top of crust and bake for 1 hour or until top turns a golden brown and center does not jiggle too much. Allow to cool before running a knife around the edge and removing from spring form pan.

serving suggestions

- Top with pineapple topping , strawberry sauce (page 66), or your topping of choice.
- For *Chocolate Cheezcake* add 2 c of Vegan chocolate chips, melted in a double boiler, to the filling while blending.

PINEAPPLE FRUIT TOPPING FOR CHEEZCAKE

10 min prep / 10 min cooking / 2 cups topping

1 c	Pineapple or other fruit juice, fresh
1 c	Pineapple or other fruit, chopped
1/3 c	Sucanat
1 ½ Tbl	Lemon, freshly squeezed
1 Tbl	Arrowroot powder, dissolved in 2 Tbl warm water
Pinch	Cinnamon powder

loving preparation

1. Place all ingredients except arrowroot in a small saucepan over medium high heat. Stir frequently with a wire whisk until tiny bubbles begin to form at the edge, approximately 5 minutes.

2. Add arrowroot mixture and cook until sauce visibly thickens, approximately 5 minutes, stirring constantly. Remove from heat and continue stirring for a few seconds.

3. Pour over cooled cheezcake.

"LIFE IS A PROMISE, FULFILL IT." - MOTHER THERESA

158

Shaka's Vegan Cheezcake with Simso's strawberry sauce (page 66)

COSMIC CURL GIRL'S CARROT CAKE

45 min prep / 1 hour cooking / 11" spring form pan

	Dry
3 ¼ C	Spelt flour
2 C	Sucanat
2 C	Carrots, shredded or grated
1 ½ C	Raisins
1 Tbl	Baking soda
¾ tsp	Cinnamon powder
¼ tsp	Sea salt, or to taste
¼ tsp	Allspice powder

	Wet
1 ¾ C	Carrot juice, fresh
½ C	Filtered water
⅓ C	Ginger juice, fresh
⅜ C	Safflower oil
2 Tbl	Apple cider vinegar, raw
1 tsp	Vanilla extract, alcohol free

loving preparation

1. Preheat oven to 350°. Place all ***Dry*** ingredients except carrots and raisins in a large mixing bowl and whisk well.
2. Place ***Wet*** ingredients in a small bowl and whisk well. Add wet to dry, along with carrots and raisins, mix well.
3. Pour into a well oiled 11" spring form pan and bake for 60 minutes or until a toothpick comes out clean.

serving suggestion

- Ice with Cashew Crème Frosting (below) and top with chopped walnuts and/or grated carrots.

"HOW WONDERFUL IT IS THAT NOBODY NEED WAIT A SINGLE MOMENT BEFORE STARTING TO IMPROVE THE WORLD." - ANNE FRANK

ST. CATHERINE'S CASHEW CRÈME FROSTING

10 min prep / 2 ½ cups frosting

1 C	Cashews
⅔ C	Coconut milk, or more to achieve desired consistency
⅓ C	Dates, or to taste
½ tsp	Vanilla extract, alcohol free

loving preparation

1. Place cashews, dates and vanilla in a blender or food processor with ½ C coconut milk and process until smooth, adding coconut milk as necessary until mixture is smooth and still thick.
2. Place in refrigerator for 20 minutes or more before frosting cake. Please wait until cake is completely cooled before frosting.

BAMBOODHA'S FRUIT CRUMBLE

30 min prep / 35 min baking / 9" x 13" baking dish

Filling		*Dry*	
2 ¼ C	Dates, pitted & chopped	3¼ C	Rolled oats
2 C	Apple juice, fresh	2 C	Spelt flour
1 C	Blueberries, fresh or frozen	¾ C	Sucanat
½ C	Raisins	½ C	Pecans, finely chopped
½ C	Walnuts, chopped	½ tsp	Cinnamon powder
¼ tsp	Cinnamon powder	⅛ tsp	Nutmeg
⅛ tsp	Cardamom powder		

Wet

½ C	Safflower oil
½ C	Filtered water
1 ½ tsp	Vanilla extract, alcohol free

loving preparation

1. Preheat oven to 350°. Place **Filling** ingredients in a medium sized pot and cook over medium low heat until juice is absorbed and dates are softened, approximately 15 minutes, stirring frequently. Be careful not to burn. Remove from heat.
2. Place 2 ¼ C of rolled oats, ½ C sucanat and remaining **Dry** ingredients in a large mixing bowl and mix well. Place **Wet** ingredients in another bowl and whisk well. Add wet to dry, mix well. Place ⅔ of this mixture in a well oiled 9"x 13" casserole dish and press down firmly. Bake in oven for 10 minutes. Remove from oven and pour filling mixture on top of this.
3. Add ½ C of rolled oats and ¼ C sucanat to remaining flour and oat mixture and mix well. Process slightly in a food processor and crumble on top of filling. Bake in oven until golden brown, approximately 25 minutes.

serving suggestions

- Allow to cool slightly before slicing. May be enjoyed cold or warm. Top with Maple Whip (page 172) or Vanilla Coco Cream (page 175).
- Please use only organically-grown dried fruits.

variations

- Many variations are possible. Experiment with different nuts or berries.
- Substitute raisins with other chopped dried fruit, or fresh pear or apple.
- Substitute different flavored fruit juices for apple juice.

"IF YOU ARE PATIENT IN A MOMENT OF ANGER, YOU WILL ESCAPE A HUNDRED DAYS OF SORROW." - CHINESE PROVERB

MAGDALENE'S MAPLE GINGER BLISS COOKIES

25 min prep / 10 min cooking / 10 medium cookies

	Wet		*Dry*
½ C	Sucanat	1 1/3 C	Spelt flour
⅓ C	Safflower oil	2 tsp	Flax seeds, ground
3 Tbl	Maple syrup	2 tsp	Arrowroot powder
2 Tbl	Ginger juice, fresh	½ tsp	Baking powder
4 tsp	Molasses	½ tsp	Cinnamon powder
4 tsp	Applesauce, sugar free	¼ tsp	Sea salt
		Pinch	Allspice powder
		Pinch	Cardamom powder

loving preparation

1. Preheat oven to 400°. Mix *Wet* ingredients together in large bowl. Sift together *Dry* ingredients in separate bowl. Add dry to wet and mix together well. Refrigerate dough for 10 minutes.
2. Form cookies with approximately 2½ Tbl of dough on a well oiled cookie sheet and bake for 10 minutes. Let cookies cool completely before enjoying.

variations

⌇ Add ¼ C of cocoa powder to dry ingredients for *Chocolate Bliss*. Top with chocolate chips before baking.

"LOVE IS OUR GUIDE" - SAMADHI LOTUS

CHANDI'S CAROB COUSCOUS PIE

15 min prep / 20 min cooking / 6" pie

	Crust		*Filling*
1 ½ C	Filtered water	2 C	Carob chips, Vegan
¾ C	Couscous	12.3 oz	Silken tofu, firm
½ C	Sucanat	¼ C	Maple syrup
3 Tbl	Carob powder	3 Tbl	Almond butter
1 Tbl	Almond butter	1 ½ tsp	Vanilla extract, alcohol free
1 tsp	Vanilla extract, alcohol free	⅛ tsp	Cinnamon powder
		Pinch	Cardamom powder

loving preparation

1. Combine **Crust** ingredients in a medium sized sauce pan and whisk together over low heat until all liquid is dissolved and the couscous is completely cooked, approximately 10-15 minutes, stirring occasionally. Place mixture in a well oiled 6" spring pan and allow to cool.
2. Place carob chips in double boiler on medium high heat until chips are melted, stirring frequently. Combine with other **Filling** ingredients in the food processor and process until smooth. Pour over crust in the spring pan and allow to completely cool in the refrigerator before garnishing, approximately 20 minutes.

serving suggestions & variations

- Garnish with minced roasted pecan, strawberries, carob chips, toasted coconut, mint leaves etc. Try replacing carob chips and powder with chocolate. Try replacing almond butter with other nut butters like cashew or macadamia. Of course, don't forget to top with the Maple Tofu Whip (page 172).
- Replace tofu with equal amount of ripe avocado for a soy-free dessert.

DA KINE NO BAKE CHOCOLATE COOKIES

20 min prep / 8-10 cookies

2 C	Chocolate or Carob chips, Vegan
½ C	Raisins
¼ C	Pecans or macadamia nuts, toasted (page 194)
½ C	Coconut flakes, toasted (page 194)
¼ C	Almond or peanut butter
2 Tbl	Maple syrup
1 tsp	Vanilla extract, alcohol free
1/8 tsp	Cinnamon powder
Pinch	Cardamom powder

loving preparation

1. Place chocolate chips in double boiler on medium high heat until chips are melted, stirring frequently. Place in a large bowl.
2. Set aside ¼ C of the toasted coconut to sprinkle on top of cookies. Add remaining ingredients to the melted chocolate and mix well.
3. Shape cookies and place on a parchment paper lined or well oiled baking sheet. Top with remaining ¼ C coconut. Refrigerate until cool.

"I HAVE AN EXISTENTIAL MAP. IT HAS 'YOU ARE HERE' WRITTEN ALL OVER IT." - STEVEN WRIGHT

Kukulkan

164

MAYAN WONDER BARS

20 min prep / 15 min cooking / 12-2 ½" squares

1 ½ C	Almond butter		½ C	Sunflower seeds, toasted (page 194)
½ C	Maple syrup		¾ C	Pumpkin seeds, toasted
½ C	Brown rice syrup		¼ C	Hemp seeds
¼ tsp	Cardamom powder		½ C	Pecans or macadamia nuts, toasted & chopped
¼ tsp	Cinnamon powder			
½ C	Quinoa, toasted (page 194)			

loving preparation

1. Preheat oven to 350°. Mix almond butter, syrups and spices in a large mixing bowl. Add remaining ingredients and mix well.
2. Spread on a well oiled 9"x 13" baking dish and bake until golden brown, approximately 15 minutes. Allow to cool completely before slicing.

variation

↝ 🪷 *Live Mayan* Omit brown rice syrup and quinoa. Add a dozen raw, crushed cacao beans and form into bars. Refrigerate instead of baking.

Temple of the Jaguar, Tikal, Guatemala

HABIBI'S HALVAH

20 min cooking / 30 min cooling / 8" x 8" pan

2 c	Chocolate chips
2 c	Raw tahini (the thickest consistency available)
3 Tbl	Agave nectar
1 tsp	Vanilla extract, alcohol free
Pinch	Cinnamon powder
Pinch	Cardamom powder

loving preparation

1. Melt the chocolate chips in a double boiler according to instructions on page 157.
2. Combine remaining ingredients in a large mixing bowl. Stir in melted chocolate, transfer to an 8"x8" pan and refrigerate until thick, from 30 minutes to a few hours depending upon the thickness of the tahini used.

variations

➷ Add ½ c of toasted pumpkin seeds or pistachio nuts, chopped fine, before refrigerating and mix well.

THE BLISS OF KRISHNA TROPICAL RICE PUDDING

15 min prep / 35 min cooking / 2 servings

½ c	White basmati rice
1 c	Coconut milk
2 ½ c	Soy milk, vanilla flavor
1/3 c	Sucanat
3 Tbl	Maple syrup, or to taste
¼ c	Pistachio or macadamia nuts, toasted until golden & chopped, (page 194)
1/3 c	Raisins
½ tsp	Cinnamon powder
¼ tsp	Cardamom powder
¾ tsp	Vanilla extract, alcohol free
•	Mint leaves, for garnish

loving preparation

1. Place rice, coconut milk and 2 c of soy milk in a 3 qt pot and cook over medium heat until rice is cooked, approximately 30 minutes, stirring occasionally.
2. Remove from heat, add remaining ingredients, including the second portion of soy milk and mix well.

serving suggestion

➷ Garnish with a mint leaf and some chopped toasted nuts. Can be served warm or cold.

"TRUE KNOWLEDGE EXISTS IN KNOWING THAT YOU KNOW NOTHING." - SOCRATES

Gateway to the temple of Aphrodite,
Aphrodisias, Turkey

MALAMA AINA MANGO GINGER BARS

35 min prep / 30 min cooking / 6-8 servings

	Crust		*Topping*
4 C	Rolled oats	2 C	Dates, pitted & firmly packed
1 large	Mango, peeled, chopped small (1 C)	1 small	Lemon, zested (½ tsp)
¾ C	Sucanat	1/3 C	Ginger juice, fresh
½ C	Spelt flour	¼ C	Coconut milk
½ C	Ginger juice, fresh	2 Tbl	Flax seeds, ground
½ C	Safflower oil	1 Tbl	Arrowroot powder, dissolved in 2 Tbl filtered water
¼ C	Maple syrup	½ C	Pecans or macadamia nuts, toasted & chopped (optional)

loving preparation

1. Preheat oven to 350°. Combine all *Crust* ingredients in a large mixing bowl, mix well and let sit for 10 minutes. Spread a ½" thick layer on a well oiled, or parchment paper-lined cookie sheet. Bake for 30 minutes, remove from oven and allow to cool.
2. While crust is baking, place all *Topping* ingredients, except arrowroot mixture, in food processor and process until smooth. Place the topping mixture in a 3 qt pot and cook on medium heat until it begins to bubble on the edges, approximately 7 minutes, stirring frequently. Add arrowroot water mixture and stir constantly until topping thickens, approximately 4 minutes.
3. Pour on top of baked crust, top with toasted nuts and allow to cool before serving.

BARAKA'S BAKLAVA

25 min prep / 25 min cooking / 8" x 8" pan

16	Phyllo sheets, spelt
1 ½ C	Walnuts
1 ½ C	Macadamia nuts or pistachio nuts, toasted
½ C	Agave nectar
¼ C	Brown rice syrup
2 Tbl	Rose water
½ tsp	Cinnamon powder
¼ tsp	Cardamom powder
¼ tsp	Nutmeg, ground
¼ tsp	Allspice powder
¼ tsp	Clove powder
½ C or more	Corn oil

loving preparation

1. Preheat oven to 350°. Chop nuts until fine, combine with agave nectar and remaining ingredients except corn oil & phyllo in a large mixing bowl and mix well.
2. In an 8"x8" baking pan, layer 6 full sheets of phyllo, brushing each sheet with oil. Fold sheets to fit pan. Place ½ nut mixture over phyllo then fold 4 more phyllo sheets, brushing each with oil. Add second ½ nut mixture and then a third layer of six sheets of phyllo, brush with oil.
3. Bake for 25 minutes and enjoy.

"ALTHOUGH THE WORLD IS FULL OF SUFFERING, IT IS FULL ALSO OF THE OVERCOMING OF IT." - HELEN KELLER

MYSTERIUM TREMENDUM MINT CHOCOLATE CHIP COOKIES

25 min prep / 15 min cook / 8 large cookies

	Dry			*Wet*
2 c	Spelt flour		⅔ c	Maple syrup
1 c	Vegan chocolate chips		⅔ c	Safflower oil
1 c	Walnuts, chopped		2 Tbl	Filtered water
¾ c	Rolled oats		1 tsp	Peppermint extract
½ tsp	Sea salt			
¾ tsp	Baking soda			
⅛ tsp	Cinnamon powder			
Pinch	Nutmeg, ground			

loving preparation

1. Preheat oven to 350°. Place **Dry** ingredients in a large mixing bowl and mix well. Combine **Wet** ingredients in another large bowl. Add wet to dry and mix well. Refrigerate for 15 minutes. Place 8 scoops on a well oiled or parchment paper-lined baking sheet and flatten slightly with hand. Space evenly so cookies have room to spread.

2. Bake until golden brown, approximately 10 minutes. Allow to cool before enjoying.

variations

- Replace walnuts with toasted pecans or macadamia nuts.
- Replace chocolate chips with carob chips or dried fruits.
- Add 2 Tbl of cocoa or carob powder to above.
- Try adding 1 Tbl spirulina.

"UNLESS SOMEONE LIKE YOU CARES A WHOLE AWFUL LOT, NOTHING IS GOING TO GET BETTER. IT'S NOT." - DR. SEUSS

Clockwise: Da Kine No-Bake Cookies, Mysterium Tremendum Mint Chocolate Chip Cookies, Mayan Wonder Bars

EMAHO'S OIL-FREE MUFFINS

20 min prep / 30 min cooking / 8 muffins

Dry		*Wet*	
3 ¼ C	Spelt flour	1 C	Pineapple juice, fresh
½ C	Coconut flakes	1 C	Pineapple, ½" chop
¾ tsp	Baking soda	¾ C	Banana, mashed
¾ tsp	Baking powder	¾ C	Maple syrup
½ tsp	Cinnamon powder	½ tsp	Vanilla extract, alcohol free
¼ tsp	Sea salt	¼ tsp	Lemon zest

loving preparation

1. Preheat oven to 350°. Mix all *Dry* ingredients in a large mixing bowl.
2. Combine *Wet* ingredients in another bowl. Add wet to dry and mix well.
3. Pour batter into well oiled muffin cups until each is ¾ full. Bake until a toothpick placed in the center of the muffin comes out dry, approximately 30 minutes.

variations

- ↬ Many variations are possible. Try adding ¼ C of finely chopped nuts.
- ↬ Replace pineapple with other fruit or berries.
- ↬ Replace pineapple juice with apple juice or other fruit juices. Replace blended bananas with apple sauce or puréed papaya.
- ↬ Replace banana with grated zucchini or carrots.
- ↬ Other standards include a maple walnut, carrot raisin or pumpkin allspice muffin.
- ↬ Replace coconut with rolled oats.

Mt. Ararat, Turkey

"MY BARN HAVING BURNED TO THE GROUND, I CAN NOW SEE THE MOON." - ZEN HAIKU

IMMORTAL CHOCOLATE BANANA CUSTARD

25 minutes cooking / 3 servings

24.6 oz	Silken tofu, firm
5 Tbl	Maple syrup
¼ C	Almond butter
1 tsp	Vanilla extract, alcohol free
Pinch	Cinnamon powder
Pinch	Cardamom powder

2 C	Chocolate chips, melted in a double boiler (page 157)
1½ C	Banana, mashed

Garnish

2 Tbl	Toasted coconut
3	Mint leaves
3	Strawberries

loving preparation

1. Place all ingredients except chocolate, banana and toasted coconut in a food processor and process until smooth. Remove ½ of the mixture and set aside.
2. Add banana to processor with remaining mixture and process until smooth. Remove from processor and pour into 3 parfait glasses.
3. Place melted chocolate chips and the base mixture that was set aside in the processor and process until smooth. Pour over banana mixture and garnish with toasted coconut, a strawberry and a mint leaf.

variations

- Replace chocolate chips with carob chips.
- Replace chocolate chips and bananas with other seasonal fruit.
- Replace tofu with avocado.

Stonehenge Stone Circle, England

"TO SEE A WORLD IN A GRAIN OF SAND AND HEAVEN IN A WILD FLOWER. HOLD INFINITY IN THE PALM OF YOUR HAND AND ETERNITY IN AN HOUR." - WILLIAM BLAKE

171

PREM'S PUMPKIN PIE

20 min prep / 1 hour cooking + pumpkin cooking time / 9" pie

1 recipe	Spelt Pie Crust (page 158)	3 Tbl	Molasses
1 medium	Pumpkin (1 ¾ C cooked)	2 Tbl	Arrowroot powder
¾ C	Almond butter	½ tsp	Vanilla extract, alcohol free
¼ C	Soy milk	¼ tsp	Cardamom powder
¼ C	Maple syrup	¼ tsp	Allspice powder
¼ C	Sucanat	¼ tsp	Nutmeg, ground
		⅛ tsp	Clove powder

loving preparation

1. Preheat oven to 350°. Cut pumpkin in half and remove the seeds. Place face down on a well oiled or parchment paper lined baking pan. Bake until a knife easily goes through the skin and the flesh of the pumpkin, approximately 45 minutes.
2. While pumpkin is baking, prepare **Crust** and press into the bottom and sides of a 9" pie pan. Bake for 10 minutes. Remove from oven and set aside.
3. Scoop out 1 ¾ C pumpkin, place in food processor or blender with remaining ingredients and process or blend until smooth.
4. Pour mixture into pie crust and bake until top is firm to touch, approximately 1 hour. Filling may puff up and rise above crust line as it bakes. It will fall back down as it cools.

serving suggestions

↝ Serve with Maple Tofu Whip Topping (below).

snack idea

↝ Be sure to save your pumpkin seeds for the best snack ever. Clean well, baste in shoyu with a pinch of cumin and chili powder. Bake at 400° for 15-20 minutes, stirring occasionally.

MAMA'S MAPLE TOFU WHIP

12.3 oz	Silken tofu
2-3 Tbl	Maple syrup or agave nectar, or to taste
2 tsp	Lemon juice, fresh squeezed
½ tsp	Vanilla extract, alcohol free
Pinch	Cardamom powder
Pinch	Cinnamon powder

loving preparation

1. Place all ingredients in a food processor or blender and process until smooth.

serving suggestion & variation

↝ Serve with Pumpkin Pie, Fruit Crumble (page 161) or Couscous Pie (page 163). Will enhance the flavor of most treats.
↝ Replace tofu with 1 ½ C soaked cashews.

"FOLLOW YOUR BLISS. FIND WHERE IT IS AND DON'T BE AFRAID TO FOLLOW IT." JOSEPH CAMPBELL

ETERNAL BLISS BALLS

30 minutes / 3-4 servings

1 c	Dates, pitted
¾ c	Almonds, soaked (page 202)
¼ c	Sunflower or pumpkin seeds, soaked (page 202)
¼ c	Macadamia nut butter, tahini or almond butter, raw
¼ c	Raisins, soaked in 1 c of filtered water
1 ½ Tbl	Flax seeds, soaked in 1 Tbl water until liquid is absorbed
1 ½ tsp	Carob powder, raw
1 ½ tsp	Spirulina powder
¼ tsp	Cinnamon powder
⅛ tsp	Cardamom powder

loving preparation

1. Place dates and almonds in a food processor and process until smooth. Place in a large mixing bowl with remaining ingredients and mix well with hands.
2. Form into 2" balls and roll in shredded coconut or dried coconut flakes to cover.

STAR LOTUS PERSIMMON PARFAIT

45 minutes / 1-2 servings

Filling

2 large	Persimmon, ripe (1 ½ c)
1 c	Almonds, soaked & peeled (page 194)
½ c	Dates, pitted
1 Tbl	Almond butter, raw
Pinch	Cinnamon powder
Pinch	Cardamom powder
Pinch	Nutmeg, ground
•	Coconut water to desired consistency

Topping

¼ c	Walnuts or pecans
3 small	Dates, pitted
1 tsp	Coconut, shredded
Pinch	Nutmeg, ground

loving preparation

1. Place filling ingredients in blender or food processor and process until smooth. Pour into 2 parfait glasses. Please note, the strength of the blender will determine how much liquid is required to reach a smooth consistency. As usual, we recommend a VitaMixer.
2. Place nuts in food processor and pulse chop. Add dates and coconut and pulse process until chopped well. Sprinkle on top of filling and enjoy. Dust with a pinch of nutmeg.

variations

↳ Replace persimmon with other fruit such as banana, berries, papaya, mango, cherimoya, atemoya or sapote. Replace almonds with other soaked nuts or seeds. Create a multilayered parfait by making three batches using a different colored fruit in each batch.

🪷 DREAM WEAVER'S LIVE PIE CRUST

20 minutes / 8" to 9" pie crust

4 c	Pecans, or other nuts
1 ½ c	Dates, pitted
¼ tsp	Cinnamon powder

⅛ tsp	Ginger powder (optional)
Pinch	Nutmeg, ground
Pinch	Cardamom powder
Pinch	Sea salt

loving preparation

1. Place nuts in food processor and chop fine. Add spices and pulse a few times to evenly distribute. Add dates and process until the mixture either balls up or keeps pushing up the side and not falling back into the center.
2. Using hands (it helps to keep fingers moistened with water) press the mixture into an 8" pie pan or spring form pan.
3. Fill with one of the following fillings.

variations

❧ Many variations are possible depending upon the nuts and seeds used. The dates may be replaced with raisins or other dried fruit. Try adding 1 Tbl of spirulina powder for a tasty way to include this nutrient in your diet.

serving suggestion

❧ Excellent when served with hazelnuts.
❧ If you use a spring form pan, sides may be decorated with shredded coconut or chopped nuts.

Lake Atitlán, Guatemala

"YOUR VISION WILL BECOME CLEAR ONLY WHEN YOU LOOK INTO YOUR HEART.

WHO LOOKS OUTSIDE, DREAMS. WHO LOOKS INSIDE, AWAKENS." - CARL JUNG

🪷 LOTUS LIVE PIE FILLINGS

20 min prep / 8" pie

Carob Chai Live Pie

3 ½ C	Banana (mashed)
¼ C	Carob powder, raw
1½ Tbl	Psyllium powder
½ tsp	Cinnamon powder
⅛ tsp	Ginger powder
⅛ tsp	Cardamom powder
Pinch	Anise powder
Pinch	Clove powder

Okinawan Purple Sweet Potato Pie

3 large	Okinawan purple sweet potato, peeled & grated (5 C)
2 C	Dates, pitted
¼ tsp	Nutmeg, ground
¼ tsp	Cardamom powder
¼ tsp	Allspice powder

St. Claire's Carrot Pie

5 C	Carrots, peeled & grated
2 C	Dates, pitted
1½ Tbl	Psyllium powder
¼ tsp	Ginger powder
¼ tsp	Cinnamon powder
•	Raisins, shredded carrots & coconut, for garnish

Tropical Bliss Out Pie

3 C	Banana, mashed
1 C	Macadamia nuts or cashews
¾ C	Dates, pitted
¾ C	Tropical fruit (papaya, mango, cherimoya) or berries
1½ Tbl	Psyllium powder
2 tsp	Lemon juice, fresh squeezed
½ tsp	Cinnamon powder
¼ tsp	Cardamom powder

loving preparation

1. Pick a pie filling. Place all of its ingredients in a food processor and process until smooth. Pour into pie crust and refrigerate until it sets and becomes more firm. Garnish creatively with fresh or dried fruits, shredded coconut and chopped nuts.

variations

- For the *Tropical Bliss Out Pie*, layers of fresh fruit such as mango, papaya, persimmon or other fruit may be placed in pie crust before adding filling. Top with a layer of Star Lotus Live Parfait (page 173) as a creamy topping.
- For a live dessert sauce to drizzle over pies, blend 1 C of cashews or macnuts, soaked and drained with ½ C of berries, and a few dates to sweeten. Coconut water may be added until desired consistency is reached.
- Coconut water may also be blended with coco meat and a few dates for a 🪷 *Live Coco Cream Sauce*. Flavor with a pinch of cinnamon and cardamom and serve over pie.
- Live pie decorating presents a wonderful opportunity to express the abundance of the Earth. They lend themselves to colorful and creative designs. Different fruits will create different and colorful fillings and sauces.

REJOICE

breakfast
juice &
smoothies

TOFU SCRAMBLE

GREEN BANANA OMELET

BUCKWHEAT PANCAKES

THREE GRAIN PORRIDGE

HEMP GRANOLA

BANANA BREAD

LIVE GRANOLA FUNK

LIVE OATMEAL

LIVE SUNFLOWER FIG DELIGHT

PAPAYA SUNRISE SMOOTHIE

CARROT VEGGIE JUICE

COCO TONIC

LEMON GINGERADE

ALMOND MILK

GREEN GOD SMOOTHIE

WHEATGRASS TONIC

MAPLE CAYENNE LEMONADE

FRESH NONI JUICE

WAKANTANKA TOFU SCRAMBLE

15 min prep / 15 min cooking / 2 servings

2 Tbl	Safflower oil
1 C	Onion, diced
2 tsp	Garlic, minced
1 lb	Tofu, extra firm, crumbled small
½ C	Tomato, diced
1 tsp	Turmeric

1 tsp	Sea salt, or to taste
1 tsp	Paprika
¾ tsp	Black pepper, ground to taste
½ tsp	Nutritional yeast
Pinch	Cayenne pepper
1 Tbl	Nama shoyu, or to taste

loving preparation

1. Place oil in a large sauté pan on medium high heat. Add onion and garlic and cook until onions are soft, approximately 5 minutes, stirring frequently.
2. Add tofu. Cook for 5 minutes, stirring occasionally. Add remaining ingredients and cook for 5 minutes, stirring occasionally.

serving suggestions

Top with a sprinkle of Fakin' Bacon bits and a dollop of Vegan Sour Crème (page 196).

variations

- Try adding ¼ C arame, soaked until soft (approximately 10 minutes) and drained well.
- Experiment with adding ¼ C veggies such as grated carrots or zucchini.
- *Indian* Add ½ tsp curry and ½ tsp cumin powder.
- *Mexican* Add 1 tsp chili powder, 1 tsp jalapeño, seeded and minced and ½ tsp cumin powder.
- *Italian* Add 1 tsp basil, fresh minced, 1 tsp parsley, fresh minced and ½ tsp oregano.

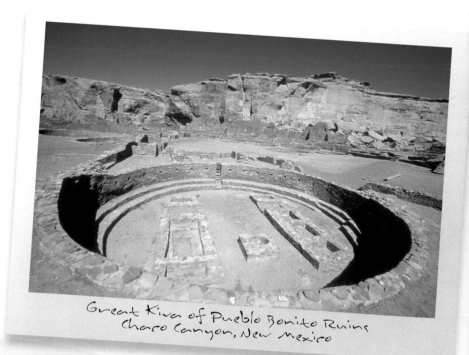

Great Kiva of Pueblo Bonito Ruins
Chaco Canyon, New Mexico

"ONE THING WE KNOW: OUR GOD IS ALSO YOUR GOD. THE EARTH IS PRECIOUS TO HIM." - CHIEF SEATTLE

VITAL ITAL GREEN BANANA OMELET

30 min prep / 40 min cooking / 2 servings

Omelet

6 medium	Green bananas (3 C mashed)
½ C	Spelt flour
1 tsp	Baking powder

Veggie Topping

½ C	Cilantro, chopped
½ bunch	Green onions, sliced
½ C	Carrots, grated

Nut Cheez

2 C	Cashews, macadamia or pine nuts
6 Tbl	Olive oil
3 Tbl	Lemon juice, fresh squeezed
5 medium	Garlic cloves
¼ C	Nama shoyu, or to taste

loving preparation

1. Cut the ends off the green bananas and score up the sides. Place the scored bananas in a 3 qt pot, cover with water, boil until you can easily poke a fork through them, approximately 20 minutes. Drain the water from the bananas and allow them to cool a few minutes.
2. Remove peels (which should come off easily) and place bananas in a large mixing bowl. Mash with a fork or masher. Add flour and baking powder to bananas and knead into a dough. Separate dough into 2 pieces. Roll into balls. Flour the counter and roll the balls into 6" rounds.
3. Combine cashews, lemon, shoyu, garlic and 6 Tbl oil in a food processor and process until smooth.
4. Heat a heavy skillet on medium heat until hot. Pour a small amount of oil onto skillet and fry omelet on one side until golden, approximately 3 minutes. Flip and cover ½ of cooked side with Nut Cheez, green onion, carrots and cilantro. Fold over like an omelet and cover. Flip and cook until golden brown on both sides. Serve hot.

serving suggestion

- Serve with a dollop of Sour Crème (page 196) and Salsa (page 24) or try with Mango Chutney (page 23).

"UNTIL THE PHILOSOPHY THAT HOLDS ONE RACE SUPERIOR AND ANOTHER INFERIOR, IS FINALLY AND PERMANENTLY DISCREDITED AND ABANDONED, THE DREAM OF LASTING PEACE... WILL REMAIN BUT A FLEETING ILLUSION, TO BE PURSUED AND NEVER ATTAINED." - H.I.M. SELASSIE

BENEVOLENT BUCKWHEAT PANCAKES

15 min prep / 10 min cooking / 12 pancakes

Dry

1 c	Buckwheat flour
1 c	Spelt flour
3 Tbl	Sucanat
1 Tbl	Flax seed, ground
1 Tbl	Baking powder
½ tsp	Baking soda
½ tsp	Sea salt

Wet

1 ¼ c	Filtered water
¾ c	Soy milk
2 Tbl	Safflower oil
2 Tbl	Apple sauce, unsweetened
Pinch	Cinnamon powder

loving preparation

1. Place the **Wet** ingredients in a large mixing bowl and mix well. Combine the **Dry** ingredients in another bowl and mix well. Combine all ingredients in one bowl.
2. Lightly oil a heavy skillet or large sauté pan with safflower oil and heat on medium high heat until skillet is hot, approximately 1-2 minutes. Pour batter, forming 6" pancakes.
3. Cook until edges of pancakes become firm and bubbles start to appear, approximately 3 minutes. Flip to other side and cook for another 3 minutes or until golden brown. Flip again if necessary until both sides are evenly cooked.
4. Add a small amount of oil in between batches, if necessary, to prevent sticking.

serving suggestions

- Top with Strawberry Sauce (page 66), Maple Tofu Whip (page 172) or maple syrup, and enjoy.

variations

- For **Wailing Wall Waffles**, pour batter into a heated, lightly-oiled waffle press, cook until golden brown.

GRANDMOTHER'S THREE GRAIN PORRIDGE

15 min prep / 20 minutes cooking / 2 servings

1 ½ c	Filtered water
¼ c	Quinoa
¼ c	Millet
¼ c	Amaranth

loving preparation

1. Bring water to a boil in a 3 qt pot. Add remaining ingredients, reduce heat to simmer, cover and cook until all liquid is absorbed, approximately 15 minutes, stirring occasionally. Remove from heat.

serving suggestions

- Add coconut milk, soy milk or rice milk to desired consistency.
- Add sweetener such as maple syrup, agave nectar, rice syrup, etc.
- Try adding 1 Tbl nut butter, 1 Tbl flax oil, dried fruits, toasted nuts, seeds or coconut.

Mt. Alban, Oaxaca, Mexico

MARLEY'S HEMP GRANOLA

15 min prep / 30 min cooking / 2-3 servings

Dry
3 c	Rolled oats
1 c	Pecans or other nuts, chopped
1 c	Spelt flour
½ c	Hemp seeds
½ tsp	Sea salt
½ tsp	Cinnamon powder
¼ tsp	Cardamom powder
Pinch	Allspice powder
Pinch	Ginger powder

Wet
¾ c	Safflower oil
¾ c	Maple syrup
1 tsp	Vanilla extract, alcohol free

loving preparation

1. Preheat oven to 350°. Combine **Dry** ingredients in a large mixing bowl and mix well.
2. Place **Wet** ingredients in a small bowl and whisk well. Stir all ingredients together.
3. Place on a well oiled baking sheet and bake until golden brown, approximately 30 minutes, stirring occasionally to break granola up into small chunks. Remove and let sit 5 minutes to crisp up.

BANANANANDA BREAD

15 min prep / 1 hour cooking / 5" x 9" loaf pan

Dry
2 c	Spelt flour
½ c	Walnuts, chopped
4 tsp	Baking powder
½ tsp	Cinnamon powder
¼ tsp	Sea salt, or to taste
¼ tsp	Nutmeg, ground

Wet
1 c	Banana, mashed
½ c	Maple syrup
½ c	Apple sauce, sugar free
½ c	Date pieces
¼ c	Safflower oil
½ tsp	Vanilla extract, alcohol free

loving preparation

1. Preheat oven to 350°. Place **Dry** ingredients in a large mixing bowl and mix well.
2. Combine **Wet** ingredients in another bowl, add dry ingredients and mix well. Pour into a well oiled 5" x 9" loaf pan and bake for one hour, or until a toothpick comes out dry. Be careful not to burn top.

serving suggestion

- For a blissful treat, pour thick Coco Cream (page 175) over warm banana bread.

variations

- Add 1 c of chocolate or carob chips to above. Replace walnuts with other nuts or seeds or dried fruits such as banana chips.

"...FIRST WE RECEIVE THE LIGHT, THEN WE IMPART IT. THUS WE REPAIR THE WORLD." - THE KABBALAH

QUEEN ESTHER'S LIVE GRANOLA FUNK

4-6 hr soaking / 20 min prep / 8 hr dehydrating / 2-3 servings

2 c	Buckwheat Groats, Raw	Pinch	Cardamom powder
1 c	Dates or raisins, tightly packed	Pinch	Nutmeg, ground
1 c	Filtered water	Pinch	Ginger powder
Pinch	Cinnamon powder	Pinch	Sea salt, or to taste

loving preparation

1. Place buckwheat groats in a large mixing bowl with 4 c of filtered water. Allow to sit in a cool dry place for 4-6 hours, draining, rinsing, refilling water at least once. Drain well and place in a large mixing bowl.
2. Soak 1 c of dates in 1 c of filtered water for 1 hour. Place both in a blender with spices and salt, blending until smooth.
3. Add date mixture to buckwheat groats and mix well, making sure that all groats are coated. Spread on a Teflex dehydrating sheet and dehydrate at 115° for 8 hours, or until mixture is dry, stirring every couple of hours to ensure even drying.

serving suggestions

~ Enjoy with Almond Milk (page 188), adding banana, raisins or other dried fruit, or soaked nuts and seeds as a live way to start the day.

"TO BE FREE IS NOT MERELY TO CAST OFF ONE'S CHAINS, BUT TO LIVE IN A WAY THAT RESPECTS AND ENHANCES THE FREEDOM OF OTHERS."
– NELSON MANDELA

LIGHT OF LIGHTS LIVE OATMEAL

20 min prep / overnight soaking / 2 servings

5 medium	Calimyrna figs, dried, soaked in 2 c filtered water
1 c	Fig soak water
1 c	Steel cut oats, soaked in 4 c of filtered water
⅛ tsp	Cinnamon powder
Pinch	Allspice or nutmeg, ground

loving preparation

1. Place oats in a bowl with 4 c of filtered water and put in a cool dry place. Soak for one or two nights, changing water once a day. Rinse and drain well.
2. Place figs in a bowl with 2 c of filtered water and put in a cool dry place. Soak overnight, pour 1 c of soak water into a food processor or blender with oats, figs and spices. Blend until just smooth.

serving suggestions

- Serve with soaked raisins, nuts, seeds and your favorite nut milk.
- Try other combinations of grains and dried fruits such as buckwheat and raisins.

SWANDANCER'S SUNFLOWER FIG DELIGHT

15 minutes / 2 servings

¾ c	Sunflower seeds
1 c	Calimyrna figs, soaked in 2 c filtered water overnight
1 ¼ c	Soak water, or to taste
Pinch	Cinnamon powder
Pinch	Cardamom powder

loving preparation

1. Rinse seeds and soak according to instructions on page 202. Drain well.
2. Place all ingredients including soak water from figs in a blender and blend until smooth.

serving suggestions

- For an energizing live way to begin the day, try with sliced bananas, soaked raisins and other soaked nuts and seeds. Keeps fresh for two days.

variations

- Replace sunseeds with pumpkin, almond or sesame seeds. Replace figs with other fig varieties or other dried fruits.

YOU ARE BEAUTIFUL

185

ETERNAL SUNRISE SMOOTHIE

15 minutes / 16 oz

1 c	Almond milk (page 188), fresh coconut milk, rice or soy milk, or fresh fruit juice, to desired consistency
½	Banana, fresh or frozen
1 medium	Papaya (¾ c)
2 cubes	Frozen orange juice
2	Frozen strawberries

loving preparation

1. Place all ingredients in a blender and blend until smooth, adding additional liquid to reach desired consistency.

variations

- Experiment with different berries or fruits, including mango, cherimoya, sapote, atemoya, soursop or any of your favorites.
- Add small amounts of soaked nuts and seeds such as almonds, pumpkin seeds, sunflower seeds or macadamia nuts.

notes

- Utilize an ice cube tray for easy smoothie creation by pouring various fruit juices into cubes and freezing until solid.
- Bananas and other fresh peeled fruit may also be frozen for later use in smoothies, it is always good to keep both on hand.

PURE & SIMPLE CARROT VEGGIE JUICE

20 minutes / 16 oz

1"	Ginger, peeled
1 bunch	Italian Parsley (1 oz juice)
10-15 medium	Carrots (15 oz juice)

loving preparation

1. Juice items in juicer in above order.

variations

Experiment with different veggies and ratios to discover your optimal combination.

- **Carrot Beet Juice** Juice 5-6 medium carrots, 2 small beets and 1 small bunch of spinach.
- **Spicy Mixed Green Vegetable Juice** Juice 2 cucumbers, 3 stalks celery, ½ bunch kale, ½ bunch spinach, a pinch of cayenne.
- For **Sweet Nectar of the Gods**, place juice in blender and blend with ½ avocado.

"TO LOVE ANOTHER PERSON IS TO SEE THE FACE OF GOD" – VICTOR HUGO

AZUL SKIES COCO TONIC

10 minutes / 1-2 servings

2 ½ c	Coconut water
1 c	Ice
¾ c	Young coconut meat (optional), or to taste
½ tsp	Lime juice, fresh squeezed, or to taste
3-4	Dates, or to taste
Pinch	Cayenne and /or chili powder (optional)

loving preparation

1. Place all ingredients in a blender and blend until smooth.

AMBER'S GINGERADE ELIXIR

10 minutes / ½ gallon

½ gallon	Filtered water
¾ c	Sucanat, or to taste
¾ c	Lemon juice, fresh squeezed
1/8 c	Ginger juice, fresh

loving preparation

1. Place sucanat in ½ gallon container. Add lemon and ginger juice. Mix well and allow sucanat to dissolve before adding water. Add water, mix well and refrigerate until chilled.

serving suggestions

- Serve iced with 2-3 crushed mint leaves and a thin lemon wedge.
- Add 6 mint leaves to container.

variations

- Try replacing sucanat with agave nectar or try using ¼ c stevia leaves steeped in lemonade until desired sweetness is attained and then strain well.
- For *Lavender Rosemary Gingerade*, place 2 ½ Tbl lavender flowers in ½ c hot water and allow to infuse for 8 minutes, strain well and add to above with a fresh rosemary stalk placed in container.
- For *Lilikoi Lemonade* replace ginger with ¾ c of lillikoi juice.

"I WANT TO BE WHERE IT'S NOT HAPPENING, THAT'S WHERE IT'S HAPPENING." - STAR LOTUS

BODACIOUS ALMOND DATE MILK

15 minutes for 2 servings

1 C	Almonds (1 ½ C soaked), blanched
2 ½ C	Filtered water
¼ C	Dates, chopped
Pinch	Cinnamon powder
Pinch	Cardamom powder

loving preparation

1. Soak, rinse and peel almonds according to method discussed on page 194. Place in a blender with remaining ingredients and blend until smooth. For optimal flavor, strain through a cheez cloth before serving.

variations

~ Sweetness may be varied by adding more or less dates or by experimenting with other dried fruits. Other soaked nuts or seeds can replace or be used in combination with the soaked almonds. Try adding nutritional powerhouses such as spirulina, chlorella or other green powder super foods.

GREEN GOD SMOOTHIE

5 minutes for 20 oz

2 ½"	Frozen banana piece
4 cubes	Frozen coconut milk
4 cubes	Frozen papaya
2 - 3	Dates, pitted
1 Tbl	Spirulina powder
•	Almond milk, fresh coconut milk, rice or soy milk, or fresh fruit juice, to taste

loving preparation

1. Place all ingredients in a blender and blend until smooth. Add additional liquid to attain desired consistency.

variations

~ Smoothies are a great way to introduce protein and beneficial supplements and oils into your diet. Great smoothies can be created by adding any combination of the following, to taste: 1 Tbl of flax, borage or hemp oil, 1 Tbl of lecithin granules, 1 tsp nutritional yeast and/or 2 Tbl nut butter.

WHA HEY GURU'S WHEATGRASS COOLER

30 minutes for 2-3 servings

1 oz	Wheatgrass juice, fresh
2 C	Apple, pear or watermelon juice, fresh
½ C	Filtered water
2 Tbl	Hibiscus flowers, dry
1 Tbl	Lime juice, fresh squeezed
Pinch	Stevia powder, or to taste

loving preparation

1. Soak hibiscus flowers in filtered water for 10-15 minutes. Drain well and add liquid to remaining ingredients, stir well and enjoy. Delicious served over ice.

"GOD IS A COMEDIAN PLAYING TO AN AUDIENCE AFRAID TO LAUGH." - VOLTAIRE

MIRACULOUS MAPLE CAYENNE LEMONADE

5 minutes / 2 servings

4 c	Filtered water
1 large	Lemon, freshly juiced (approximately ¼ c)
3 Tbl	Maple syrup, grade B, or to taste
¼ tsp	Cayenne pepper, or to taste

loving preparation

1. Combine all of above and mix well. May be enjoyed cold or warm.

note

- This is a very refreshing tonic based upon the Master Cleanser Formula developed by Stanley Burroughs.

FIRE OF PELE NONI TONIC

10 minutes / ¾ cup

¼ c	Noni juice, fresh
½ c	Filtered water
2 Tbl	Lime juice, fresh squeezed
1-2 pinches	Stevia powder

loving preparation

1. Combine all ingredients in a glass and stir well.
2. For homemade noni juice, place whole noni fruit in a sealed jar and leave in a warm sunny space until liquid forms, approximately 3 days or longer. Strain and use as needed.

The goddess Pele in flow, Big Island of Hawaii

"WHERE ARE YOU SEARCHING FOR ME FRIEND? LOOK HERE AM I RIGHT WITHIN YOU.

NOT IN TEMPLE, NOR IN MOSQUE, NOT IN CASBAH NOR KAILAS, BUT HERE RIGHT WITHIN YOU AM I." - KABIR

12

vegan
natural
food
preparation

preparation basics...
in the beginning

This chapter provides a brief introduction to some of the basic cooking and food preparation techniques involved in Vegan World Fusion Cuisine. For a more in-depth study of these matters, please view our website at www.veganfusion.com and consider signing up for our on-line Vegan chef certification program.

mise en place...
create the space

Before beginning any preparation, create a clean "work" space. Play your favorite music, bring in some flowers and make your environment as pleasant as possible. Have all ingredients prepared and ready to be used before beginning the cooking process. Complete your cycles. Wipe down cutting boards and attempt to keep a clear space.

equipment

The more comfortable you are with your kitchen utensils and appliances, the more inspired and motivated you will be to prepare your own food. If your means allow, we recommend the following items to start you on your journey.

A high quality chef knife is a must; this is one of your most trusty companions... a good, sharp knife will make all the difference in the world (we prefer ceramic knives), cutting board (we like wood), blender (like a Vitamixer or other strong blender), wooden utensils, strong and firm spatulas and whisks, metal or glass mixing bowls, cast iron or stainless steel pots and pans (no aluminum or Teflon), steamer, colander and strainers, basting brush, measuring cups and spoons, and baking sheets.

Other items that will expand your repertoire include a food processor, a seed grinder for spices, a juicer (a Green Power or Champion works well) and a dehydrator. Items like a mandolin and a vegetable spiralizer will increase the creativity of presentation and is recommended in live food preparation to create veggie versions of pasta. Please check out our website for more information.

preparing vegetables

You will feel tremendous satisfaction if the vegetables you are using in the recipes are from your own organic garden. A local organic farm is the next best, so please support your local farmer's market. Avoid commercially grown and genetically modified foods at all costs. Rinse veggies well with filtered water, discarding any spoiled parts. Soak nonorganic foods in a tub or sink with vegetable washes to assist in removing unwanted pesticides and chemicals.

shelf life...

For maximum nutrition, flavor and freshness, we always recommend eating foods as soon as possible after preparing them. The recipes in this book will generally keep for at least two to three days if stored properly. Certain items like dressings will keep for longer, up to a week.

the way... techniques
cutting

Different terms are used to refer to various shapes and sizes depending on how you slice your food. *Mince* is the finest that can be cut by hand. *Dice* is slightly larger, ¼" uniform pieces. *Chop* is larger than dice and is usually a ½" square. *Slices* are thin pieces and can be of different shapes depending upon the size of the item. *Julienne* are long and thin strips à la matchsticks!

steaming

Steaming involves using a steamer basket, either bamboo or stainless steel. Vegetables are placed in the basket, the basket is placed in a pot of water with a lid. The water boils and the vegetables are cooked by the steam that is generated by the boiling water. A small steamer basket fits well in a 3 quart pot and can provide countless quick and easy steamed veggie medleys.

If several vegetables are used, place the firmer vegetables that take longer to cook, like yams, carrots, cauliflower, etc. in the steamer first and steam for a few minutes. Add other vegetables like broccoli, green beans, red bell peppers, mushrooms, purple cabbage, zucchini or snow peas, keeping all veggies vibrant and just cooked until tender. Please do not overcook or run out of steam water. Check periodically until you discover the best timing that works for you.

steam sautéing

Steam sautéing may be used by those wishing to eliminate the use of heated oils in their diets. Water or stock is used instead of oil in the initial cooking stages. Place a small amount of water or stock in a heated pan , add vegetables and follow the recipes. Add small amounts of water at a time if necessary to prevent sticking. Lemon juice or nama shoyu may also be mixed in with the water for added flavor. Many of the recipes rely on a partial use of this method. A small amount of oil is used to get things going and enhance the flavor—the water or stock does the rest of the cooking.

A note on measurements: Generally 1 c of vegetables will yield 1 c of cooked vegetables, if not overcooked. Regarding leafy greens, the more tender greens—such as spinach—will vary in volume from 1 cup raw to ½ cup or less steamed.

roasting vegetables

Roasting brings out a wonderfully rich flavor and creates a grounding effect. Preheat oven to 400°. Place vegetables in a casserole dish or on a baking sheet. The veggies can be marinated, mixed with olive oil and spices, or simply cooked in water and their own juices. Cook until just soft, stir occasionally to make sure veggies are getting evenly cooked.

For **roasted garlic**, you can peel the garlic and roast the cloves as mentioned above. Another method involves slicing the top ½" portion off the stem of a bulb of garlic and placing it in a very small baking dish, sliced side up, topped with olive oil, a pinch of Celtic salt and fresh ground pepper and 1 tsp of minced fresh herbs, baking until a knife can easily pass through the garlic, approximately 35 minutes. Squeeze garlic out of bulb and use as a spread for toast or flax crackers, or to enhance the flavor of other spreads, stir frys and casseroles.

roasting bell peppers

Preheat oven to 400°. Rinse peppers and place on a well oiled baking sheet. Place in oven and cook until skin of peppers is charred and bubbly, approximately 35 minutes. Remove from oven and place in a covered bowl for 10 minutes. Peel off skin and remove seeds. Gently rinse under cold water if necessary. May also be roasted over an open flame.

193

"BEING VEGAN HELPED ME REALIZE I CAN SAY AND DO WHAT I BELIEVE IS RIGHT. THAT'S POWERFUL."

- ALICIA SILVERSTONE

roasting tofu or tempeh

Tofu and tempeh cubes can be marinated, roasted and then stored for a couple of days to be used in salads, stir frys (Kung Pao Tofu, page 124) or on their own as a snack. Cubes can be cut into different sizes, depending upon the dish, from ¼" to 1". Place in any one of the marinades on the following page and roast until golden brown. A convection oven will provide a crisper crust. Broiling in your oven will also provide a savory flavor.

toasting nuts, seeds, spices & grains

Toasting brings out a depth of flavor that enhances dishes. Toasting can be done in a sauté pan. For this method, place item in pan, turn heat to high and cook until item turns golden brown, stirring constantly. This method is good for spices, grains and small quantities of nuts or seeds. Another method involves preheating an oven to 375°. Place items to be toasted on a dry baking sheet, and leave in oven until golden brown, stirring frequently and being mindful not to allow item to burn. This method is best for nuts, seeds and shredded coconut.

grilling

Preheat a grill. Consider grilling tempeh and tofu cutlets, as well as many vegetables such as portabello mushrooms, corn, onions, baby bok choy, peppers, zucchini or eggplant. If you wish for added flavor, place items in Shoyu or Lemon Herb Marinades or come up with your own variation. Marinate items for a few minutes or even overnight. The longer an item stays in the marinade, the more of the flavor it will absorb. Baste with Basting Sauce (page 196), brushing occasionally and grilling until char marks appear and the item is heated thoroughly, flipping periodically. If using a gas grill, avoid placing items over a direct flame. To grill ulu, boil until tender, approximately 30 minutes, slice into cutlets and follow directions above.

blanching

This involves dipping an item in boiling water and then placing immediately into ice water. This helps stop the cooking process and keeps a fresh color to vegetables.

blanching almonds

We blanch almonds to remove their skins. Timing is important, especially for live food dishes. Drop soaked almonds in boiling water, remove after 10 seconds, drain and rinse well under cold water before removing skins. Skins will easily pop off after blanching. The longer the almonds are left in the water, the less "live" they will be.

magical marinades

Creating marinades is both fun and rewarding. Below are a few of our favorite marinades. For live dishes, place your prepared vegetables in marinade for a minimum of one hour before serving. For cooked dishes, place items in marinade for a minimum of 15 minutes. The longer it sits in the marinade, the more of its flavors it will acquire.

MAGICAL MARINADES
10-15 minutes for ¾-1 ¼ cups

Creamy Tahini Marinade

¾ C	Filtered water
4 tsp	Nama shoyu
¼ C	Tahini or other nut butter, raw
2 Tbl	Lemon juice, fresh squeezed
½ tsp	Garlic, minced
½ tsp	Ginger, peeled & minced (optional)
1 tsp	Herbs, minced (basil, parsley, cilantro or your favorite)
Pinch	Cayenne pepper

Nama Shoyu Marinade

½ C	Filtered water
1 tsp	Nama shoyu
1 tsp	Maple syrup
2 tsp	Herbs, minced (basil, parsley, cilantro, rosemary, sage, dill, thyme or others of your choosing)
½ tsp	Balsamic vinegar
½ tsp	Mustard powder
½ tsp	Apple cider vinegar, raw
Pinch	Cayenne pepper
2 Tbl	Olive oil (optional)
½ tsp	Garlic, minced (optional)
½ tsp	Ginger, peeled & minced (optional)
½ tsp	Turmeric root, peeled & minced (optional) or pinch of dry powder

Lemon Herb Marinade

½ C	Filtered water
2 Tbl	Lemon or lime juice, fresh squeezed
1 tsp	Nama shoyu
2 tsp	Herbs, minced

loving preparation

1. For **Creamy Tahini Marinade**, place all ingredients in a blender and blend until smooth. This marinade is good for cutlets that will be crusted (Blue Corn Crusted Tempeh, page 122), and/or baked (Baked Tofu Sandwich, page 89).

2. For **Nama Shoyu** or **Lemon Herb Marinade**, place ingredients in a bowl and whisk well. These marinades are good for items like grilled or sautéed veggies, tofu, tempeh or ulu. **Lemon Herb Marinade** is especially suited for simple and Live Food items.

variations

Different spices may be added to each of the above to create ethnic flairs.

- **Indian** 1 tsp cilantro, minced, ¼ tsp cumin and ½ tsp curry.
- **Italian** 1 tsp fresh or ½ tsp each basil and parsley, ½ tsp fresh or ¼ tsp dry oregano and thyme.
- **Mexican** 1 tsp cilantro, minced, ½ tsp chili powder,¼ tsp cumin powder.

condiments

Making your own condiments adds another degree of satisfaction to the process and is a more sustainable, lower impact approach to food preparation. Use these recipes when the item is called for throughout this book. If you prefer to purchase ready made items, experiment with the many brands available to find the quality that works best for you.

BABU'S BASTING SAUCE

5 minutes preparation / 2 c of sauce

2 c	Olive oil
2 Tbl	Basil, fresh minced
2 Tbl	Italian parsley, fresh minced
1 Tbl	Thyme, fresh minced
1 Tbl	Garlic, fresh minced, or ginger, peeled and minced (optional)
2 tsp	Paprika

preparation

1. Combine all ingredients in a bowl, mix well. Use for grilling & basting. May also be used in place of olive oil in any recipe.

J.J'S VEGAN MAYONNAISE

10 minutes / 3 ½ cups

2 ¼ c	Safflower oil
1 c	Soy milk
1 Tbl	Maple syrup or agave nectar
¾ tsp	Sea salt, or to taste
2 - 2 ½ tsp	Apple cider vinegar, raw or lemon juice, fresh squeezed
½ tsp	Dijon mustard

preparation

1. Combine all ingredients except vinegar or lemon juice in blender, blending until smooth. Slowly add vinegar or lemon juice until liquid thickens.

SHANTI'S SOUR CRÈME

10 minutes for 2 cups

2 c	Vegan mayonnaise, see above
1 ½ Tbl	Lemon or lime juice, fresh squeezed
1 ½ tsp	Green onion (the green part) or chives, minced
½ tsp	Dill, fresh, minced (or ¼ tsp dry)

preparation

1. Combine all ingredients in a bowl and mix well.

AMMA'S SOY MILK

1 hour for ½ gallon

1 c	Soy beans, sorted, rinsed & soaked in 2 c of filtered water overnight.
5 c	Hot filtered water for blending (almost boiling)
1-2 Tbl	Maple syrup or agave nectar, to taste
1 ½ tsp	Vanilla extract, alcohol free
¼ tsp	Sea salt, or to taste
4 c	Cool water, filtered

preparation

1. Rinse & strain soaked soy beans. Place ½ of beans & 2 ½ c hot water in large blender or Vitamixer, blending until smooth, approx. 2-3 minutes. Repeat with remaining beans in 2 ½ c hot water.

2. Strain mixture, saving liquid in a large pot. Strain a second time through a fine stainless steel strainer, ensuring as much liquid is removed as possible. The solid matter, okara, can be used in any recipe calling for crumbled tofu. A third straining through cloth may be necessary.

3. Add remaining ingredients including filtered water to liquid, mix well, transfer to a jar & allow to cool to room temperature before refrigerating.

note & variations

- Lasts for up to 3 days if properly cooled and refrigerated.
- Add 1 Tbl of carob powder to above for a carob soy milk.
- Use okara for a great ricotta by adding fresh minced basil, parsley, dried spices such as oregano, thyme, a small amount of tahini, salt, pepper to taste and nama shoyu (optional).

CAMPAÑERO'S CHILI SAUCE

20 minutes / 4 cups

½ lb	Silken tofu
½ C	Safflower oil
¼ C	Nama shoyu, or to taste
¼ C	Ancho chilis, soaked & seeded
¼ C	Sundried tomatoes, soaked in 1 ¾ C hot water until soft
1 ¾ C	Sundried tomato soak water
1 ½ Tbl	Lime juice, fresh squeezed
2 Tbl	Cilantro, minced
1 tsp	Jalapeño pepper, roasted, seeded & minced
½ tsp	Black pepper, ground to taste
•	Sea salt, to taste

preparation

1. Place all ingredients in a blender and blend until smooth. Use as sauce for grilled tofu, Tempeh Mexicana (page 117) or Whole Enchilada Casserole (page 136).

NIÑOS DE CHIAPAS SPICE MIX

15 minutes preparation

1 part	Chili powder
1 part	Garlic powder
1 part	Ginger powder
1 part	Red pepper flakes

preparation

1. Mix all ingredients well in a small bowl. Place in small jar and use for spicy dishes. Add a little water and use as chili paste.

LOTUS CURRY PASTE

15 minutes preparation / ½ C

1 small	Lime leaf
1 Tbl	Shallot, minced
1 Tbl	Chili pepper, hot variety, minced
1 Tbl	Lemongrass stem, minced
2 tsp	Ginger, peeled & minced
1 tsp	Garlic, minced
½ tsp	Curry powder
¼ tsp	Coriander powder
¼ tsp	Sea salt, or to taste

¼ tsp	Black pepper, ground to taste
2 Tbl	Sesame oil
•	Coconut milk, fresh, to taste

preparation

1. Blend all ingredients in a blender, adding sesame oil until smooth consistency is attained. Store refrigerated in a jar and use as needed. Lasts up to a week or longer if refrigerated.

PICKLED GINGER

15 minutes / 2 cups

2"	Ginger root, peeled, sliced paper-thin
¼ tsp	Sea salt
½ tsp	Sucanat
3 Tbl	Apple cider vinegar, raw
¼ C	Filtered water

preparation

1. Place all ingredients except ginger in a small mixing bowl & whisk well. Add ginger, cover bowl and refrigerate at least a 1-2 days before use.

GOMASIO

5 minutes / ¼ cup

¼ C	sesame seeds, toasted
1 ½ tsp	sea salt

preparation

1. Mildly crush sesame seeds in mortar & pestle or spice grinder, slowly adding salt. Lightly dust any finished dish with gomasio.

CATSUP

15 minutes / 2 cups

1 C	Sundried tomatoes, soaked in 1 C filtered water
1 C	Fresh tomato, chopped
2 Tbl	Apple cider vinegar, raw
½ tsp	Maple syrup or agave nectar
Pinch	Cayenne pepper

preparation

1. Soak sundried tomatoes a minimum of 15 minutes. Blend all ingredients together until smooth.

Coco Info: the story of the perfect food

Known as the "tree of life" or *niu* in Hawaiian, the coconut palm (cocos nucifera) has been a staple in tropical climates for centuries. The gelatinous flesh and juice of young or green coconuts can be consumed straight from the shell, while the flesh of more mature coconuts are blended together to make coconut creams and milks. Experiment with texture and flavor while you try these recipes.

Young green coconuts, at about six months of age, have a gelatinous center, with a texture similar to a melon, which can be scooped out with a spoon. It has a fresh, fruity almost nutty flavor, not overly sweet. This is called the jelly, which as the coconut 'dries' becomes the meat. The older the coconut, the drier the meat, until it is like the dark brown coconut you find in the market. Try to locate young green cocos, at Asian or Latin markets and you will see the difference. Also, check www.veganfusion.com for additonal sources.

To open young coconuts, carefully slice off the top with a large sharp serrated knife. Drain off any juice, then, using a hammer, tap around the edges to crack a large top off. The flesh can now be pried off carefully with a large tablespoon or wooden knife. Coconuts are both tasty and nutritious, being an optimum food. Much has been written about green cocos, and you can learn much more at our site, www.veganfusion.com. The water of the green coco is the highest form of minerals and electrolytes available anywhere. This is why you feel so content and pleasantly energized when you eat one.

VANILLA MILKSHAKE

15 minutes / 2 servings

3 nuts	Coconut jelly
3 nuts	Coconut water
½ bean	Vanilla, fresh
1 Tbl	Agave nectar
1 c	Ice

loving preparation

1. Drain the water from three green coconuts. Remove the coconut jelly from all three coconuts. Combine equal amounts of milk and jelly and blend with vanilla bean and agave nectar. Add 1 c of ice and blend until creamy. Vary the amount of coco water to create different textures.

varations

- You have now mastered making coconut cream. You may freeze for pie fillings and ice cream.
- You may vary liquid content to create rich desserts. You may place in an ice cube tray, freeze and blend to create gelatos.
- To make the chocolate variety add 10-12 raw cacao beans and blend

note

- Try not to overblend. The raw cacao in coconut cream actually are the original chocolate chips! Drink while fresh.

serving suggestion

- Add nutmeg and cinnamon as topping for holiday nog or use as a sauce for a fruit salad.

198

"ALWAYS REMEMBER THAT YOU ARE UNIQUE, JUST LIKE EVERYONE ELSE." - ANON

RUBY LIGHT'S LIVING PAD THAI

1 hour preparation / 6-8 servings

"Noodles"

3 c	Young coconut pulp, julienned (about 4-5 coconuts)

Fruits & Vegetables

1½ c	Zucchini, julienned
1 c	Red cabbage, thinly sliced
1½ c	Carrots, julienned
1/3 c	Red onion, diced
1½ c	Granny Smith apple, julienned
¼ c	Yellow bell pepper, julienned
¼ c	Red bell pepper, julienned
½ c	Mung bean sprouts, julienned
¼ c	Cilantro leaves
½ c	Cucumber, julienned
1 Tbl	Lime juice, fresh
1½ tsp	Sea salt, or to taste

Tamarind Sauce

2 Tbl	Tamarind purée
2 Tbl	Maple syrup
1 clove	Garlic
1 Tbl	Nama shoyu
1½ Tbl	Serrano chili, minced
1 Tbl	Olive oil

Almond Chili Sauce

½ c	Almond butter
1 Tbl	Ginger, minced
2 Tbl	Lime juice
2 Tbl	Maple syrup
1 clove	Garlic
½ Tbl	Nama shoyu
1	Thai dragon chili, minced
1 Tbl	Sesame oil
¼ c	Coconut water

Garnish

1 Tbl	Sesame oil
½ Tbl	Nama shoyu
1 Tbl	Maple syrup
1 c	Cashews, whole, raw
2 Tbl	Black sesame seeds

loving preparation

1. To prepare *Young Coconut "Noodles"* crack coconuts, or cut off the tops. Drain water into a separate container. Set aside. Gently lift coconut pulp from the wood with a large tablespoon or wooden paddle. Clean and cut into thin strips. Set aside.

2. To prepare the *Fruits & Vegetables* place zucchini, cabbage, carrots, red onion, apple, pepper, sprouts, whole cilantro leaves and cucumber in a bowl. Toss with 1 Tbl lime juice and sea salt.

3. To prepare *Tamarind Sauce* place tamarind purée, 2 Tbl maple syrup, 1 clove garlic, 1 Tbl Nama shoyu, Serrano chile, and 1 Tbl olive oil in a food processor. Purée until smooth. Set aside.

4. To prepare *Almond Chili Sauce* place almond butter, ginger, 2 Tbl lime juice, 2 Tbl maple syrup, 1 clove garlic, ½ Tbl shoyu, Thai dragon chili and 1 Tbl sesame oil into a food processor. Gradually add coconut water until desired consistency is reached.

5. To prepare *Garnish* place 1 Tbl sesame oil, ½ Tbl shoyu, and 1 Tbl maple syrup in a bowl with cashews, whisk together. Toss with sesame seeds.

6. To assemble, toss coconut noodles and julienned fruits and vegetables with tamarind purée. Place on plates and drizzle with almond chile sauce. Garnish with cashews.

soup stock

Soup stock adds depth to dishes and is a great way to use vegetables for maximum yield. It may be made from many vegetables. It is a versatile and wonderful ingredient to have on hand. Use it for sauces, sautéing, consommés, a warm broth or use it in any of the recipes calling for vegetable stock.

If shoyu is included in the stock, and the stock is used for recipes in this book, the amount of shoyu or salt listed in the recipe needs to be decreased.

AKASHIC SOUP STOCK
20 min prep / 40 min cooking / 10-12 cups

16 c	Filtered water
2 ½ c	Onion, chopped
1 ¼ c	Carrots, chopped
1 c	Celery, sliced
1 c	Parsnip, sliced
¾ c	Italian parsley, roughly chopped & lightly packed
¼ c	Garlic cloves, fresh (14 medium)
2 Tbl	Thyme, fresh, chopped
2 Tbl	Olive oil
1 tsp	Black peppercorns, whole
3	Bay leaves (optional)
¼ c	Nama shoyu

loving preparation

1. Place oil in a large stock pot on medium high heat. Add onion, carrot, celery and cook for 5-10 minutes, stirring constantly.
2. Add the remaining ingredients and allow to simmer over medium heat for 40 minutes. Strain and use as needed in recipes. The longer you simmer your stock, the more concentrated and flavorful it will become.

notes & variations

- Soup stock can be made from many vegetables. Some veggies to consider include potatoes, celery, carrots, onions, parsley, parsnip, zucchini, leeks and garlic.
- Many avoid using vegetables that become bitter such as bell peppers, radishes, turnips, broccoli, cauliflower and brussels sprouts. It is not necessary to add dry herbs or spices to a stock as it becomes flavorful unto itself.
- For a simple stock, save clippings and scraps of vegetables used in preparing other recipes. Place in a large, thick-bottomed stock pot on low heat and simmer until all veggies are completely cooked and their flavor has been fully imparted to the broth. Experiment with different vegetables and herbs until you discover your favorite combinations. Strain well, add salt and pepper to taste. Use as the liquid component in your recipes to create a deeper, more enhanced flavor.
- May be frozen and defrosted for future use. Some pour broth into ice cube trays, freeze and use as needed.

"WHEN THE FIVE SENSES AND THE REASON ARE STILL, AND REASON ITSELF RESTS IN SILENCE, THEN BEGINS THE PATH SUPREME." – KATHA UPANISAD

ulu, ancient wonder food
of the future

One of our favorite local ingredients here on Kauai is the *ulu* or "breadfruit". Ulu has its origin in ancient Polynesia and presently grows abundantly here on the Island. It can create many different flavors depending upon its ripeness and the method of preparation. Given its great versatility and abundant yield it has the potential to be one of the staple crops of the future. Before it fully ripens, try it grilled as a cutlet (page 194), or baked and mashed like a potato. When ripe it may be baked as the only base for a flour and sugar free cake. When fully ripe it is simply divine as a creamy live pudding. No matter how it's prepared, you are sure to enjoy this local island delicacy.

BRADDAH'S ULU CAKE
30 min prep / 40 min cooking / 5-7 servings

1 medium	Ulu, sweet ripe flesh, mashed (4 c)
4 small	Apple bananas, semi-mashed (1 c)
1 c	Walnuts, chopped
½ c	Date pieces
1 Tbl	Baking soda
1 tsp	Cinnamon powder
1 tsp	Sea salt
¼ tsp	Nutmeg, ground

loving preparation

1. Preheat oven to 350°. Cut open ripe ulu and spoon out flesh. Place all ingredients in a bowl and stir well. Pour into a lightly oiled 8" x 8" square baking pan.
2. Bake until top browns and cake pulls away from sides of the pan, approximately 40 minutes.

serving suggestion

☞ Top with Maple Whip (page 172) or Strawberry Sauce (page 66).

variations

☞ Add 1 c chocolate chips or dried cherries. Experiment with using other dried fruits and nuts.

WASABI MASHED ULU
30 minutes / 3 servings

3 c	Ulu or potatoes, mashed
1 c	Coconut milk
2 Tbl	Filtered water
2 tsp	Wasabi powder
1 Tbl	Green onion or chives, diced
½ tsp	Sea salt, or to taste
¼ tsp	Black pepper, ground to taste
Pinch	Cayenne pepper

loving preparation

1. Cook ulu according to instructions on page 146. Mash well in a large mixing bowl with remaining ingredients.

"I LIVE IN THE MOMENT MORE THAN I REALIZE." - STAR LOTUS

life begets life
living world fusion cuisine

Represented in this cookbook is just a small portion of the many delicious living foods recipes created in ten years of testing and development experience by the chefs of The Blossoming Lotus. In order to create these recipes, there are some important principles that need to be learned, including soaking, sprouting, dehydrating, culturing and the preparation of nut and seed milks and cheezes.

soaking

Soaking nuts, seeds, grains or beans releases enzyme inhibitors, allowing the sprouting process to occur. This is said to activate the life force inherent in the food. This in turn is passed on to us as we partake of that food.

To soak an item, rinse it well in a strainer and then place in a bowl or jar with filtered water well above the item being soaked. This is because as the seeds, nuts or grains soak, they will absorb the liquid and expand. Soak for the time listed in the following chart. Rinse and drain well. Soaked and drained nuts and seeds will last for three days if refrigerated.

Some items, such as buckwheat groats, chickpeas and wheatberries benefit from having the soaked water changed twice a day to prevent spoiling.

sprouting

Witness the miracle of life as your soaked seeds and nuts start to sprout. The life force continues to develop through the sprouting process, and each ingredient has an optimal time for harvest. Refer to the following chart in order to properly sprout an item.

Here is a simple method to get you started. Follow the previously mentioned soaking instructions. Place seed, nut or grain in a mason jar with a mesh screen or cheesecloth secured with a rubber band. Place jars on a 30 to 45 degree angle on a dish rack in a dark place or place item in a sprouting bag or

tray. Allow to sit for 12 to 24 hours. Rinse and drain twice a day until the cute little sprout "tails" appear.

Place sprouts in an airtight container in the refrigerator to stop the sprouting process.

dehydrating

Dehydrating is the slow process of low temperature "cooking" with air circulation that removes liquid and moisture from your dish. Live food preparation involves dehydrating various soaked grains, nuts, seeds and fruits to create crackers, live pizza and pie crusts, breads and treats. It is said to maintain the enzyme quality of the foods as long as you do not exceed 115° when dehydrating. Please see Dehydrated Flax Crackers (page 30), Live Greek Pizza (page 113) and Manna Bread (page 112) for some examples. Also great for making tasty treats such as dehydrated bananas with nut butter filling or veggie burgers. Please come visit us at www.veganfusion.com to check for our latest live kitchen creations.

soaking & sprouting chart

Item	Hours Soaking	Days Sprouting	Comments
Almonds	8	1-2	Try to always have soaked almonds available for snacks, patés & nut milks.
Alfalfa (¼ Cup Seed=5 Cups Sprouts)	6	4-5	Place in sunny location after 3rd day & remove hulls while rinsing. Be sure to rinse and drain well & not over-sprout.
Aduki Beans	10	3-4	Use like mung beans.
Barley	12	2	Great as breakfast cereal, also makes great milk.
Black Beans	24	3-4	Most popular for Mexican dishes.
Broccoli Seeds	8	5-6	Place in sunny location after 3rd day & remove hulls while rinsing. A personal favorite for salads.
Buckwheat	½	2	A wonderful micro green for salads, be sure to use raw buckwheat. Kasha will not sprout.
Chia Seeds	2-4	-	Spread mixture evenly on a hemp cloth to sprout.
Clover	6	5-6	Place in sunny location after 3rd day & remove hulls while rinsing. Great in salads and for live hummus.
Fenugreek	12	2-3	Delicious in Indian dishes. Reputed to be a digestive aid.
Flax Seeds	½	-	Soak preparation for flax crackers and for baking as an egg replacement.
Garbanzo Beans (Chickpeas)	48	3-4	Great in salads and for live hummus.
Kamut	12	2-3	Excellent for breads and cereals.
Lentil Beans	8	1-2	Use green, yellow or red—popular in salads and for their spicy taste.
Mung Bean	10	3-4	Be careful to keep clean.
Oat Groats	12	2	Use only unhulled oats. Great in cereal and milks.
Peas	12	3	Use sparingly in salads.
Pumpkin Seed (Pepita)	8	-	Live food staple, great as an all-around snack.
Quinoa	2-4	1-2	Nutty addition to live casseroles, cereals and crackers.
Rye	10	3	Used in breads.
Sesame Seeds	4-6	-	Used extensively in live food preparation, including desserts.
Spelt Berries	12	2-3	Great in breads and cereals.
Sunflower Seeds	12	1-2	Popular sprout for salads and cereals.
Walnuts, Cashews, Hazel Nuts	6	-	Please soak and rinse all nuts a minimum of one hour before using.
Wheat Berries	12	2-3	Breakfast cereal, source for Rejuvelac, manna bread.
Wild Rice	24-48	-	Rinse frequently, use in wild rice salads.

"BE THE CHANGE YOU WISH TO SEE IN THE WORLD." - GANDHI

nut & seed milks and cheezes

Nut milks are incredibly easy to make and are a staple in a live food diet. The filtered product from the milks may become the base for your Nut Cheez. We like to use almonds, walnuts, macadamia and pine nuts as they seem to impart a creamy texture to the dish.

SIMPLE ALMOND CHEEZ

1 c	Almonds, soaked & blanched
2 c	Rejuvelac or coconut water
1 Tbl	Light miso
2 Tbl	Scallions, minced
1 tsp each	Basil, thyme & oregano, minced
1 tsp	Ume boshi paste

loving preparation

1. Blend all ingredients in a food processor. Pour mixture into a jar, cover opening with cheesecloth, secure tightly with a rubber band and allow to ferment for 3 to 4 hours. Turn jar upside-down in a bowl to make for a drier cheez and to remove the "whey" (use whey in a sauce or dressing to impart tartness).

"TO A SINCERE STUDENT, EVERY DAY IS A FORTUNATE DAY." - ZENGETSU

culturing

There are many health benefits attributed to cultured or fermented foods such as improved digestion, nutrition and overall enjoyment. Some well-known favorites are sauerkraut, kim chee and nut and seed cheezes. Check out Shekina's Sauerkraut (below) and Conquering Lion Cashew Cheez (page 29) for some enjoyable ways to include these beneficial items in your diet.

SHEKINA'S SAUERKRAUT

15 min prep / 2-3 days culturing / 4 cups

1 large	Green cabbage
2 tsp	Ginger, fresh minced
1 tsp	Dill, fresh
½ tsp	Sea salt

loving preparation

1. Peel off outer layers of cabbage and set aside. Coarsely grate or finely chop cabbage and place in a 1 gallon glass jar. Cover with outer layer cabbage leaves. Place a smaller glass jar filled with water on top of the cabbage to weigh contents down. Cover with a cloth.
2. Allow this mixture to sit for approximately two to three days in a dark warm place. Check after the second day. It should have a slightly fermented taste but should not be gray or moldy. When ready, place in a container with salt, dill and ginger.

variations

- Replace green cabbage with purple cabbage. Replace dill with other fresh herbs or spices. Replace ginger with fresh minced garlic.

rice & grain dishes

Grains are complex carbohydrate foods that are filled with fiber and nutrition. As such, they are the staple food for many of the world's cultures. They promote energy and are rich in minerals and B-vitamins, and are fun to cook with as well.

Whole grains contain an oil that can become rancid and attract insects if not stored correctly. To store grains, it is recommended to keep them in a tightly sealed container in a cool, dry location. They can be stored in a refrigerator for up to four weeks and in a freezer for up to six months. Cooked grains may be kept in the refrigerator for up to three days and in the freezer for up to six months.

Many grains may also be soaked and sprouted, therefore enjoyed in their live state. These sprouts may also be dehydrated and ground into flour for live food baking to create flour and then used in baking.

Today we have the benefit of being able to enjoy incredible grains such as buckwheat, millet, quinoa and barley. Additionally it is easy to create or purchase pastas made with these life-giving grains. Please try to eliminate as much processed wheat as possible from your diet.

cooking grains

Simply follow these instructions and you will always have perfectly cooked grains.

- Rinse the grain thoroughly and drain the excess water.
- Bring the measured amount of grain and liquid (either vegetable stock or filtered water) to a boil. You may wish to add a dash of sea salt.
- Cover with a tight-fitting lid, reduce heat to low and simmer for the recommended time. Since the grain is being steamed, do not lift the lid until the grain is finished cooking.

The following chart is provided to give you an approximate cooking time and yield of some of the more common grains. Cooking times may vary depending upon altitude and stove cooking temperatures. The grain is generally finished cooking when it is chewy and all of the liquid is absorbed.

grain cooking chart

Grain	Liquid/cup of Grain	Approx. Cooking Time (Minutes)	Approx. Yield (Cups)	Comments
Amaranth	2.5	25	2.5	Ancient grain of Aztecs, higher in protein and nutrients than most grains.
Barley, pearled	3	45	3.5	Good in soups and stews.
Buckwheat	2	15	2.5	Hearty, nutty flavor. When toasted its called Kasha. Can be used as a breakfast cereal.
Corn Meal	3	20	3.5	From ground corn, a staple of Native Americans. Use in Corn Bread or grits.
Couscous	1.5	15	1.5	A North African Staple made from ground semolina.
Kamut	3	60	3	A type of wheat that many with wheat allergies are able to tolerate.
Millet	2.5	20	3	A highly nutritious grain that is used in casseroles, stews and cereals. Especially tasty with flax oil.
Oats				
Steel Cut	3	30-40	3	
Groats	3	60	3	A versatile grain that is popular as a cereal, for baking and for milks.
Rolled	3	10	3	
Quick	2	5	2	
Polenta	3	10	3	A type of Corn Meal-used in Italian Cooking. To cook, bring liquid to a boil. Reduce to simmer and whisk in polenta, stirring until done.
Quinoa	2	20	2.5	Ancient grain of the Incans. High in protein and nutrients. Has a delicate, nutty flavor.
Rice				
Brown Basmati	2	35-40	2.25	Rice has a high nutrient content and is a staple in many of the world's cultures, to say the least. Basmati Rice has a nutty flavor and is used in Indian cooking. We prefer brown short grain rice, for its taste and nutritional value.
White Basmati	1.5	20	2	
Brown Long Grain	2	45	3	
Brown Short Grain	2	45	3	
Wild	3	60	4	
Rye				
Berries	4	60	3	A staple grain throughout Europe. Used as a cereal, or ground to make breads including pumpernickel.
Flakes	3	20	3	
Spelt	3.5	90	3	Spelt is the most pure and ancient form of wheat. It contains much more protein and nutrition than wheat and Is Infinitely more digestible.
Teff	3	20	1.5	From Ethiopia, smallest grain in the world, main ingredient for injera flatbread.
Wheat				
Whole	3	120	2.75	Primary bread grain. Bulghur is used in Mid Eastern dishes, such as Tabouleh. Cracked may be used as a cereal.
Bulghur	2	15	2.5	
Cracked	2	25	2.5	

legume cooking chart

Legume	Liquid/cup of legume	Approximate cooking time (hours)	Approximate yield (cups)	Comments
Aduki/Adzuki Beans	3¼	45 min	3	Tender red bean used in Japanese & macrobiotic cooking.
Anasazi Beans	3	2	2	Means "the Ancient Ones" in Navajo language, sweeter and meatier than most beans.
Black Beans (Turtle Beans)	4	1¼	2½	Good in Spanish, South American and Carribean dishes.
Blackeyed Peas	4	1¼	2	A staple of the American South.
Garbanzo Beans (Chickpeas)	4	3-4	2	Used in Mideastern & Indian dishes. Puréed cooked garbanzos form the base of hummus.
Great Northern Beans	4	1½	2	Beautiful, large white bean.
Kidney Beans	4	1½	2	Medium sized red beans. Most popular bean in the U.S., also used in Mexican cooking.
Lentils	3	45 min	2¼	Come in green, red and French varieties. Member of pea family used in Indian Dahl dishes and soups.
Lima Beans	3	1½	1¼	White Bean with a distinctive flavor and high in nutrients.
Baby Limas	3	1½	1¾	
Mung Beans	3	45 min	2¼	Grown in India and the Orient. Used in Indian Dahl dishes. May be soaked and sprouted and used in soups and salads.
Navy Beans (White Beans)	4	2½	2	A hearty bean used in soups, stews and cold salads.
Pinto Beans	4	2½	2	Used in Mexican and Southwestern cooking. Used in soups and as refried beans in burritos.
Split Peas	3	45 min	2¼	Come in yellow and green variety. Do not need to be soaked. Used in soups and Indian dahls.
Soy Beans	4	3+	2	Versatile, high protein bean that is widely used in the Orient. May be processed into tofu, tempeh, miso, soy milk, shoyu and soy "cheez".
Soy Grits	2	15 min	2	Use as part of tasty breakfast cereal, or in baking.

Note: These times are for cooking dry beans. Please reduce cooking time by 25% when beans are soaked.

"I HAVE NO DOUBT THAT IT IS A PART OF THE DESTINY OF THE HUMAN RACE, IN ITS GRADUAL IMPROVEMENT, TO LEAVE OFF EATING ANIMALS." - HENRY DAVID THOREAU

legume dishes

Legumes are considered to be a highly nutritious addition to the diet. They are a high fiber, low calorie, low fat, low sodium and cholesterol-free food. They are also relatively high in protein, amino acids, vitamins and minerals.

Before you cook beans, it is recommended to clean thoroughly, rinse well and soak overnight. This is said to improve digestibility and to reduce gas. Other methods for improving digestibility include adding some fennel seeds, a handful of brown rice or a few strips of the sea vegetable kombu to the beans while cooking. If you forget to soak the beans over night, a quick method is to bring beans and four times the amount of water to boil, remove from heat, cover and allow to sit for a few hours.

After soaking the beans or boiling them in this fashion, discard the soak water, add the measured amount of vegetable stock or filtered water to a thick bottomed pot, bring to a boil, cover, reduce heat to simmer and cook until tender.

Do not add salt to the cooking liquid, it can make the beans tough. Beans are done cooking when they are tender, but not mushy. They should retain their original shape.

sweet mystery of life,
at last I've found you...

Many people believe that eating foods with refined white sugar can lead to certain health problems, including emotional disorders, obesity, diabetes and tooth decay. It is believed that since refined sugars are missing the nutrients that are contained in naturally sweet whole foods, the body is drained of its own store of minerals and nutrients in its efforts to metabolize the sugar.

Vegan natural food preparation makes use of various naturally occurring and minimally processed sweeteners. These sweeteners are superior to white sugar but it is still believed that most of them need to be used in moderation.

The following chart indicates how much of a sweetener is needed to replace one cup of white, refined sugar. The chart indicates how much liquid to delete from the recipe to maintain its consistency if the sweetener is a liquid.

Waimea Canyon, Kauai, Hawaii

"STUDY NATURE, LOVE NATURE, STAY CLOSE TO NATURE. IT WILL NEVER FAIL YOU." - FRANK LLOYD WRIGHT

sugar conversion chart

Sweetener	Replace one cup of refined sugar with	Reduce liquids by	Comments
Agave Nectar	¾ c	⅓	Excellent choice because of its "low glycemic index," a natural extract from this famous Mexican cactus.
Barley Malt Syrup	¾ c	¼	Roughly half as sweet as honey or sugar. Made from sprouted barley and has a nutty, caramel flavor.
Brown Rice Syrup	1 c	¼	A relatively neutral flavored sweetener that is roughly half as sweet as sugar or honey. It's made from fermented brown rice.
Blackstrap Molasses	½ c	¼	This syrup is a liquid by-product of the sugar refining process. It contains many of the nutrients of the sugar cane plant. Has a strong, distinct flavor.
Date Sugar	⅔ c	0	A granulated sugar produced from drying fresh dates.
Fruit Syrup	1 c	¼	The preferred method of sweetening involves soaking then blending raisins and dates with filtered water to create a sweet syrup. Try ½ cup raisins with 1 cup water and experiment to find desired sweetness.
Honey	¾ c	⅛	An extremely sweet nectar made by bees when they return to the hive with the pollen of flowers. Raw and unfiltered honey contains many healthful nutrients. It comes in a variety of flavors depending upon the type of flowers the bee harvested. Please do not heat honey.
Maple Syrup	¾ c	⅛	Forty gallons of sap from the maple tree are needed to create one gallon of maple syrup. It is mineral rich and graded according to color and flavor. Grade A is the mildest and lightest, Grade C is the darkest and richest. Good for baking.
Sucanat	1 c	0	Abbreviation for "Sugar Cane Natural". It is a granular sweetener that consists of evaporated sugar cane juice. It has approximately the same sweetness as sugar. It retains most of the vitamins and minerals of the sugar cane.
Stevia (powdered)	1 tsp	0	Stevia is a plant that originates in the Brazilian rainforest. The powdered form is between 200 and 400 percent sweeter than white sugar. It is noncaloric, does not promote tooth decay and is said to be an acceptable form of sugar for diabetics and those with blood sugar imbalances. For baking conversions, please see our web site.

quick and easy...

Random musings on tasty snacks, elixirs and the wonder of it all

The following are some simple ideas for delicious meals, snacks, treats and finger foods.

❧ **Living Waters Coco Bliss** Drink water of a fresh coconut, add a pinch of cayenne pepper and sea salt, split open and spoon out the meat. Enjoy with a splash of lime.

❧ **Chrissy's Smoked Coco from Heaven** Place hulled coconut in coals of campfire until blackened and charred, open coconut and scoop out meat. Meat can also be scooped out and grilled.

❧ **Golden Rule** Toasted pita triangles with Hummus (page 20).

❧ **Transcendental Tofu** Grilled tofu, wrapped in lettuce, Peanut Dipping Sauce (page 21).

❧ **Santosha Crudite** Raw veggies in slices or sticks, usually served with a dip—using jicama, carrots, celery, bell pepper and cucumber sticks and slices for dipping into Cashew Cheez (page 29), Hummus (page 20) or Paté (page 28).

❧ **La Dolce Vita** Add minced fresh herbs to Vegan cream cheez, stuff in small roma or cherry tomato and top with fresh basil. Serve cold or bake in the oven until warm. Or use cream cheez spread as a filling for wraps and sandwiches.

❧ **Ahimsa's Arame** Soak 1 cup arame, drain, add ½ of an avocado, diced, 2 scallions, diced, 1 grated carrot, 1 tablespoon olive or flax oil, ½ teaspoon of raw apple cider vinegar and a pinch of sea salt and cayenne pepper.

❧ **The Radical Mystery Meal** Contemplate the ontological and radical mystery of being while enjoying steamed vegetables over rice or quinoa, with a salad. Serve with dressing or sauce of choice, or simply add flax oil, nutritional yeast, sea salt or shoyu.

❧ **Alavu Pancake Delight** Leftover buckwheat pancakes used for lunch with an almond butter, jelly and banana filling.

❧ **Izzi's Pono Grinds** Brown rice, olive oil and nutritional yeast with a dash of shoyu.

❧ **Amrita's Coco Candied Yams** 2 medium yams, steamed or baked in an oven until soft, mashed with ½ C coconut milk, 2 Tbl maple syrup or agave nectar and a pinch of the following: cinnamon, cardamom, nutmeg, allspice and sea salt.

❧ **Dulcinea's Dulse** Try this sea vegetable as a tasty salty snack on its own or sprinkle as topping for salads. Also try lightly baking in oven until crisp and serving on a sandwich with lettuce, tomato, vegan mayo and other fixings as a D.L.T.

ᔑ *Sage I and Judah's Choice* Popcorn with olive oil, nutritional yeast and sea salt. Add an optional dash of garlic, cayenne or spirulina.

ᔑ *Primal Scream Frosties* Frozen fresh fruit run through a Champion juicer with the blank installed. Try bananas, mango, coconut or papaya. Mix with nut butters and top with chopped nuts. Need we say more.

ᔑ *O No Godzilla* Shitake mushrooms marinated in red wine vinegar for ten minutes and pan-seared on a hot cast iron skillet. Serve with peanut dipping sauce as part of a vegan pupu platter.

ᔑ *Vigil's Very Good Fruit Kanten* This is the original "jello." Place 2 cups of fruit juice in a saucepan on medium heat. We like grape or berry juice. Cook until juice begins to simmer. Whisk in 2 Tbl of agar flakes and continue whisking until agar dissolves, approximately 5 minutes. Remove from heat, add 1 cup of berries or bite-sized pieces of fruit, a pinch of cinnamon, nutmeg and cardamom. Pour into a medium bowl or shaped molds and refrigerate until chilled and solid, approximately 2 hours.

ᔑ *Babe's Blessed Tempeh Strips* Slice tempeh into ¾" strips and place in a shallow dish. In a small bowl, combine 2 Tbl shoyu, 1 Tbl filtered water, 3 drops liquid smoke, a pinch each of garlic powder, chili powder, paprika and fresh ground black pepper. Whisk well and pour over tempeh strips. Allow to marinate for 5 minutes. Bake on a well oiled baking sheet at 400° for 10 minutes, flip tempeh and cook until slightly crispy, approximately 10 minutes.

ᔑ *Will's Union Dip* Sour Crème (page 196) mixed with natural powdered onion soup mix as a dipping sauce for chips and veggies.

ᔑ *Axum's White Bean Tarragon Salad* Use 1 ¾ C cooked white beans, 1 ½ tsp minced tarragon, 2 tsp fresh squeezed lemon juice, sea salt to taste, ground black pepper to taste, 1 ½ Tbl flax oil and ¼ tsp shoyu. Substitute different beans and herbs such as black beans & cilantro, cannaleni beans and basil, etc.

ᔑ *Don Quixote's Artichoke* Cut off top of artichoke, open up top and pour in a little olive oil, garlic powder and salt. Steam until a leaf can easily be removed, approx. 35-40 minutes. Serve with a simple dipping sauce including 3 Tbl olive oil, 1 tsp balsamic vinegar, 1 tsp minced fresh herb, sea salt and fresh black pepper to taste.

John Galt's Stuffed Potatoes Bake potato, open it, fluff and fill with steamed veggies and Sour Crème (page 196) or topping of your choice. Try topping with Cheez Sauce (page 100).

Abba's African Hot Sauce Use 1 c filtered water or stock, 8-10 assorted, chopped hot peppers (habañero, serrano, jalapeño, etc., about ½ cup), 1 medium diced green bell pepper (about ¾ cup), 1 ½ tsp minced garlic, ½ cup shallots or diced green onions, ¼ cup tomato paste, 2 Tbl raw apple cider vinegar, 1 tsp fresh ground black pepper, 1 tsp sea salt, ¼ tsp cardamom powder, ¼ tsp cayenne powder. Place all ingredients in a blender and blend until smooth. Place into a small saucepan on low heat and cook for 20 minutes, stirring frequently. ¡Cuidado! Es muy caliente.

Laxmi's Latkes Use 2 medium russet potatoes, cleaned and coarsely grated, 2 Tbl ground flax seed, ¼ cup diced onions, ½ tsp sea salt. Mix well in a mixing bowl. Place on a hot griddle. Serve with Sour Crème (page 196) and apple sauce. For a colorful treat, can easily be made with yams or Okinawan purple potatoes.

Jimbo's Miso Dissolve 1 Tbl of miso paste in a bowl with 1½ c hot water. Add ½ of an avocado, diced, and enjoy.

Deva's Dipping Platter Flax crackers, served with an olive tapenade, diced avocado and salsa of choice, or top crackers with Live Food Paté (pages 28 & 32) and serve with Cashew Cheez (page 29).

One Hand Clapping Miso Soup Use 2 c hot filtered water, ¼ c natto chutney miso paste or your favorite variety, ¼ c diced extra firm tofu, 2 Tbl diced green onion, 1 crumbled nori sheet, 2 Tbl arame or hijiki (optional) soaked in hot water until soft and drained. Add water to a 3 qt pot and bring to a boil. Remove from heat. Add miso and whisk well. Add remaining ingredients and gently stir. Please do not boil once miso has been added. Make your own miso bowl. Ten thousand combinations are possible with this recipe.

Native Nick's Lemongrass Miso To the above recipe add 3 c water and 1 stalk of lemongrass, chopped into three or four pieces, and bring to a boil. Reduce heat to simmer and cook for 5 minutes. Remove lemongrass stalks, add shoyu to taste and enjoy. Individualize the above recipe by adding ½ c assorted vegetables. Add udon or soba noodles for a heartier meal.

Milarepa's Maki Roll Spread Preheat a grill. Cut 1 small green papaya in half, scoop out the seeds and place in a large pot of boiling water. Cook until papayas are soft with some firmness. Remove from water, slice into cutlets, and place in Lemon Herb Marinade (page 195) for 5 minutes. Place on grill and grill each side for 5 minutes, basting periodically with Basting Sauce (page 196). Chop a few cutlets into small pieces to measure 1 c for this recipe. Place in a food processor with 1 ½ Tbl Vegan Mayo (page 196), ½ tsp Agave nectar or maple syrup, ¾ tsp Mirin and a pinch of Cayenne pepper, pulse process until slightly smooth with some chunkiness. This may be used as a spread for nori rolls or wraps. Yields ¾ c and takes 20 minutes to prepare.

"IN THE CENTER OF THE CASTLE OF THE SOUL, OUR OWN BODY, THERE IS A SMALL SHRINE IN THE FORM OF A LOTUS FLOWER... WITHIN CAN BE FOUND A SMALL SPACE. THIS SMALL SPACE WITHIN THE HEART IS AS GREAT AS THE UNIVERSE. THERE IS A LIGHT THAT SHINES BEYOND ALL THINGS ON EARTH, BEYOND US ALL, BEYOND THE HEAVENS, BEYOND THE UNIVERSE. THIS IS THE LIGHT THAT SHINES IN THE LOTUS HEART." - CHANDOGYA UPANISHAD

sample menus

Our cookbook is designed with the heavier dishes at the beginning of each chapter and are devoted to lightness and simplicity as you progress to assist you in gravitating towards your optimal diet. The following sample menus list the dishes that are most suited for each particular stage of your path.

light
the hearty vegan

appetizers, snacks & spreads

B.B.Q. tempeh kebobs, antipasto, hummus, guacamole, salsa, sour crème, Vegan mayonnaise

soups

Minestrone, potato leek, broccoli bisque, unchicken noodle, coco purple potato, roasted squash

dressings

Thousand island, green goddess, toasted pecan, caesar

sauces

Thai coconut, marinara, mushroom gravy, roasted squash, cranberry

salads & sides

Tuna-free tempeh, egoless egg, corn bread stuffing, purple potato salad, coleslaw, herb roasted potatoes

wraps & sandwiches

Tempeh reuben, grilled portabello, TLC, baked tofu sandwich, burrito, taro burger

breads, pizza and pasta

Macaroni and cheez, spicy Thai noodles, soba and peanut sauce, calzone, corn bread, pad thai

tempeh, tofu & seitan

Tempeh chili, tempeh mexicana, tofu cacciatore, tempeh stroganoff, chicken free seitan salad, holiday loaf, broccoli and garlic seitan, maple glazed seitan

casseroles, grains & beans

Enchilada casserole, shepherds pie, grilled veggie lasagna, ulu lasagna, spanikopita, coconut rice, mung dahl

desserts

Kava brownies, chocolate cake, no bake cookies, mint chocolate chip cookies, rice pudding, pumpkin pie, tofu cheezcake, banana chocolate pudding, baklava

breakfast, juices & smoothies

Green banana omelet, tofu scramble, granola, buckwheat pancakes, lemon gingerade.

lighter
everyday vegan

appetizers, snacks & spreads

Hummus, baba ganoush, summer rolls, chutney, stuffed mushrooms, guacamole, salsa, wasabi mashed ulu

soups

Mideast chickpea, black barley corn, black bean, roasted red pepper and pine nut, split pea and roasted parsnip, gazpacho, miso soup, soup stock

dressings

Miso tahini, red pepper vinaigrette, sesame shitake, maple balsamic, cilantro lime

sauces

Black bean, curry, roasted red pepper, carrot ginger

salads & sides

Acorn squash with wild rice pilaf, Jamaican jerk plantain, kale and yam, roasted root veggies, tropical ratatouille, bindi masala, couscous salad, asparagus with red pepper & dill

"ALL SORROWS ARE DESTROYED UPON THE ATTAINMENT OF TRANQUILITY.." – BHAGAVAD GITA

wraps & sandwiches

Hummus wrap, nori roll, buckwheat neatballs

breads, pizza & pasta

Himalayan stuffed bread, pasta primavera, thai peanut pizza, Jamaican roti, spelt chapati

tempeh, tofu & seitan

Sweet and sour tofu, kung pao tofu, tempeh stir fry, pistachio blue corn crusted tempeh, seitan paella, Mexican seitan and black beans, seitan with sundried tomatoes and pine nuts

casseroles, grains and beans

Black rice polenta, asparagus risotto, peas and collards, buckwheat pilaf, multigrain rainbow casserole, kasha varnishkes, barley corn salad, chana masala

desserts

Carrot cake, ginger bliss cookies, fruit crumble, carob couscous cake, mayan wonder bars, halvah, oil free muffins, ulu cake

breakfast, juices & smoothies

Three grain porridge, granola, banana bread, papaya smoothie

lightest
living foods

appetizers, snacks & spreads

Guacamole, salsa, cashew and other Nut Cheezes, pates, sunflower seed dip, chard rolls, flax crackers

soups

Corn chowder, miso, carrot ginger, chilled melon

dressings

Lemon herb, cucumber mint, papaya seed ranch, tomato basil, flax

sauces

Live tomato, live almond

salads and sides

Live fettucini alfreda, green papaya salad, arame salad, sauerkraut, pickled ginger

wraps & sandwiches

Live veggie sandwich, collard club

breads, pizza & pasta

Live ethnic pizzas, manna breads, live pad thai

casseroles, grains & beans

Rainbow paté, live lasagna, live tabouli, live sprouted quinoa

desserts

Bliss Balls, live parfait, live fruit pies, frosties

breakfast, juices & smoothies

Live granola, live oatmeal, live fig and seed, green god smoothie, carrot veggie juice, almond milk, wheatgrass tonic, noni juice, maple cayenne lemonade

enter the mystic

fasting: Please consider giving your body a periodic break from food. This ancient art of cleansing and healing is more thoroughly covered at our web site www.veganfusion.com.

breatharian: Breathe in… breathe out… be light.

217

"WHEN HUMANS PARTICIPATE IN CEREMONY, THEY ENTER A SACRED SPACE. TIME TAKES ON A DIFFERENT DIMENSION. EMOTIONS FLOW MORE FREELY. THE BODIES OF PARTICIPANTS BECOME FILLED WITH THE ENERGY O LIFE, AND THIS ENERGY REACHES OUT AND BLESSES THE CREATION AROUND THEM. ALL IS MADE NEW, EVERYTHING BECOMES SACRED." - SUN BEAR

resource guide

this is the healing
of the nations

vegan education

www.veganfusion.com is the official web site for this book. A comprehensive guide to recipes, nutrition and the whole approach to the vegan lifestyle. You will also find information regarding products, sustainability, healing and activism.
Web: www.veganfusion.com Toll Free: (888) 44-LOTUS

Vegan Action a nonprofit grassroots organization dedicated to educating people about the many benefits of a Vegan lifestyle. Visually pleasing, comprehensive web site where one can find definitions, campaigns, resources, etc.
Web: www.vegan.org Address: P.O. Box 4288, Richmond, VA 23220 Tel: (804) 502-8736

Earth Save educates people about the effects our food choices have on the planet, our health and all life, and encourages a shift toward a plant based diet.
Web: www.earthsave.org E-Mail: information@earthsave.org
Toll Free: (800) 362-3648

The Vegetarian Resource Group VRG is a non-profit organization dedicated to educating the public on vegetarianism (i.e. health, nutrition, ecology, ethics and world hunger). VRG publishes the Vegetarian Journal. VRG also produces and sells cookbooks, other books, pamphlets and article reprints.
Address: P.O. Box 1463, Baltimore, MD 21203 Tel: (410) 366-8343 Web: www.vrg.org. E-mail: vrg@vrg.org.

GetVegan.com a growing collective based in Southern California that aims to promote ecological consciousness, sustainable living practices and animal rights. Their site contains tons of great info from recipes, news articles and literature to health products and related links.

Web: www.getvegan.com Mailing Address: P.O. Box 3307, Beverly Hills, CA 90212

Vegan Essentials is the place to shop for vegan clothes, shoes, cosmetics and so much more. Check them out online.
Web: veganessentials.com

HappyCow.org is the definitive global guide to vegetarian and vegan dining, loaded with a wealth of relevant information.
Web: www.happycow.org

www.vegan.org Comprehensive site with great ideas on going vegan.

Highland Veggies is a British based website supported by the Vegetarian and Vegan Societies. Contains vegetarian and great Vegan info in such areas as nutrition, health and animal rights.
Web: www.highlandveggies.org

Natural Zing is a vegan, raw and organic food and health products retailer. The site contains copious amounts of Vegan information as well as tips on how to be green.
Web: www.naturalzing.com.

VegEats.com is an international guide to dining, veggie and Vegan style. You can find recipes, restaurants, mailing lists and lots of links.
Web: www.vegeats.com

VegDining.com is another dining guide which includes an international search option, a monthly veggie restaurant

"A REDUCTION IN BEEF AND OTHER MEAT CONSUMPTION IS THE MOST POTENT SINGLE ACT YOU CAN TAKE TO HALT THE DESTRUCTION OF OUR ENVIRONMENT AND PRESERVE OUR NATURAL RESOURCES. OUR CHOICES DO MATTER. WHAT'S HEALTHIEST FOR EACH OF US PERSONALLY IS ALSO HEALTHIEST FOR THE LIFE SUPPORT SYSTEM OF OUR PRECIOUS BUT WOUNDED PLANET." - JOHN ROBBINS

contest and the opportunity to purchase a VegDining card for discounts at participating veggie restaurants.
Web: www.vegdining.com

www.beacondv.org is a discussion group site on Vegansim.

living foods

Living and Raw Foods is the largest online community dedicated to educating the world about the power of raw and Live Foods. This site is jam packed with information, classifieds, personals, books, homepages and much more.
Web: www.living-foods.com

www.rawfood.com has the most information, product selection and wisdom regarding live food products anywhere.

www.rawtimes.com is an online publication of anything raw, be it politics or food. Very informative and amusing.

www.sunfood.net This site is dedicated to the promotion of the raw food Vegan way of life. You will find articles regarding raw foodism, vegetarianism, living foods, and other aspects of natural living. Subscribe to *Just Eat an Apple* magazine, consult raw recipes, link to other raw Vegan sites.

www.rawfoodsnews.com A magazine about the raw and living foods community: breaking news, the science, interviews, testimonials, etc.

organic, sustainability & permaculture'

One Love Gardens is a community based organic fruit farm located on the mystical, magical island of Kauai. One Love provides a place to learn the principles of permaculture design, organic farming and self-sustainability, along with the daily practice of living with like-minded individuals in harmony with the land and each other. Contact them to learn more about internships, work-trade exchanges or for more information.
Tel: (808) 823-9791 E-mail: onelovegardens@hotmail.com

Center for Vegan Organic Education A non-profit education and research organization getting the word out about Vegan organic gardening techniques. Soil conditioners for sale online. Web: www.veganorganiced.org
Address: P.O. Box 13217, Burton, WA 98013. Tel: (206) 463-4520 E-mail: info@Veganorganiced.org

Barking Frogs Permaculture Center in Florida has courses and consulting available. Web: barkingfrogspc.tripod.com

221

Organic Gardening find out where to get your soil tested, manage pests without using chemicals, and read vegetable and flower growing guides. Regional monthly almanacs and magazines available.
Web: www.organicgardening.com

Avant-Gardening A site advocating organic gardening as a medium for creative expression and spiritual growth. Information on composting, soil building, permaculture principles, botany, companion and intensive planting and more.
Web: www.avant-gardening.com

Organic Trade Association OTA's mission is to encourage global sustainability through promoting and protecting the growth of diverse organic trade. Great site for tons of info on anything from public policy, U.S. legislation, definitions, market trends, food safety, GMO's, etc. Check it out!
Web: www.ota.com

World-Wide Opportunities on Organic Farms WWOOF is an association helping those who wish to volunteer on organic farms internationally. Become a member on-line.
Address: P.O. Box 2675, Lewes BN7 1RB, London, England Web: www.wwoof.org

GE Food Alert Campaign Center is a coalition of seven organizations commited to testing and labeling genetically engineered food.
Address: 1200 18th Street, NW, 5th floor, Washington, DC 20036 Toll Free: (800) 390-3373 Toll-Free Fax (800) 390-4751 California Address: 3435 Wilshire Boulevard, #380, Los Angeles, CA 90010 Tel: (213) 251-3680 Fax: (213) 251-3699 Web: www.gefoodalert.org

Organic Consumers Association The OCA is a grassroots non-profit public interest organization dealing with issues of food safety, industrial agriculture, genetic engineering, corporate accountability, and environmental sustainability. OCA is the only organization focused exclusively on representing the interests of U.S. consumers. Tons of information on their site.
Address: 6101 Cliff Estate Rd, Little Marais, MN 55614
E-Mail: staff@organicconsumers.org Activist or Media Inquiries: (218) 226-4164 Fax: (218) 353-7652
Web: www.organicconsumers.org

Earthflow is an all natural approach to permaculture design, offering garden tours and training programs, including permaculture courses.
Web: www.earthflow.com

environmental groups

Greenpeace is an international non-profit organization. Greenpeace focuses on the most crucial worldwide threats to our planet's biodiversity and environment. They campaign to stop climate change, protect ancient forests, save the oceans, stop whaling, say no to genetic engineering, stop the nuclear threat, eliminate toxic chemicals, and encourage sustainable trade. Their website has information on these topics, breaking news, campaign info and even jobs.
Web: www.greenpeace.org

Sacred is a non-profit organization specifically aimed at saving the California redwood forest through direct action and campaigns against the MAXXAM Corporation based in Houston, TX.
Web: www.sacredredwood.org Address: P.O. Box 980751 Houston, TX 77098-0751. Tel: (713) 858-0074.
E-mail: info@sacredredwood.org

Natural Resources Defense Council the NRDC is an environmental action group with over one million members working to safeguard the American continents' natural systems. It is touted as America's most effective advocate for the environment.
Web: www.nrdcwildplaces.org Mailing Address: NRDC, 40 West 20th St., NY, NY 10011

222

Green Restaurant Association the GRA is a national non-profit organization, promoting fair worker treatment and providing services in research, consulting, education, marketing and community organizing. Utilizing a collaborative strategy that involves restaurants, manufacturers, vendors, grassroots organizations, government, media, and restaurant customers, the GRA's model provides a convenient way for all sectors of the restaurant industry, which represents 10% of the U.S. economy, to become more environmentally sustainable.
Web: www.dinegreen.com Tel: (858) 452-7378 E-mail: gra@dinegreen.com Mailing Address: The Green Restaurant Association, 3660 Ruffin Rd. Suite E, San Diego, CA 92123

The Sierra Club The Club is America's oldest, largest and most influential grassroots environmental organization. Join their action network, find out about local and national outings, shop at their store, read their news releases, browse their magazine, investigate their political programs.
Web: www.sierraclub.org Address: 85 Second St, 2nd Floor, San Francisco, CA 94105 Tel: (415) 977-5500

The Permaculture Activist reports the work of grassroots landscape designers and social change artists from around the world. It's a quarterly magazine and resource guide for permaculture. Check them out online.
Web: www.permacultureactivist.net

Friends of the Trees Society is a wonderful grassroots nonprofit organization founded and directed by Michael Pilarski. It offers workshops, courses, events and education on permaculture and wildcrafted and organically-grown botanicals. Contact them via their website.
Web: www.friendsofthetrees.net

Public Interest Research Group the PIRG is an alliance of state-based, citizen-funded organizations that advocate for the public interest. The mission of PIRG is to provide result-oriented activism to protect the environment, develop a fair marketplace and encourage a responsive, democratic government. Look for your state's PIRG on their web site.
Web: www.pirg.org

Forests Forever carries out a program of citizen education and mobilization through direct-contact grassroots organizing. Their mission is to protect and enhance the forests of California. Check out where they are coming from!
Web: www.forestsforever.org Address: 50 First Street, Suite 401, San Francisco, CA 94105 Tel: (415) 974-3664

GMO-Free Kauai is a grassroots organization created to raise awareness and educate the public about the health, economic, and environmental risks of Genetically Engineered and Modified Organisms. Hawaii, including Kauai, is one of the top two states in the country for open-air GMO field testing. Visit their site for more info and other GMO links on their site or call them directly for local meeting times. Stop GMO testing now!
Web: www.higean.org/kauai Tel: (808) 651-9603 E-mail: gmofreekauai@care2.com

Rainforest Action Network is working to protect tropical rainforests around the world and the human rights of those living in and around those forests. RAN protects the rainforests and supports the rights of their inhabitants through education, grassroots organizing, and nonviolent direct action. Their website 223

"OH, NIGHT THAT GUIDED ME, OH, NIGHT MORE LOVELY THAN THE DAWN, OH, NIGHT THAT JOINED BELOVED WITH LOVER, LOVER TRANSFORMED IN THE BELOVED!" - ST. JOHN OF THE CROSS

Rio Preto Falls, Brazil

has a great page for kids and teachers too! You can e-mail or contact them the old fashioned way, by mail.
Web: www.ran.org E-mail: rainforest@ran.org Address: RAN 221 Pine St., Suite 500, San Francisco, CA 94104 Tel: (415) 398-2732

Children of the Earth United educates the public on ecological concepts and aims to provide a forum for people to share knowledge and ideas. Learn about Animals, Plants, Ecology, Nature, Environmental Issues, Native Wisdom, Nature Centers, etc. This is a great site for kids of all ages.
Web: www.childrenoftheearth.org

animal rights groups

People for the Ethical Treatment of Animals PETA, the largest animal rights organization in the world, is dedicated to establishing and protecting the rights of all animals. "PETA operates under the simple principle that animals are not ours to eat, wear, experiment on, or use for entertainment." Visit their raw and undiluted web site!
Web: www.peta.org Address: 501 Front St. Norfolk, VA 23510 Tel: 757-622-PETA (7382) Fax: 757-622-0457 E-mail: info@peta.org

Animal Concerns Community This community serves as a clearinghouse for information on the Internet related to animal rights and welfare. Check out their site for a myriad of related resources.
Web: www.animalconcerns.org Address: EnviroLink Network, P.O. Box 8102, Pittsburgh, PA 15217

The American Society for the Prevention of Cruelty to Animals The ASPCA provides effective means to prevent animal cruelty in the U.S. The ASPCA offers national programs

in humane education, public awareness, government advocacy, shelter support, and animal medical services and placement.
Web: www.aspca.org Address: 424 E. 92nd St, New York, NY 10128-6804

Farm Animal Reform Movement FARM is an organization advocating a plant based diet and humane treatment of farm animals through eight grassroots programs. Sponsors of the Great American Meat-Out, it is operated by a mere staff of eight. Wonderful people with a wonderful site, they have a great links page posted.
Web: www.farmusa.org Address: P.O. Box 30654, Bethesda, MD 20824

The Humane Society of the U.S. the HSUS wishes to create a world where humans relate to animals with compassion. "We seek a truly humane society in which animals are respected

© David S. Holloway / Apix

for their intrinsic value, and where the human-animal bond is strong." Visit their profound site.
Web: www.hsus.org Address: 2100 L Street, NW, Washington DC 20037 Tel: (202) 452-1100

Animal Aid is the UK's largest—and one of the world's oldest—animal rights groups. Exposes and campaigns against animal cruelty and abuse in all its forms. They promote a cruelty-free lifestyle, including vegetarianism/Veganism.
Address: The Old Chapel, Bradford Street, Tonbridge, Kent, TN9 1AW, UK E-mail: info@animalaid.org.uk Tel: +44 (0) 1732 364546 Fax: +44 (0) 1732 366533

world peace and hunger organizations

The Jane Goodall Institute celebrates the prospect of peace on Earth through a variety of initiatives and projects. The JGI aims specifically to improve quality of life for the chimpanzee population and recognizes the need to advance the power of individuals to take informed and compassionate action to improve the environment of all living things. Their own action towards this goal is the Roots & Shoots Global Peace Initiative, which inspires youth to make the world a better place through project-based learning. Read more about JGI on their web site.
Web: www.janegoodall.org U.S. Address: 8700 Georgia Ave Suite 500, Silver Spring, MD 20910-3605 Tel: (301) 565-0086 Fax: (301) 565-3188

The Seva Foundation offers programs that are developed in a way that builds self-reliance and are based on a vision of the connection between spirit, culture and health. They are dedicated to finding skillful means to relieve suffering through compassion in action. Seeking long-term solutions that will support cultural sustainability.

Address: 1786 Fifth Street, Berkeley, CA 94710 Phone: (510) 845-7382 Fax: (510) 845-7410 Orders: 1 (800) 223-7382 E-Mail: admin@seva.org Web: www.seva.org

The World Council of Religious Leaders is to serve as a resource to the United Nations, countries and other organizations, offering the collective wisdom and resources of the various faith traditions toward the creation of world peace. Check out their ongoing initiatives such as International Day of Peace, the World Youth Peace Summit, and the Women's Partnership for Peace on their web site.
Web: www.milleniumpeacesummit.org Address: Secretariat, 301 E. 57th Street, 3rd Floor, New York, NY 10022 Tel: (212) 593-6438 Fax: (212) 593-6345 Press Office: (212) 715-1571 E-mail: info@millenniumpeacesummit.org

World Peace Foundation WPF seeks to advance the cause of peace through study, analysis and the advocacy of wise action. WPF examines the causes and cures of civil conflict. They are currently active in the problems of Cyprus, the Sudan and Sri Lanka. WPF seeks to resolve conflicts as well as to study them.
Web: www.worldpeacefoundation.org Address: 79 John F. 225

Kennedy Street, Cambridge, MA 02138 Tel: (617) 496-9812 Fax: (617) 491-8588 E-mail: world_peace@harvard.edu

Mahatma Gandhi Canadian Foundation for World Peace seeks to universally share knowledge of Mahatma Gandhi's beliefs and philosophies. This web site also serves as a vehicle for news from live feeds worldwide and as a gateway of information on nonviolence, international development, anti-terrorism, peace research and education, publications and human rights. Web: www.gandhi.ca E-mail: info@gandhi.ca Phone: (780) 492-5504 Fax: (780) 492-0113 Address: P.O. Box 60002, University Postal Outlet, Edmonton, AB, Canada T6G 2S4

Religious Tolerance is a megasite fostering peace among all nations and religions. Religious tolerance means extending freedom to all peoples of all religions, though you may disagree with their beliefs or practices. Support these good folks. Web: www.religioustolerance.org

www.belief.net is the largest site on the internet for pan-cultural religious tolerance, supporting a global vision for understanding and dispelling myths about faiths and beliefs.

Creating Peace is a site created for one single purpose—to promote the idea of a peaceful world and to cultivate the quality of peace in everyday life. It offers various simple meditations to help improve life on a personal level. Peace begins with each individual. Web: www.creatingpeace.net

www.nonviolence.org is a virtual new media organization, started by one person, Martin Kelley. It has won attention from the mainstream and continues to be one of the most highly-visible and visited peace websites. Web: www.nonviolence.org Address: The Nonviolence Web, P.O. Box 38504 Philadelphia, PA 19104 Tel: (215) 681-0783 E-Mail: nvweb@nonviolence.org

Food Not Bombs is an all volunteer organization dedicated to nonviolence. Each chapter recovers food that would otherwise be thrown out and makes fresh hot vegetarian meals that are served in city parks, at peaceful protests and other events to anyone without restriction. Check out their site to see how to set up a Food Not Bombs chapter in your area. Web: www.foodnotbombs.net Address: A Food Not Bombs Menu, P.O. Box 744, Tucson, AZ 85702-0744 Toll Free: (800) 884-1136

The Hunger Site is a leader in online activism and fights to end world hunger. This site is power packed with information regarding hunger, peaceful activism to eradicate starvation. Web: www.thehungersite.com Address: The Hunger Site, One Union Square, 600 University Street, Suite 1000, Seattle, WA 98101-4107

Care initially founded to provide help to WWII survivors, is one of the world's largest private international humanitarian organizations. Their goal is that every person enjoys at least the minimum standards required to live in dignity and security. Web: www.careusa.org

The Hunger Project is an organization committed to end world hunger sustainably. Working in Africa, Asia and Latin America, this global movement's highest priority is the empowerment of women. Web: www.thp.org Address: 15 East 26th Street, New York, NY 10010 Tel: (212) 251-9100 Fax: (212) 532-9785

World Hunger Year WHY, founded by the late Harry Chapin, gets to the root causes of hunger and poverty by promoting grass-roots, community-based solutions to create self-reliance, economic justice and food security. Web: www.worldhungeryear.org Address: World Hunger Year, 505 Eighth Ave., Suite 2100, New York, NY 10018-6582 Tel: (212) 629-8850 Fax: (212) 465-9274 E-Mail: why@worldhungeryear.org

"I'O NALANI, THE UNIVERSAL SPIRIT, SAYS THAT WE—HUMAN KIND—ARE ALL OF HAWAI'I, WE'RE ALL HAWAI'IAN. THERE IS NO SEPARATION. YOU HAVE TO KNOW WHO YOU ARE AND WHERE YOU COME FROM TO UNDERSTAND WHY YOU ARE DOING THE WORK YOU DO. WE ARE ALL CONNECTED. IN REALITY THERE IS NO SEPARATION. IN OFFERING ALOHA WE SAY, 'COME SHARE MY SPACE, COME SHARE MY BREATH'." - PUNA DAWSON

"THE GEM CANNOT BE POLISHED WITHOUT FRICTION, NOR MAN PERFECTED WITHOUT TRIALS."

- CHINESE PROVERB

Glossary

Here is a brief description of some of the items used in Vegan World Fusion Cuisine. For more comprehensive and current information, please check out our web site at www.veganfusion.com.

Agave Nectar
Excellent sweetener that is a natural extract from this famous cactus.

Apple Cider Vinegar (raw and unfiltered)
This type of vinegar preserves many of its nutrients and is considered by many to have beneficial healing qualities.

Arame
A sea vegetable high in calcium, protein, iron and other vitamins and minerals. It is delightful in salads and stir fries, once it is soaked a minimum of 10 minutes and drained well.

Arrowroot
A powdered starch made from the root of the arrowroot plant. Used as a thickener in sauces, soups and desserts. Dissolve an equal amount of arrowroot with cold water before adding to mixture being thickened.

Barley Malt Syrup
A sweetener that is roughly half as sweet as honey or sugar. Made from sprouted barley and has a nutty, caramel flavor.

Black Barley
Highly nutritious heirloom grain that has a nutty taste and chewy texture. *To obtain more information on where to purchase this exotic grain, please visit our website.*

Black Rice
A deep purple when cooked, black rice (*sweet* or *forbidden* variety) has a nutty taste and soft texture, and is high in iron and other nutrients.

Brown Rice Syrup
A relatively neutral flavored sweetener that is roughly half as sweet as sugar or honey. It's made from fermented brown rice.

Buckwheat
An incredible, highly nutritious grain and one of our favorites. Raw *groats* are used in Live Food preparation. The roasted groat is *kasha.* It imparts a nutty, wholesome flavor.

Cacao Beans
The seeds of the cacao tree and the source of chocolate. The nutrient-rich power food of the Aztecs, Incans and Mayans.

Capers
A peppercorn-sized flower bud of a Mediterranean bush, it is usually sundried and pickled in a vinegar brine. Imparts a tangy, salty flavor to dishes.

Carob
Also referred to as St. Johns Bread or Honey Locust, may be used as a wonderful alternative to cocoa powder.

Celtic Sea Salt
See sea salt.

Chickpeas
Also known as *garbanzo beans*, they are a great transition food. Great as sprouts, on salads, in hummus or falafel.

Daikon
Literal translation "large root," this white Japanese radish is sweet, crisp and juicy. Delicious grated in salads and wraps.

Dulse

This sea vegetable is a high source of iron. Sprinkle flakes on salads, soups or steamed veggies or snack on whole strips.

Flax seeds

This small seed is packed with omega-3 fatty acids (EFAs) and other nutrients such as calcium, iron, niacin and omega-3 fatty acids. It can be ground and used in baking to replace eggs. Pressed into oil, it is great over salads. They make great live crackers when soaked, sprouted, mixed with veggies and spices, then dehydrated.

Hijiki

A calcium-rich sea vegetable which is also high in iron and protein. Tastes great in salads, soups or sprinkled over entrées once soaked a minimum of 30 minutes and drained well. Hijiki adds a strong sea flavor to dishes.

Kelp

Kelp is a regular part of the normal diet in many parts of the world such as Japan and Hawaii. We like to use it liberally as a seasoning as it is a good source of folic acid and iodine, as well as many other valuable vitamins and minerals.

Kombu

The quintessential seaweed, wide and flat, is a good source of calcium, iron, protein, and vitamins A, B1 and B2. We add it while cooking beans to bring out the flavor of the bean and increase digestibility. It is also popular soaked well and mixed with sea vegetables, salads, soups and stews.

Lemongrass

Popular in Thai and Vietnamese cooking. Imparts a wonderful lemon flavor and has many positive nutritional benefits.

Lime Leaf

The bay leaf of Southeast Asia, the Kaffir lime leaf is added to stocks and soups and removed before serving. It is a must for hot and sour dishes.

Liquid Smoke

Purified water that has been infused with the flavor of smoked wood. It adds a unique, smoky flavor to dishes. Only a small amount is necessary.

Mirin

A sweet, Japanese rice cooking wine that many use as a 'secret ingredient' to add depth and a unique flavor to a variety of dishes.

Miso

A salty paste made by fermenting soybeans, grains and other beans. It varies in color from light varieties such as mellow miso, shiro miso or chickpea miso—to the darker ones, such as brown rice, hatcho, red or barley. The lighter varieties are usually fermented for a shorter period, are more delicately flavored and sometimes sweet. The darker varieties are heavier and saltier. Miso is used in many recipes, including dips, dressings, sauces and spreads. The procedure for adding it to soups involves removing a small amount of broth from the soup, dissolving the miso paste into this broth and then returning the miso mixture to the soup after the miso is dissolved. Please do not boil miso, it destroys the enzymes.

Nama Shoyu

See *shoyu.*

Nori

A highly nutritious sea vegetable delivering calcium, iron and other vitamins and minerals. It is most commonly found wrapped around rice in a maki roll, sushi style. We love using it in our Live Food sushis and soups.

Nutritional Yeast

A plant-based culture consisting of up to 50% protein, very high in B vitamins, generally grown in petrie dishes on molasses. In cooking it is used to create a "cheezy" flavor and is wonderful as a topping for salads, popcorn and steamed vegetables. Please do not confuse with baking yeast.

"I JUST HAVE THIS ABSOLUTE BELIEF THAT HUMANS ARE MOVING AWAY FROM CRUELTY TOWARDS A TIME WHEN WE CAN TRULY LIVE IN HARMONY WITH NATURE. WHEN WE UNDERSTAND THAT THERE IS A SPIRITUAL POWER AROUND US FROM WHICH WE CAN DRAW STRENGTH. THAT IS WHERE I BELIEVE HUMAN DESTINY ULTIMATELY IS TAKING US. I JUST HOPE WE HAVE TIME." - DR. JANE GOODALL

Oils

Of the oils, flax and *borage* are our favorites. Many wish to avoid heating oils. If you do use an oil in sautéing, we recommend coconut, safflower or peanut oil.

Phyllo (Fillo)

A paper-thin sheet pastry dough. It may be shaped and baked to form a flaky crust for desserts and samosas. We recommend a spelt variety.

Quinoa

An ancient Incan grain power packed with complete protein, lysine and other amino acids. Also a great source of calcium, iron, phosphorus, a variety of B vitamins and vitamin E. This nutty grain is delicious.

Saffron

The most precious and expensive spice in the world. It imparts a bright orange-yellow color and fragrant, exotic aroma. Please use only the strands when following the recipes.

Sea Salt

Evaporated sea water, higher in minerals than commercially processed sea salt. Celtic salt is unrefined, with a high mineral content. This light grey salt is naturally harvested off the coast of France. It is the most highly regarded form of salt. Not all sea salts are created equal, so use the coarsest grind available for highest mineral content.

Seitan

Seitan, originating in Ancient China, is sometimes referred to as "meat of wheat" or "Buddha food". It is basically a wheat gluten dough that has been cooked in a broth with different types of seasonings. Seitan can be used in recipes the same way the animal product would be used, with little or no adjustments to the recipe and is very high in protein. Seitan may be stored in the refrigerator for approximately one week when out of its packaging or it may be frozen for longer term storage.

Shoyu

Japanese for *soy sauce*, we use Nama shoyu because it is wheat-free and unpasteurized. Considered a live food, it is the "champaigne of the soy sauces." Please use sparingly, can alter taste and color of dish considerably.

Soy Milk

A popular soy-based milk with a nutty taste, this animal milk alternative is made using cooked soy beans. In addition to our homemade version (page 196), there are many brands and many different flavored soy milks with which you can experiment.

Spelt

A highly nutritious and ancient grain that is in the wheat family and yet is generally tolerated by those with wheat allergies. It has a slightly nutty flavor and may be used to replace whole wheat flour in baked goods and pastas.

Spirulina

A freshwater, blue-green algae concentrated with proteins and nutrients like beta carotene and vitamin B. It is great in live pie fillings and crusts, smoothies, or sprinkled on salads. A true superfood.

Sucanat

Abbreviation for "Sugar Cane Natural". It is a granular sweetener that consists of evaporated sugar cane juice. It has approximately the same sweetness as sugar, but is much more nutritious.

Sunchoke

The *Jerusalem artichoke* is the tuber of a plant from the sunflower family. It has a nutty, Earthy flavor, has many health benefits including a good source of inulin. It may be enjoyed grated raw in salads or roasted in cubes.

Tahini

A paste made from finely ground sesame seeds, used in Middle Eastern and Mediterranean cooking. Imparts a creamy, buttery consistency to many dishes. The consistency of this product varies according to brand. A tremendous source of calcium, we use it for milks, sauces, dressings, soups and spreads. Try making yours fresh.

Tamari

A traditional Japanese soy sauce made without wheat. See *Shoyu.*

Tamarind

A tropical fruit widely used in drinks and sauces. The pulp has a pleasing sweet and sour flavor, rich in B vitamins and calcium. Popular as a chutney in Indian cuisine, and in drinks.

Tempeh

Tempeh is originally from Indonesia. It consists of soy beans fermented in a rice culture, then cooked. Many different varieties are created by mixing the soy bean with grains such as millet, wheat or rice together with sea vegetables and seasonings. Tempeh has a heavier texture than tofu. It usually has a mild, slightly fermented flavor. Its color is usually white with a few dark gray spots. As with tofu, it may replace the animal product in traditional meat based dishes. It needs to be thoroughly cooked either through steaming, sautéing, baking, grilling, etc. For storage, tempeh may be frozen or refrigerated. At the Lotus, we love tempeh burgers and stirfries. Some believe it is the best way to enjoy soy.

Textured Vegetable Protein (TVP)

A soy-based product that adds a hearty texture to dishes such as chilis, sloppy joes and casseroles. We consider this to be a transition food.

Tofu

Tofu, which is processed soy bean curd, has its origins in Ancient China. It is commercially sold in a number of different forms including extra firm, soft and silken. Each different form lends itself to a particular type of food preparation. The silken style may be blended and used to replace dairy products in puddings, frostings, dressings, creamy soups and sauces. The soft type may be used cubed in soups or puréed in sauces, spreads or dips. The firm style may be scrambled, grated in casseroles or cubed in stir fries. The extra firm style may be grilled or baked as cutlets, or it may be cubed and roasted. Extra firm tofu may also be steamed and used in steamed veggie dishes. Always make sure your tofu is as fresh as possible.

Ume Boshi Plum Paste

A Japanese plum that is salted, pickled and aged for many years. Imparts a tangy, salty flavor to many dishes. Great when used as a spread in Nori Rolls.

Wakame

A beautiful green seaweed popular in Asia, used in soups, salads and noodle dishes. It is high in calcium, iodine, magnesium and iron.

Wasabi

A condiment traditional to Japanese cuisine. It is a ground root that is pungent, bright green and horseradish-like in flavor. When combined with water, it forms a pungent pasty condiment served with nori maki rolls.

"LET THE BEAUTY WE LOVE BE WHAT WE DO. THERE ARE
THOUSANDS OF WAYS TO KNEEL AND KISS THE EARTH"

- RUMI

About The Blossoming Lotus

Located in the heart of Kapaa Town, Kauai, The Blossoming Lotus Restaurant is creating cuisine many say is the finest they have ever experienced. Celebrating international food, music, art and the wonder of nature, we delight in serving the Island community and world-wide travelers alike.

Our Vegan World Fusion Cuisine menu is an evolving creation of the many talented and gifted Chefs of the Lotus. Respect for the Earth and the principles of nonviolence guide us to utilize the abundance of the plant kingdom in all of our recipes.

This unique Vegan cuisine is inspired, healthful and incredibly delicious... just ask any one of our elated guests. Better yet, come visit our restaurant, bakery, juice bar and beautiful Island and you will experience for yourself how a gourmet meal can be both healing and transformational.

The Blossoming Lotus offers catering for retreats, weddings and gatherings on the Island of Kauai. For more information, please call 808 822-7678 or visit our website at www.blossominglotus.com. While on the Island, you might also want to consider our renowned personal chef services.

We offer products and educational services both online at www.veganfusion.com and in the tropical paradise setting that is our home.

The long term vision of The Blossoming Lotus is to bring the healing vibration cultivated on Kauai to communities around the globe, planting lotus seeds wherever the soil is fertile. Our restaurant model fosters community growth, supports local farmers, musicians and artists, and is a vortex of positive and loving vibrations for all to experience. Vegan World Fusion Cuisine is a celebration of the gift of life.

"It has been said, and I quote from Ecclesiastes, 'to everything there is a season, a time for every purpose under the heaven.' It is my professional opinion that your Blossoming Lotus Restaurant and Cookbook could not be more perfectly timed. America, and the world for that matter, are approaching reality regarding how we should be eating. You are on the crest of this wave. Your time has come!"

George A. Naddaff
Founder, Boston Chicken

in the Garden with...

Amy Archbold Food photographer and photographer of Kauai people and places. Amaya is a resident artisan of Kauai exploring the art of living and loving on this beautiful garden island. She is ever thankful for the mystic dance of creation and prays that one day all of humanity may find itself joyfully poised in a mandala of peace. And yet for now may the rhythms of life rage on, and in the words of Merl Saunders "let's take care of this Earth so we have someplace to boogie!" amayananda@yahoo.com.

Esther Heckman Food stylist. Kauai resident artist, creative chef, and laughing wanderer. She lives devising, revising, creating and experiencing the results. Always present at her side, her deft and clever assistant, Filbert. devashakti@whale-mail.com.

Gabriel Zingaro Co-Founder, Managing Member, Blossoming Lotus, LLC. Editing and wisdom contributions. A cornerstone of The Blossoming Lotus, Gabriel dreams of a world where business is conducted for the benefit of all beings, the Earth and future generations. A father of two children, Gabriel is motivated to heal the planet and its people through creating sustainable business models born of integrity and compassion, redefining profit as something everyone receives. Business becomes a global network of shared resources and people working for a collective whole. We are all neighbors living on planet Earth.

Jessyka Murray Co-Founder Blossoming Lotus, LLC. Lead recipe tester. Editing. Resource Guide and Glossary Development. By creating and serving delectable vegan delights, Jessyka seeks to awaken humanity to the simple joys of a natural, whole foods diet. Her deep passion for sustainable lifestyles and community living guided her in the development of our resource guide and glossary. It is an extension of her love and caring for the Earth and all of its children. Where there has been no path, this banyan tree momma has created one. Mahalo ke akua.

Star Rinaldi is a yogi, visionary artist and the creative force behind www.starlotus.com. Having healed herself by practicing nonviolence and the Vegan diet, she holds an enlightened vision of peace and harmony for all Creation. With a sincere desire for a World without borders, Star realizes that ahimsa is the foundation for a Global healing. She is one of the many inspirations behind the art and writings you view in this book. Artwork on page 173.

Dr. Jane Goodall, DBE through her kindness contributed the Foreword text. She is the founder of the Jane Goodall Institute, a UN Messenger of Peace, an internationally recognized scientist, peace keeper, wildlife and environmental spokesperson. Her list of publications includes two overviews of her work at Gombe — *In the Shadow of Man* and *Through a Window* — as well as two autobiographies in letters, the spiritual autobiography *Reason for Hope* and many children's books. *The Chimpanzees of Gombe: Patterns of Behavior* is the definitive scientific work on chimpanzees and is the culmination of Dr. Jane Goodall's scientific career. She has been the subject of numerous television documentaries and is featured in the large-screen format film, *Jane Goodall's Wild Chimpanzees*, 2002. www.janegoodall.org.

Martin Gray These photographs of sacred sites from around the world were provided by Martin Gray, an anthropologist and photographer specializing in the study of global pilgrimage traditions. During the past twenty years, Martin has traveled extensively in more than 80 countries to visit, research and photographically document over 1,000 holy and magical places of both ancient and contemporary religions. Many hundreds more of Martin's photographs as well as detailed writings on sacred sites, pilgrimage, archaeoastronomy, sacred geography, ecopsychology, Earth mysteries and related subjects may be found on his highly visited web site at www.sacredsites.com. Martin also presents beautiful slide shows around the world and his lecture schedule is available on this web site, along with a free newsletter and links to related web sites. Photos on pages 10, 15, 37, 47, 48, 76, 80, 90, 93, 99, 101, 112, 116, 119, 122, 132, 138, 141B, 142, 157, 166, 170, 171, 178.

Tim O'Rielly A photojournalist who has traveled extensively through Guatemala, Mexico, Brazil, Hawaii, China and India to photograph cultures and the spirit of the people. For more info, contact Tim at (858) 272-1947 or at perennialimages@yahoo.com. Some of his photos can be found on pages 7, 41, 53, 61, 117, 141A, 147, 162, 165, 174, 182, 224, 229, 237A, 244.

Jennifer Jonak An award-winning photographer from the San Francisco Bay Area who specializes in nature and wildlife photography, particularly endangered species and habitats. She has been published in numerous books and magazines, including Nature's Best, Time Magazine, The Washington Post, and Outdoor Photographer. Her work has also been featured on group display in the Smithsonian Museum of Natural History. Jenny has been a vegetarian for 17 years. You can see more of her work at www.jonak.com and her photos on pages 29 and 160.

Michael Edwards "Eternal Life" pages 9 & 14, and "Kuklakan" on page 164. Michael is a transformative visionary artist, graduate of the Chicago Art Institute, and bachelor of pharmacology with over 25 years experience in color, light and sound expression. He has been immersed in studies of West African and Native American culture, music and ceremony for many years. E-mail imagodeiarts@yahoo.com or visit www.imagodeivisionaryarts.com.

Francene Hart "Forest Cathedral" on page 94. Reverence for the natural environment, and experiencing the interconnectedness between all things has long guided Francene to create watercolor paintings of beauty and spirit. " My artmaking acts as a bridge between everyday reality and a metaphorical world of healing, continuity, and transformation. This comes from my heart. It is my intention to create works that express the joy and gratitude I feel for the honor of being part of this earthwalk." www.francenehart.com or email hartart@haii.net.

Adam Prall Book design, layout & typography by Hawaii Link Design, with many thanks to Yuko and Sydney Yamane for their contributions. He is a surfer/designer whose obsession with computer design began at age ten and can now be found gracing magazines, books, TV, CDs and computer screens worldwide. www.hawaiilink.net or e-mail adam@hawaiilink.net. (808) 246-9300.

Chefs and Managers of The Blossoming Lotus Recipe development and testing by Jessyka Murray, Amber Fox, Jennifer Murray, Gia Baiocchi, Kaya and Nadia Rathje, Sean "Seitan King" Leary. Management and leadership by Chris Vaughn and Jeremy Mohlenkamp.

Recipe Testing Kelly Hardaway, Angela Sunshine, Hannah Weiss, Aquarius Mitchell, Shari Gab and Danielle Rinaldi.

Recipe Editing & Computer Entry Shari Gab.

Sundaram Sundaram is a yogi/photographer whose great love is Santana Dharma, the "Eternal Religion," kept for all the world by the Himalayan sages and great masters of India, and photographing their endlessly unfolding expressions of spirituality. Photos on pages 42, 78, 86 & 149.

Kauai's Hindu Monastery Open daily from 9 AM to noon, with weekly guided tours. Visitor details and directions can be found at www.saivasiddhanta.com/hawaii/visiting.html or by phoning the monks at (808) 822-3012. Photos on pages 17, 26, 89, 215, 232, 245.

Eleawani Esther Felix Born and raised in Switzerland, in 1997, Spirit called her to the Hawaiian Islands where she found home on beautiful Kauai. www.eleawani.com or eleawani@yahoo.com. Photos on pages 189, 210.

Danielle Rinaldi An imaginative and visionary Vegan and live food chef, Danielle is well known for her creative style. With a true passion for creating original, tasty and healing dishes, she has a variety of different outlets which include personal chef services and small-scale Vegan catering. Please contact her at daniellethevegan@hotmail.com to learn more.

Cricket Harmony "Breathing for the Benefit of All Beings" on page 106. Cricket Harmony lives on Kauai where she grows organic food, studies hula, and enjoys being auntie to her Kaua'i keiki. Her mandala-like art appears in multimedia, murals, paintings and drawings. They reflect her love for the mother Earth and passion to spread peace. E-mail unityfire888@yahoo.com or visit www.rainbowphoto.com.

Dave Orchid "Azure Bay" on page 151, "Sinai Buddha" on page 105 and "Orchids of Simeera" on page 205. Dave Orchid is a 45 year old digital visionary artist that resides in the country in Southern Oregon. Please take a break from life and visit my website at www.runningwildonline.net.

Prop Donations by Lotus Galleries, Kauai. www.jewelofthelotus.com, sacred art and gems from around the world, and Jungle Girl www.junglegirl.com, Kauai island funk and flash.

Healing and Transformational Staff Massages provided by Ken Solin at Solin Massage (808) 651-6979.

Blossoming Lotus Logo Design by Thomas Wolfe. www.wolfestudios.com.

©2004 Thousand Petals Publishing

give thanks

We give thanks for all of our teachers, family, friends and fellow travelers. We celebrate you and feel deep gratitude for your loving kindness and support. It is a gift to be able to share this timeless wisdom.

Here on Kauai, we strive to be a living example of the pristine beauty, healing and hope that emanates from our Garden Island Home. We are now living in a modern age with all of the resources and knowledge necessary to create peace and sustenance for humanity. May this book inspire and uplift you to make this dream a reality.

Malama Aina. May love and respect for the Earth and all of its inhabitants be generated in the hearts of All.

Recipe Index

"UNTIL HE EXTENDS THE CIRCLE OF COMPASSION TO ALL LIVING THINGS, MAN WILL NOT HIMSELF FIND PEACE." - ALBERT SCHWEITZER

"WE MUST FACE THE PROSPECT OF CHANGING OUR BASIC WAYS OF LIVING. THIS CHANGE WILL EITHER BE MADE ON OUR OWN INITIATIVE IN A PLANNED WAY, OR FORCED ON US WITH CHAOS AND SUFFERING BY THE INEXORABLE LAWS OF NATURE." - JIMMY CARTER

Swordfish, Ben Bimstein, Master Ice Carver and Chef

Full Name Index

"IF YOU DON'T RISK ANYTHING, YOU RISK EVEN MORE." – ERICA JONG

"IN THIS PURE LAND THERE ARE MANY FRAGRANT LOTUS
BLOSSOMS, AND EACH BLOSSOM HAS MANY PRECIOUS
PETALS, AND EACH PETAL SHINES WITH INEFFABLE BEAUTY.
THE RADIANCE OF THESE LOTUS BLOSSOMS BRIGHTENS
THE PATH OF WISDOM, AND THOSE WHO LISTEN TO
THE MUSIC OF THE HOLY TEACHING
ARE LED INTO PERFECT
PEACE."

– BUDDHA

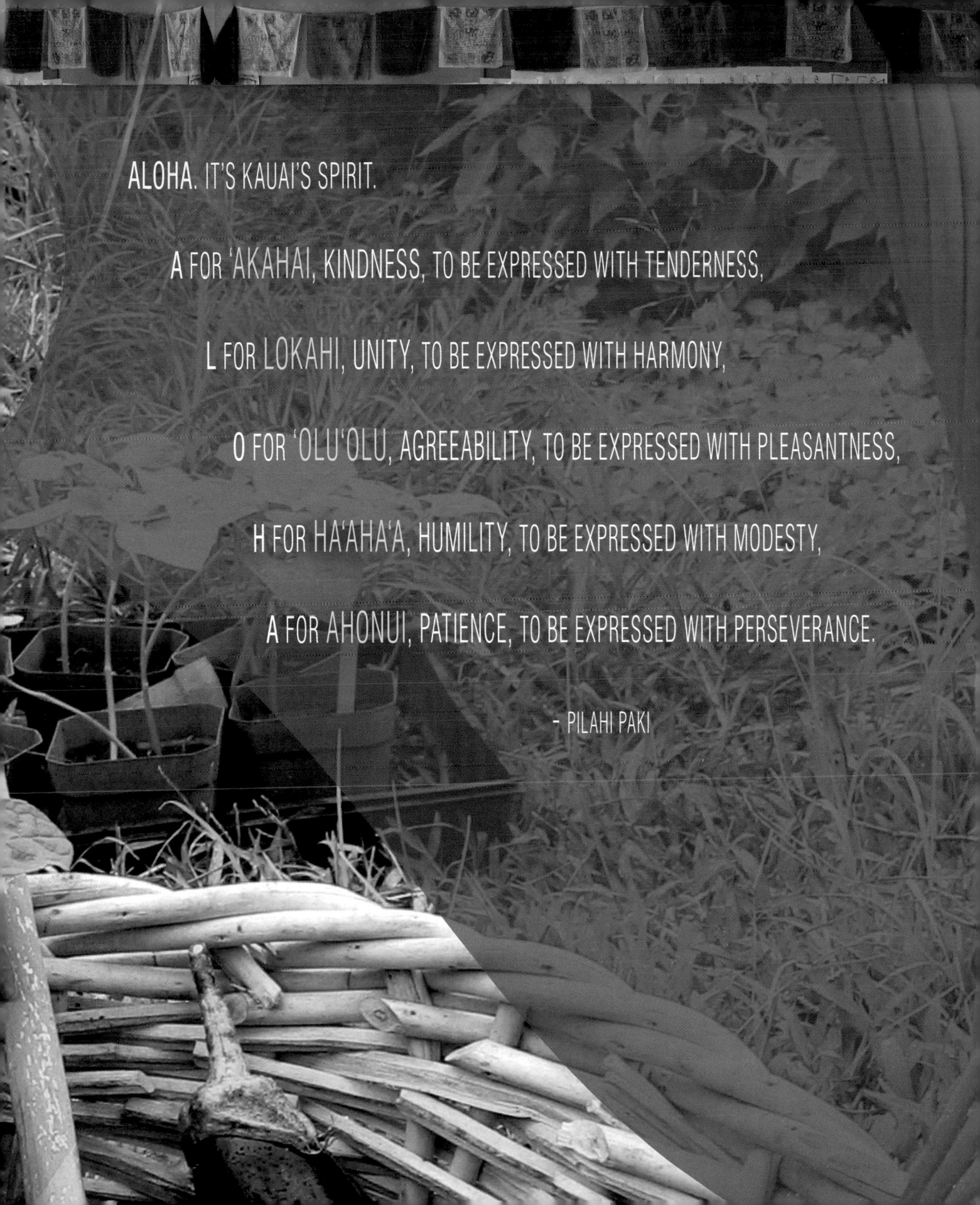

ALOHA. IT'S KAUAI'S SPIRIT.

A FOR 'AKAHAI, KINDNESS, TO BE EXPRESSED WITH TENDERNESS,

L FOR LOKAHI, UNITY, TO BE EXPRESSED WITH HARMONY,

O FOR 'OLU'OLU, AGREEABILITY, TO BE EXPRESSED WITH PLEASANTNESS,

H FOR HA'AHA'A, HUMILITY, TO BE EXPRESSED WITH MODESTY,

A FOR AHONUI, PATIENCE, TO BE EXPRESSED WITH PERSEVERANCE.

– PILAHI PAKI